MEANING, UNDERSTANDING, AND PRACTICE

Meaning, Understanding, and Practice

Philosophical Essays

BARRY STROUD

OXFORD
UNIVERSITY PRESS

Great Clarendon Street, Oxford OX2 6DP
Oxford University Press is a department of the University of Oxford.
It furthers the University's objective of excellence in research, scholarship,
and education by publishing worldwide in

Oxford New York

Athens Auckland Bangkok Bogotá Buenos Aires Calcutta
Cape Town Chennai Dar es Salaam Delhi Florence Hong Kong Istanbul
Karachi Kuala Lumpur Madrid Melbourne Mexico City Mumbai
Nairobi Paris São Paulo Singapore Taipei Tokyo Toronto Warsaw

and associated companies in Berlin Ibadan

Published in the United States
by Oxford University Press Inc., New York

First published 2000

British Library Cataloguing in Publication Data

Data available

Library of Congress Cataloging in Publication Data
Stroud, Barry.
Meaning, understanding, and practice : philosophical essays / Barry Stroud.
Includes bibliographical references and index.
1. Meaning (Philosophy) 2. Comprehension (Theory of knowledge) 3. Necessity
(Philosophy) 4. Thought and thinking. 5. Wittgenstein, Ludwig, 1889–1951. I. Title.
B840 .S872000 121′.68—dc21 99-059017

ISBN 0-19-825034-7

1 3 5 7 9 10 8 6 4 2

Typeset by Best-set Typesetter Ltd., Hong Kong
Printed in Great Britain
on acid-free paper by
T. J. International Ltd
Padstow, Cornwall

CONTENTS

INTRODUCTION

Collected here are thirteen essays published in almost as many different journals and anthologies over many years, more than half of them since 1990. I bring them together in the hope of making them more easily available in one place and providing each with whatever new light might be cast upon it by its juxtaposition with the others. They are arranged chronologically, and deal with different but related topics, with several themes or concerns reappearing throughout. Parts of some of the essays overlap with parts of others, in a few cases quite closely, but I have left them all as they originally appeared, hoping that each still contributes enough to stand on its own. I thank the original publishers for permission to reprint them here.

Five of the essays are exercises in the interpretation of the philosophy of Wittgenstein; at least that many others put ideas found in Wittgenstein to work in understanding philosophical issues of meaning, understanding, necessity, and the intentionality of thought.

Some of the earlier papers touch on questions about the nature and source of necessary truth, something I worked on for years in the 1960s and early 1970s. I thought I had come to see how and why none of the accounts of necessity then available could be right, but I had nothing better of my own to put in their place. Part of my interest had been in a priori knowledge, and on that question I think I did make progress. In papers presented in a number of places in the late 1960s I argued against the Kantian view that the necessary truth of something we know is a 'sure criterion' of its being known a priori, and even against the view that we have any a priori knowledge at all. None of that was published, at least in print, while necessity remained unexplained. Advance of a different kind began when I found it increasingly difficult even to formulate a clear question about necessary truth which I could see I had been trying to answer.

One way of putting it had been in terms of the 'source' of necessity. It seems obvious enough that some facts about us and the world we live in are somehow responsible for our being able to do what we do and think as we think, including our thinking of some things as necessarily so. But all those facts will be broadly speaking contingent, and their role in our thoughts about necessity could not be understood in a way that reveals the things we regard as necessarily so to be really contingent after all. That would deny what was to be explained. If the necessity is preserved, those contingent facts alone could not explain it. In particular, our acceptance of certain 'conventions', whether they be conventions of language or of something else, could not explain the necessity of the things we regard as necessarily so. Nor, I think, could it even account for our acceptance of them.

In holding something to be necessarily so we regard its opposite as impossible. It might seem natural, then, to seek the source of the limits of our acknowledging something as a possibility, and to find it somehow in our clear understanding of the state of affairs we regard as necessarily so. Understanding something is a matter of having grasped correctly what it involves or what it means. So from necessity it is easy to move to questions of understanding and meaning. But how well do we understand those notions themselves? Can they bear the weight that would then be put upon them? Would a correct understanding of them explain the "must" with which one thing must be true if another is, or we must accept a conclusion if we accept premisses which imply it?

What can be expected of a philosophical account of one's understanding of the meaning of something is a question running through many of these essays. How far can we get in explaining the phenomena of meaning and understanding 'from outside' them, as it were, without attributing intentional attitudes or supposing that anything means anything or is understood in a certain way to those whose understanding is being accounted for? This is basically a question of reduction, the prospects of which in this case seem to me hopeless. It that is so, what follows, both for our understanding of one another, and for human understanding in general? It seems as if even the very general contingent facts which make language and communication possible must themselves be understood in intentional terms in order to be seen to have that role.

For any words to have meaning, or to be understood as having certain meanings, some words must be used in certain ways, to do something or other. Sounds or marks do not possess meaning all on their own. Someone's meaning or understanding something by a certain word on a certain occasion could then perhaps be explained as the person's engaging in a certain practice or conforming to the way that word is used; without some such practice the word would have no meaning at all. But that would account for the person's meaning or understanding that word in a certain particular way only if the description of the general practice says or implies what that word is used to mean in the community in question.

Even to say that a word is regularly applied in a certain community only to things that are red, for example, is not to specify what that word means in that community. So a speaker's conformity to that practice, as described, would not indicate what he means by the word either. But to say that in the community the word is used to mean *red*, or to say of things that they are red, and that the individual speaker's performances conform to that practice, is to describe the practice in ways that attribute a certain meaning to words, or a certain understanding to speakers, in that community. If semantic or intentional terms must be used in this way in describing the practice, there will be no explanation of the idea of meaning in general solely in terms of regularities or practices non-semantically or non-intentionally described.

The idea that there is no saying what somebody means by something without making use of the idea of something's already making sense is what I believe lies at the heart of Wittgenstein's treatment of 'inner' or 'private' objects, thought to be accessible only to the person whose mind contains them. Exactly how he deals with those notions, and how this condition of our understanding the meaning of something comes into it, is the topic of two essays here. The idea is central too to his exposure of the conception of a person's understanding or meaning something by an expression as some kind of mechanism or reservoir from which the person's individual utterances or responses spring, and by which they are thereby explained. The failure to capture meaning and understanding at all in purely extensional descriptions of goings-on in the world, and the corresponding need to see them always from within an engagement with some community's understanding of them, is illustrated and developed in one way or another in most of the later essays.

The earliest, 'Wittgenstein and Logical Necessity', was published in *Philosophical Review* in 1965. It opposes the attribution to Wittgenstein of any kind of 'conventionalist' account of necessity, and brings out the role of contingent facts of what Wittgenstein calls 'natural history' in our finding the limits of acknowledged possibility to lie where they do. Conventionalism can seem called for because of Wittgenstein's denial that anything in a person's understanding of any premisses or rules he accepts forces him to accept a particular conclusion: with such 'freedom', it can seem as if only a decision could take him to a conclusion he accepts. That interpretation is resisted by showing that there being nothing of that sort in a person's having performed, or having understood things, in a certain way so far does not mean that there are no limits at all to the intelligibility of his going on in any way at all, or that there is nothing he must do in order to be performing correctly. Nor does it mean, as Kripke's 'sceptic' would later argue,[1] that there is no such thing as a person's meaning or understanding anything. The question is what accounts for the unintelligibility of sufficiently 'deviant' responses, and what resources are needed for describing a person's meaning and understanding things in the ways he does.

'Conventionalism and the Indeterminacy of Translation', which was published in *Synthèse* in 1968, focuses on a condition of success of any conventionalist account of logical truth: the presence of intelligible alternative conventions among which we can be seen (if only in imagination) to have chosen. I argue on the basis of Quine's views of translation in *Word and Object* that there are no such alternative 'conventions' available which could be seen to be the source of the truth of the elementary logical truths we accept. There are other things going on in the essay as well, some of which now strike me as confused, or at the very least unilluminating. I include it here because of what I continue to believe is right in what it says about conventionalism.

What lies behind it is the truistic observation that in order to assess the intelligibility of what conventionalism must hold to be a possibility, we can decide the question only by seeing whether *we* can make sense of it or not. That depends on the resources we now possess for making sense of anything, not merely on the abstract

[1] See Saul A. Kripke, *Wittgenstein on Rules and Private Language* (Cambridge, Mass., 1982).

thought that things could have been different. What we can even acknowledge as a possibility is to that extent a function of how much room we can find to manœuvre within what we have got now. We can start only from where we are, and proceed only by steps we can find intelligible. When pressed all the way, this would support the idea that we can make no sense of genuinely 'alternative conceptual schemes'.[2]

'Inference, Belief, and Understanding', published in *Mind* in 1979, starts from Lewis Carroll's brilliant story 'What the Tortoise Said to Achilles',[3] and takes up again the question of being 'forced' to a conclusion. The story shows that a truth's being necessary, even if it links a set of premisses with a conclusion that follows from them, will not explain any sense in which one is forced to draw that conclusion if one accepts those premisses. It shows, in effect, that if one's understanding and accepting something is understood only as one's having 'inscribed' certain sentences in one's 'notebook', as it were, then the notebook's containing what it does at any given time can never force one to accept anything that is not then inscribed in the notebook. I try to bring out the implications of this for a belief's being based on, or being a reason for, another belief. It cannot be a matter simply of the propositions believed, however many such propositions there might be thought to be in the basis.

The threat of a regress of the kind that besets Achilles imposes constraints on how someone's understanding something is best understood, and what role it can play in explaining the person's individual utterances or responses. If understanding is thought of as a certain capacity or ability, it cannot be seen as something that issues instructions to a speaker, and so guides or directs his particular utterances or responses. If that were so, those instructions in turn would have to be understood, and on this picture that would require further instructions, more guidance, *ad infinitum*. But if having the capacity is nothing more than being able to speak and respond appropriately, then it could not be what his individual performances spring from in a way that determines them and so would explain them. The importance of this regress and its implications for the proper understanding of meaning and the mind is not

[2] For this reading of the essay see Richard Rorty, 'The World Well Lost', *Journal of Philosophy* (1972).

[3] *Mind* (1895).

always clearly recognized. It is a major theme of many of these essays.

'Evolution and the Necessities of Thought' was published in L. W. Sumner, J. Slater, and F. Wilson (eds.), *Pragmatism and Purpose: Essays Presented to T. A. Goudge* (Toronto) in 1981. It asks whether we can see human knowledge as a changing product of historical, even evolutionary, processes, while continuing to believe that some things are necessarily true and could not have been otherwise. Necessary truth appears to present a difficulty that does not arise for truth alone. A conventionalist account of the 'emptiness' or 'non-factual' character of necessary truth would overcome the difficulty by making the truths we accept in some sense the product of our thinking or deciding to act in certain ways. But the essay argues that no appeal to contingent facts of our thinking or speaking in certain ways could explain the necessary truth of those things we regard as necessarily true. Attention to such facts might none the less help explain our acceptance of the necessary truths we accept, and increase our understanding of necessity by revealing more fully what we actually do with the idea, and what role it plays in all the ways we think about the world. The complex 'grammar', even the indispensability, of the idea of necessity, can be appreciated without seeking a definition or 'analysis' of it, let alone an explanation of its 'source'.

'Wittgenstein's "Treatment" of the Quest for "a language which describes my inner experiences and which only I myself can understand"' was presented in Kirchberg am Wechsel, Austria, in 1982 and published in P. Weingarntner and H. Czermak (eds.), *Epistemology and Philosophy of Science: Proceedings of the Seventh International Wittgenstein Symposium, Kirchberg, 1982* (Vienna) in 1983. It is a reaction to much that had been said and written over the years on Wittgenstein and the possibility of a 'private language'. The perversely long title in Wittgenstein's own words is my way of avoiding the hackneyed phrase "private language", which Wittgenstein almost never uses. It is worth avoiding, since by now it is widely thought to be known exactly what a 'private language' is or would be, and almost equally widely believed that Wittgenstein proved (or tried and failed to prove) the impossibility of such a thing. This short essay tries to look without preconception at what Wittgenstein actually attempts in part of the text usually thought to contain his main 'argument', and to show how and why those beliefs are mistaken. The very idea of what Wittgenstein is doing in his philosophy, or what is to be expected from his philosophical writings, is part of what is at stake. A fuller account of Wittgenstein's treatment, with detailed discussion of an impressive interpretation to the contrary, is given in the last essay in this volume, 'Private Objects, Physical Objects, and Ostension'.

'Wittgenstein on Meaning, Understanding, and Community' was also presented in Kirchberg am Wechsel seven years later and published in R. Haller and J. Brandl (eds.), *Wittgenstein—Towards a Re-evaluation: Proceedings of the Fourteenth International Wittgenstein Symposium* (Vienna) in 1990. It explains some of the consequences, and some things that are not consequences, of Wittgenstein's idea that meaning is use. A word must be used in some way in order to mean something, and someone whose use of a word conforms to the use of it in the community uses the word with that meaning. But saying what a word means is not necessarily to say anything about a community or anyone's conformity to it, and saying only that someone's use of a word is the same as that of the community is not enough to specify the meaning of that word. Since the fact of mere conformity to a practice does not suffice to determine meaning, and since nothing to be found in a person's mind could determine that he means one thing rather than another, there is a tempting inference, perhaps drawn by Kripke's 'sceptic', to the conclusion that there is no such thing as anything's meaning anything. The essay argues against that inference. The idea that meaning is nothing more than use does not restrict us to facts only about the similarity of use of merely mentioned expressions in saying what a word or a person means, even though no 'mental' objects can be brought in to help. Meaning's being indeterminate relative to a certain class of facts would have the consequence that meaning is indeterminate only if those facts were the only facts there are. But a 'community practice' view of meaning has no such implication. Some further objections to that view are briefly explored, with some speculation as to their real source.

'Quine's Physicalism', published in R. Barrett and R. Gibson (eds.), *Perspectives on Quine* (Oxford) in 1990, takes up the idea that all meaning and intentional phenomena in general are indeterminate or underdetermined relative to all the physical facts. What notion of "physical" is needed to make physicalism a substantive and challenging, or even very interesting, thesis? It must be more than the ontological claim that the only objects that exist are physical objects. It is rather that "physical" predicates are sufficient to express everything that is 'fundamentally' or 'really' so. The question is whether that can be expressed and defended in a form which someone who believes there are mental or intentional facts would be threatened by or want to deny. This is another version of the question of whether meaning's being problematic or indeterminate relative to a certain class of facts can be shown to imply that meaning is problematic or indeterminate.

The question is taken up in another way in 'Meaning, Understanding, and Translation', which was published in the *Canadian Journal of Philosophy: Supplementary Volume* 16 in 1990. It overlaps closely in its middle parts with 'Wittgenstein on Meaning, Understanding, and Community', but is sufficiently different elsewhere, I hope, to warrant its appearance here. By taking seriously the threat of regress in the idea that words or marks or representations alone are enough to account for a person's meaning or understanding something, it shows that understanding cannot be simply an ability to translate some expressions into others. But the potential regress also shows that sufficient conditions will not be found by simply adding to those expressions some other entities, even entities 'in the mind', which they somehow stand for or express. The constraints on the proper understanding of understanding or meaning something can be fulfilled by invoking only the abilities or the knowledge of speakers, without additional entities, but the abilities or knowledge in question must be more than knowledge simply of the relations among certain mentioned expressions. In saying what a speaker knows, we make use of the same kind of semantic competence which we ascribe to him. The last part of the essay tries to blunt the force of one resource of Kripke's 'sceptic': the idea that a person's meaning some particular thing is underdetermined by all possible evidence, if that evidence is describable by 'Goodmanized' predicates like "grue" or "quus".

'The Background of Thought' is my contribution to a volume of critical essays on the philosophy of John Searle (E. LePore and R. Van Gulick (eds.), *Searle and His Critics*, (Oxford)) published in 1991. It starts from the familiar regress, which shows that mental or intentional facts cannot be understood solely in terms of the presence of objects, contents, or representations alone. Searle agrees, and thinks that is equivalent to, or implies, or in any case leads one to, what he calls a 'Background' that he thinks must be there to underlie our intentional states or to 'determine the conditions of satisfaction' which make a particular intentional state the state it is. Appeal to that 'Background' is said to be essential to any account of the mind, and to involve attitudes or capacities that are 'pre-intentional', 'non-representational', but 'mental'. I struggle with the question what this 'Background' is, and what it adds to the important, but largely negative, point that representations alone are not enough.

I find the three considerations Searle explicitly gives in favour of his 'hypothesis' inconclusive at best, but it seems they are not his real reasons. I try some informed speculation about why he wants to say the things he does, but even if I were right about that (which he says I am not), it would not explain what the 'Background' is, but only why he thinks there has to be some such thing. What he says about it, taken all together, seems to me to express conflicting demands. But if there has to be such a thing, the conflicts must be avoidable somehow. I have not seen how. Searle's reply in the volume in which my essay appeared leaves me feeling as if I had to comment on something happening under a huge blanket. A lot seems to be going on there, I'm not sure why, from where I stand it is difficult to tell what it is, and for every suggestion I come up with, I'm told that is not it.

'Quine on Exile and Acquiescence' was delivered in San Marino in 1990 and published in P. Leonardi and M. Santambrogio (eds.), *On Quine* (Cambridge) in 1995. The 'exile' in question is a 'cosmic exile' who would philosophize from a position outside all conceptual schemes or linguistic forms, with no serious views of his own about reality. Quine's opposition to any such enterprise is set against his own theorizing about language. His doctrine of the inscrutability of reference seems to produce a regress of more and more expressions without our ever reaching a point (according to the theory) at which we can understand them to mean or refer to something in particular. The essay explores what sense Quine can make of our 'acquiescing in our mother tongue and taking its words at face value'. It requires understanding or knowing the meanings of our words in a way that is not simply a matter of being able to translate them into other words, and not a matter of possessing or being acquainted with some item in the mind either. Being 'at home' in our language involves an ability to knowingly use words with certain meanings, and to respond intentionally to the words of others. It would appear to be an inescapable part of our making sense of the world in the ways we do. To reject the very fact of intentionality itself, as Quine sometimes does, would leave only expressions, or sounds and marks, without end.

'Mind, Meaning, and Practice' was my contribution to *The Cambridge Companion to Wittgenstein* (H. Sluga and D. Stern (eds.) (Cambridge)) published in 1996. It overlaps considerably with 'Wittgenstein on Meaning, Understanding, and Community', and to some extent with 'Meaning, Understanding, and Translation', but it aims to be more general and more comprehensive. It gives fuller treatment to some of the topics they deal with, and makes connections with issues they do not mention. The main theme is Wittgenstein's account of how we are led to misconstrue talk of meaning, understanding, and thought—in short, the mind—by thinking that something must accompany the sounds or marks we make, or the actions we perform, in order to make them meaningful or appropriately 'mental'. Resistance to that distorted conception of the mental is to be found in a proper understanding of the idea of meaning as use, and of what is required for what Wittgenstein calls 'ostensive teaching'.

The second half of the essay is an extended discussion of the claim of Kripke's 'sceptic' that there is no such thing as someone's meaning or understanding something by a particular expression. I raise doubts about that idea as an interpretation of Wittgenstein, and try to show that it rests on the requirement that one's understanding must somehow guide or instruct one in speaking or responding, which is something Wittgenstein rejects. It is conceded that there are many descriptions of what people do or have done which do not determine what they mean by the expressions they use. But because what they mean, or their meaning anything at all, is indeterminate relative to those facts, it does not follow that there is no such thing as their meaning something. With intentional or semantical terms we can capture the fact of their meaning what they do. I try to show that if facts expressible in that way are not available to us, we cannot make the right kind of sense of the linguistic behaviour that Kripke's 'sceptic' would account for simply in terms of the 'assertibility conditions' of sentences. I end with some speculation about why such facts might be held to be unavailable for the purposes of giving a philosophical account of meaning or understanding.

'The Theory of Meaning and the Practice of Communication' was presented to a conference on the philosophy of Donald Davidson at the Instituto de Investigaciones Filosóficas in Mexico in 1997, and published in *Crítica* in 1998. It is in part a gloss on Davidson's claim that there would be no such thing as a language if the views of language of many philosophers and linguists were correct. I take the misconstruals in question to centre on the idea of linguistic competence or understanding, which has been widely seen as a matter of applying general rules or conventions to particular acts of utterance. Even with what Davidson calls a theory of meaning for a particular language, which is something that speakers of that language can be said to know, it does not follow that speakers simply apply that general knowledge to particular utterances and derive what a speaker has said. The main difficulty I identify in all such theories is that they fall foul of the familiar regress; that is why what they require would make language impossible. The difficulty bedevils any account of understanding that is required to explain how knowledge of meaning is 'delivered' to the speaker, or 'guides' or 'instructs' him, and in that way explains his individual utterances or responses. Why theorists continue to insist on that requirement is something I speculate about along the same lines as in 'Mind, Meaning, and Practice': they feel that without it there could be no satisfactory general explanation of how meaning and understanding are possible.

'Private Objects, Physical Objects, and Ostension' is to be published in D. Charles and W. Child (eds.), *Essays on David Pears and Wittgenstein* (Oxford) in 2000. It is first a close examination of Pears's account of what he calls the 'private language argument' in Wittgenstein. I give reasons to doubt it as an interpretation of Wittgenstein's texts, and reasons not to endorse the argument he finds there, whether it is Wittgenstein's or not. I then give what seems to me the best account of what is going on in the texts Pears considers, while doing justice to much of what he rightly stresses. The essay expands on and supports in more detail the reading of Wittgenstein I introduced and sketched in 'Wittgenstein's Treatment of the Quest . . .'. It emphasizes the need to understand correctly the very special philosophical enterprise that Wittgenstein engages in, and what is to be expected from his philosophical writings. It touches again on the desire to explain thought and meaning somehow 'from outside' them, and on the philosophical dissatisfactions of finding ourselves able to understand ourselves, if at all, only 'from within'.

I

Wittgenstein and Logical Necessity

Michael Dummett has described Wittgenstein's account of logical necessity as a 'full-blooded conventionalism'.[1] On this view, the source of the necessity of any necessary statement is 'our having expressly decided to treat that very statement as unassailable' (p. 329). Even faced with a rigorous mathematical proof:

> at each step we are free to choose to accept or reject the proof; there is nothing in our formulation of the axioms and of the rules of inference, and nothing in our minds when we accepted these before the proof was given, which of itself shows whether we shall accept the proof or not; and hence there is nothing which *forces* us to accept the proof. If we accept the proof, we confer necessity on the theorem proved; we 'put it in the archives' and will count nothing as telling against it. In doing this we are making a new decision, and not merely making explicit a decision we had already made implicitly. (p. 330)

This implies that it is possible for someone to accept the axioms and the rules of inference and yet to reject the proof, without having failed to understand those axioms or rules. But, Dummett objects:

> We want to say that we do not know what it would be like for someone who, by ordinary criteria, already understood the concepts employed, to reject this proof . . . The examples given in Wittgenstein's book are—amazingly for him—thin and unconvincing. I think that this is a fairly sure sign that there is something wrong with Wittgenstein's account. (p. 333)

This essay was first published in *Philosophical Review*, 74 (October 1965).

[1] Michael Dummett, 'Wittgenstein's Philosophy of Mathematics', *Philosophical Review*, 68 (1959), 324. Page numbers alone in parentheses in the text always refer to this article. Parentheses containing '*PI*' refer to sections or pages of L. Wittgenstein, *Philosophical Investigations*, tr. G. E. M. Anscombe (Oxford, 1953). Those containing '*RFM*' refer to L. Wittgenstein, *Remarks on the Foundations of Mathematics*, tr. G. E. M. Anscombe (Oxford, 1956).

Dummett is obviously on strong ground here—it seems impossible to understand this alleged possibility—but I think Wittgenstein would agree. His examples are not designed to show that we do understand this. What is important for the problem of logical necessity is to explain what makes the denial of a necessary truth 'impossible' or 'unintelligible'. It is not enough to say that it is 'logically impossible', since an explanation of logical necessity is just what is in question. Dummett appears to agree with this (pp. 328–9). In the rest of this paper I shall try to say what, according to Wittgenstein, is responsible for the unintelligibility in such cases.

In defending the claim that he is not committed to saying that everybody could infer in any way at all, Wittgenstein points out that it is essential to inferring, calculating, counting, and so forth, that not just any result is allowed as correct. If everybody continues the series as he likes, or infers just any way at all, then 'we shan't call it "continuing the series" and also presumably not "inference"' (*RFM* I, 116). General agreement among people as to the correct results of inferences or calculations and general agreement in the results that one gets oneself at different times are both necessary in order for there to be inferring or calculating at all (*RFM* II, 66, 73). The same holds for counting, continuing a series, and so on. These are all activities in which the possibility of different results at different times and places is not left open. It is just here that a calculation differs from an experiment, where people at different times and places can get different results.

These remarks suggest that the source of necessity in inferring or calculating is simply that any activity in which just any results were allowed would not be *called* 'inferring', 'calculating', and so forth. In the case of drawing logical conclusions:

> The steps which are not brought in question are logical inferences. But the reason why they are not brought in question is not that they 'certainly correspond to the truth'—or something of the sort—no, it is just this that is called 'thinking', 'speaking', 'inferring', 'arguing'. (*RFM* I, 155)

This looks like the standard claim that all necessity finds its source in definitions or in the meanings of words. In inferring, one must write down 'q' after '$p \supset q$' and 'p' because to do otherwise is to cease to infer correctly, and correct inference is just 'defined' by the laws of logic. That is what we call correct inference. This would presumably mean that, since it is possible for something else to be meant by 'correct inference', it would also be possible for something else to be the conclusion. Despite suggestions of this 'standard conventionalism' in Wittgenstein, I agree with Dummett that he does not hold such a view, although it is not always easy to see how what he says differs from it.

The main target of Wittgenstein's writings on necessity is the Platonism of Frege and the early Russell. In this respect he and the logical positivists are alike. According to Platonism it would be impossible for someone, when given the order 'Add 2', to write down all the same numerals as we do up to '1000' and then to go on '1004, 1008, . . .', and still be able to justify his going on in that way. It would be impossible because it is simply wrong, in continuing the series '+2', to write down '1004' right after '1000'; that is not, in fact, the next member of the series. So the pupil must either have misunderstood the instructions or have made a mistake. Anyone who puts anything other than '1002' is wrong and should be declared an idiot or an incorrigible if he persists in his perversity. As Frege puts it: 'here we have a hitherto unknown kind of insanity'.[2]

The conventionalist's opposition to Platonism consists primarily in showing that our present ways of inferring, counting, calculating, and so forth, are not the only possible ones. But the standard conventionalist would also reject the alleged possibility on the grounds that the description of such a state of affairs is contradictory. If the person has understood the instructions, if he has just written down '1000', and if he is to continue following the instructions, then he *must* write down '1002'. Of course, he is free not to continue the series at all, or to claim that he has been following instructions like 'Add 2 up to 1000, 4 up to 2000', and so forth, but it is logically impossible (involves a contradiction) for him to have understood the instructions correctly and to write down '1004' right after '1000'. His claiming that '1004' is the correct step is a sufficient condition of his having abandoned the ordinary sense attached to the order 'Add 2'. That it is correct to write '1002' is already contained in the meaning of those instructions, and once one has agreed to follow them, then because they mean what they do there are certain steps which one logically must take.

[2] G. Frege, *Grundgesetze der Arithmetik* (Jena, 1903), p. xvi.

The crucial notion in this conventionalistic theory is that of understanding the meaning of a word or a rule, and this is something to which Wittgenstein devotes a great deal of attention. Part of his interest in it is in the sense, if any, in which someone's having understood the instructions somehow logically guarantees that he will write down '1002' right after '1000'. If this is logically guaranteed, then it would seem that his going on '1004, 1008, . . .' could be due only to misunderstanding or to a mistake; in any event, he could not have understood correctly. But what is it to understand correctly? What determines which move is the correct one at a given point? The answer would appear to be that the way the order was meant, or what was meant by the person giving the order, determines which steps are correct. But again, Wittgenstein asks, what shows which way the order was meant? It is not the case that the teacher very quickly thought of each particular step which he wanted the pupil to take, and even if he did, that would not show that 'meaning 1002, 1004, . . .' meant 'thinking of 1002, 1004, . . .' (*PI* 692). Rather, what the order means will be shown in the ways we use it, in what we do in following it, in the ways we are taught to use it, and so on (*RFM* I, 2).

If someone who had learned to continue various series just as we do began to differ from us when he went beyond any point he had reached in his training, would it follow that he simply had not understood the instructions? If he continued to do this, must we say that he is unintelligent, perhaps idiotic? Wittgenstein tries as follows to suggest negative answers to these questions:

> If my reply is: 'Oh yes of course, *that* is how I was applying it !' or: 'Oh! That's how I ought to have applied it—!'; then I am playing your game. But if I simply reply: 'Different?—But this surely *isn't* different!'—what will you do? That is: somebody may reply like a rational person and yet not be playing our game (*RFM* I, 115)

He tries to show that not all cases of deviating from what we expect or from what we all do in continuing the series can be put down to simple misunderstanding, stupidity, or deliberate perversity on the part of the pupil. It is almost certain in any particular case we come across that some discoverable mistake has occurred, and that the pupil will come to recognize this. But *must* he do so? Is there no possibility other than those mentioned above? The example is intended to suggest that there is. But the important, and difficult, problem is to say exactly what this alleged possibility comes to. Although Frege said it would be a new kind of insanity, 'he never said what this "insanity" would really be like' (*RFM* I, 151). To see what it would be like is to understand on what our being compelled in inferring, calculating, counting, and so forth, rests.

The person who continues the series '1004, 1008, . . .' is described as 'finding it natural' to go on in that way; it 'strikes him as the same' as he has done earlier. In trying to get such a person to continue the series as we do it would no longer be useful for us to go through the training and give him the old explanations over again. And providing him with a rule precisely formulated in mathematical terms would not avoid the difficulties, since it is just the possibility of his understanding such a rule that is in question.

> In such a case we might say, perhaps: It comes natural to this person to understand our order with our explanations as *we* should understand the order: 'Add 2 up to 1000, 4 up to 2000, 6 up to 3000, and so on.'
>
> Such a case would present similarities with one in which a person naturally reacted to the gesture of pointing with the hand by looking in the direction of the line from finger-tip to wrist, not from wrist to finger-tip. (*PI* 185)

For Wittgenstein, it will not be enough to object that, if we are patient and careful, surely we could eventually get the pupil to see that he is to make the same move after '1000' as before—that he is not to change the size of the steps. He is convinced that he is making the same move, and 'who says what "change" and "remaining the same" mean here' (*RFM* I, 113)? One is inclined to reply, I think, that nobody *says* what is the same and what is different; it is just a fact that the pupil is wrong in supposing that going on '1004, 1008, . . .' is doing the same as he was in writing down '2, 4, 6, . . .'. But is there some discoverable fact of which we are aware, and which he is missing? What sort of fact is it, and how could he be brought to acknowledge it? Trying to explain to him that he has not gone on in the same way would be like trying to teach someone how to carry out the order 'Go this way' when I point in a particular direction. If that person naturally reacted to the gesture of pointing by looking in the direction of the line from fingertip to wrist, it would not be enough to say to him, 'If I point this way (pointing with my right hand) I mean that you should go *this* way (pointing with my left hand in the same direction).' Isn't every explanation of how someone should follow an arrow in the position of another arrow?[3]

Or, to choose another example, suppose we come across some people who find it natural to sell wood, not by cubic measure or board feet as we do, but at a price proportionate to the area covered by the pile of wood, and they pay no attention to the height of the pile.

> How could I show them that—as I should say—you don't really buy more wood if you buy a pile covering a bigger area?—I should, for instance, take a pile which was small by their ideas and, by laying the logs around, change it into a 'big' one. This *might* convince them—but perhaps they would say: 'Yes, now it's a *lot* of wood and costs more'—and that would be the end of the matter. (*RFM* I, 149)

This case is analogous to that of trying to get the deviant pupil to see that the next step after '1000' is really '1002'.[4] But can we describe what these people do as 'selling wood the wrong way'? Is it a way whose 'incorrectness' we could point out to them? And surely it is not logically impossible for there to be such people: the example does not contain a hidden contradiction.

The natural reply to this example is that it shows only that such people mean by 'a lot of wood' and 'a little wood' something different from what we mean by it, and similarly, as Dummett suggests, anyone who agrees with us in accepting all the steps in a proof but who then refuses to accept what we all accept as the conclusion must be blind to the meaning that has already been given to the words in the premisses or in previous proofs. It seems as if he could not remain faithful to the meanings of those words and still reject the conclusion. Dummett concludes from this that he is

[3] L. Wittgenstein, *The Blue and Brown Books* (Oxford, 1958), 97.

[4] There are some important features of the two cases as presented which are not analogous. We are imagining a single pupil who makes a single deviant move after having done exactly as we had expected up till now, whereas the example of the wood-sellers is presented from the outset as one in which we come across a whole, flourishing society. Consequently, what appears to be a sudden and inexplicable change, or an individual aberration, in the former case is not present in the latter. Furthermore, and crucially, the society of wood-sellers is not our own, but the strange pupil has apparently sprung up right in our midst. I think that these and other disanalogies can be avoided by presenting both cases in the same way from the beginning, although Wittgenstein never does this. (Some of the difficulties which these differences appear to create for the later stages of my argument were pointed out to me by Professor Stanley Cavell.)

simply *deciding* to accept some particular statement as necessary in complete isolation from everything else he has accepted. This is why Wittgenstein is called a 'full-blooded' conventionalist. The strange people Wittgenstein describes differ from us only in having 'adopted different conventions'. But does it follow from the case which Wittgenstein tries to construct that the deviant pupil simply chooses to write '1004' and that his choice makes that the correct step? Can the people in Wittgenstein's examples properly be said to differ from us only in having adopted different conventions? I think the answer is 'No'. One thing implied by saying that we have adopted, or are following, a convention is that there are alternatives which we could adopt in its place. But in the case of writing '1002' right after '1000' there appear to be no alternatives open to us. It seems impossible to understand how we could 'adopt the convention' that writing '998, 1000, 1004, . . .' is going on in the same way, or taking steps of the same size. Surely if writing '998, 1000, 1002, . . .' is not taking steps of the same size, then nothing is.

I have been trying to suggest so far that for Wittgenstein such 'alternatives' are not inconceivable or unimaginable because they involve or lead to a logical contradiction. Just as there is no logical contradiction involved in the supposition that people might sell wood, and defend their doing so, in the way described earlier, so there is no logical contradiction involved in supposing that someone might agree with us in all uses of words or in all steps of a proof up to the present, and that he should now accept something different from what we all accept as the conclusion, without being simply idiotic or deliberately perverse. Wittgenstein's examples are designed to show this; it is part of the attack on Platonism. But as long as such alternatives are inconceivable in whatever sense, it looks as if Dummett is right in pointing out that 'we do not know what it would be like for someone who, by ordinary criteria, already understood the concepts employed, to reject the proof'. And if we do not know what this would be like, how can we find at all plausible Wittgenstein's purported examples of someone who 'replies like a rational person' and yet is not 'playing our game'? So it appears that, as Dummett says, Wittgenstein's examples are 'thin and unconvincing', as they presumably must be if they are supposed to be examples of something that is unimaginable or inconceivable.

This seems to present the interpreter of Wittgenstein with a choice between two alternatives. Either Wittgenstein has not succeeded in giving any clear or intelligible examples of people whose ways of calculating, and so forth, are radically different from ours, and therefore he has not begun to support his anti-Platonistic account of logical necessity; or else he has succeeded in giving intelligible, perhaps even convincing, examples which commit him to a 'full-blooded conventionalism'. And if the latter is the case, then Dummett's successful attack on radical conventionalism will be equally successful against Wittgenstein. But this choice is not an exhaustive one. There can be plausible examples to show the possibility of ways of counting, inferring, calculating, and so forth, different from ours, but which do not imply that our doing these things as we do is solely a result of our abiding by, or having adopted, certain more or less arbitrary conventions to which there are clear and intelligible alternatives. Nor do such examples imply that 'at each step we are free to accept or reject the proof' or that 'a statement's being necessarily true is solely a result of our having decided to treat that very statement as unassailable'. But at one point Wittgenstein says:

> So much is clear: when someone says: 'If you follow the rule, it *must* be like this', he has not any *clear* concept of what experience would correspond to the opposite.
>
> Or again: he has not any clear concept of what it would be like for it to be otherwise. And this is very important (*RFM* III, 29)

If this is true, how can he hope to be successful in giving examples of what it would be like for it to be otherwise, while still maintaining that there is logical necessity in such cases? How can he have it both ways? The solution to this dilemma is to be found in the explanation of why we do not have any clear concept of the opposite in the case of logical necessity, and why Wittgenstein speaks of our not having a *clear* concept here. How could we have any concept at all?

Wittgenstein gives many examples of people whose ways of inferring, counting, calculating, and so forth, are different in significant ways from ours. As well as the wood-sellers mentioned earlier, there might be others who sell wood at a price equal to the labour of felling the timber, measured by the age and strength of the woodsman. Or perhaps each buyer pays the same however much he takes (*RFM* I, 147). Also, there might be people who measured with soft rubber rulers, or with rulers which expanded to an extraordinary extent when slightly heated (*RFM* I, 5). Or suppose that people in their calculations sometimes divided by '(n-n)' and yet were not bothered by the results. They would be like people who did not prepare lists of names systematically (for example, alphabetically), and so in some lists some names would appear more than once, but they accept this without worrying (*RFM* V, 8). Or there might be people who count, but when they want to know numbers for various practical purposes ask certain other people who, having had the practical problem explained to them, shut their eyes and let the appropriate number come to them (*RFM* V, 14). There are many more such examples, merely mentioned or briefly discussed, throughout Wittgenstein's *Remarks*.[5] They are all intended to be analogous in various ways to the 'possibility' that someone might go on '1004' right after '1000' in continuing the series '+2'.

When first presented with these examples it seems that we can understand them, and that we can come to know what such people would be like. We do not happen to do things in these strange ways, but, it seems, we could. If these examples represent clear alternatives, then why doesn't it follow that our calculating, counting, measuring, and so forth, as we do is purely a matter of convention? If this is not a matter of convention, how can these examples be perfectly intelligible to us? In suggesting answers to these questions I will have begun to show how Wittgenstein can escape between the horns of the above dilemma.

When we look more closely at the examples, are they really as intelligible as they seemed at first? For instance, consider the people who sell wood at a price proportionate to the area covered by the pile of wood and who defend their doing so in the way described earlier. Surely they would have to believe that a one-by-six-inch board all of a sudden increased in size or quantity when it was turned from resting on its one-inch edge to resting on its six-inch side. And what would the relation between quantity and weight possibly be for such people? A man could buy as much wood as he could possibly lift, only to find, upon dropping it, that he had just lifted more wood than he could possibly lift. Or is there

[5] e.g. *RFM* I, 136, 139, 152, 168; II, 76, 78, 81, 84; III, 15, 17; IV, 5; V, 6, 12, 27, 29, 36, 42, 43, 44.

more wood, but the same weight? Or perhaps these people do not understand the expressions 'more' and 'less' at all. They must, if they can say, 'Now it's a lot of wood, and costs more.' And do these people think of themselves as shrinking when they shift from standing on both feet to standing on one? Also, it would be possible for a house that is twice as large as another built on exactly the same plan to contain much less wood. How much wood is bought need have no connection with how much wood is needed for building the house. And so on. Problems involved in understanding what it would be like to sell wood in this way can be multiplied indefinitely.

If so, then so far we do not really know what it would be like for us to sell wood, and to try to justify our doing so, in the way Wittgenstein has described. And we have already noted the difficulties in trying to understand the example of continuing the series '+2'. I think the initial intelligibility and strength of Wittgenstein's examples derive from their being severely isolated or restricted. We think we can understand and accept them as representing genuine alternatives only because the wider-reaching consequences of counting, calculating, and so forth, in these deviant ways are not brought out explicitly. When we try to trace out the implications of behaving like that consistently and quite generally, our understanding of the alleged possibilities diminishes. I suspect that this would happen with most, if not all, of Wittgenstein's examples, but I do not need to prove this in general, since if my interpretation is right these examples will fulfil their intended role whether or not this point holds.

The reason for this progressive decrease in intelligibility, I think, is that the attempt to get a clearer understanding of what it would be like to be one of these people and to live in their world inevitably leads us to abandon more and more of our own familiar world and the ways of thinking about it upon which our understanding rests. The more successful we are in projecting ourselves into such a world, the less we will have left in terms of which we can find it intelligible. In trying to understand these alleged possibilities, we constantly come across more and more difficulties, more and more questions which must be answered before we can understand them. But this is not to say that we do not understand them because they are 'meaningless' or 'contradictory', or because what they purport to represent is 'logically impossible'.

Wittgenstein's examples are intended to oppose Platonism by showing that calculating, counting, inferring, and so forth, might have been done differently. But this implies no more than that the inhabitants of the earth might have engaged in those practices in accordance with rules which are different from those we actually follow. It is in that sense a contingent fact that calculating, inferring, and so forth, are carried out in the ways that they are—just as it is a contingent fact that there is such a thing as calculating or inferring at all. But we can understand and acknowledge the contingency of this fact, and hence the possibility of different ways of calculating, and so forth, without understanding what those different ways might have been. If so, then it does not follow that those rules by which calculating, and so forth, might have been carried out constitute a set of genuine alternatives open to us among which we could choose, or even among which we could have chosen. The only sense that has been given to the claim that 'somebody may reply like a rational person and yet not be playing our game' is that there might have been different sorts of beings from us, that the inhabitants of the earth might have come to think and behave in ways different from their actual ones. But this does not imply that we are free to put whatever we like after '1000' when given the instructions 'Add 2', or that our deciding to put '1002' is what makes that the correct step. Consequently, Wittgenstein's examples do not commit him to a 'radical conventionalism' in Dummett's sense. In trying to explain more fully why he is not committed to this I will return to the sense in which he can be called a 'conventionalist'.

In several places Wittgenstein describes what he is doing in some such way as this:

> What we are supplying are really remarks on the natural history of man: not curiosities however, but rather observations on facts which no-one has doubted, and which have only gone unremarked because they are always before our eyes. (*RFM* I, 141)

What facts does he have in mind here, and what role do they play in his account of logical necessity? The reason for calling them 'facts of our natural history' is to emphasize both what I have called their contingency—that is, that they might not have obtained—and the fact that they are somehow 'constitutive' of mankind—that is, that their obtaining is what is responsible for human nature's being what it is.

Part of human behaviour consists of calculating sums, distances, quantities, of making inferences, drawing conclusions, and so forth. It is a fact that we engage in such practices: 'mathematics is after all an anthropological phenomenon' (*RFM* V, 26). There are various facts which make it possible for calculating to occur at all. For example, our memories are generally good enough for us not to take numbers twice in counting up to 12, and not to leave any out (*RFM* V, 2); in correlating two groups of five strokes we practically always can do so without remainder (*RFM* I, 64); somebody who has learned to calculate never goes on getting different results, in a given multiplication, from what is in the arithmetic books (*RFM* I, 112); and so on. The inhabitants of the earth might have lacked these and other simple abilities, and if so there would be no such thing as calculating at all. In that way the possibility of calculating depends on such contingent facts. These are examples of what Wittgenstein calls the 'physical', 'psychological', and 'physiological' facts which make activities such as calculating possible (*RFM* V, 1, 15).

A contingent fact which is responsible for our calculating as we actually do is the fact that we take '1002, 1004, . . .' to be going on in the same way as putting down '996, 998, 1000, . . .'. It is a fact that we naturally go on in this way, but people might not have done so. Since they might naturally have followed the rule in a different way, our rules alone do not logically guarantee that they will not be taken or understood in deviant ways. A rule itself does not make 'strange' ways of following it impossible, since a rule is not something which stands apart from our understanding of it, and which mysteriously contains within it all of its future applications. How we naturally understand and follow the rule determines which applications of it are correct, and the way a rule is followed will depend in part on what we take to be 'going on in the same way. . . . The use of the word "rule" and the use of the word "same" are interwoven' (*PI* 225). It is because people might not share our natural reactions, or might not be in accord with us in their 'judgements of sameness' that their understanding the instructions does not rule out their taking a different step from ours at some point while still finding what they have done to be in accord with the rule. So understanding the rule in the way we do depends on such things as finding it natural to go on to '1002' right after '1000'. That we take just the step we do here is a contingent fact, but it is not the result of a decision; it is not a convention to which there are alternatives among which we could choose. And that we share any such 'judgements' at all (whatever they might be) is also a contingent fact, but without this agreement there would be no understanding of any rules at all.

> If language is to be a means of communication there must be agreement not only in definitions but also (queer as this may sound) in judgements. This seems to abolish logic, but does not do so. (*PI* 242)

Those described as 'not playing our game' are the people who are not in accord with us in the 'judgements' on which the possibility of language and communication rests. Wittgenstein's examples of the possibility of people like this serve to bring out the contingency of the fact that, as things are, we are in accord in these 'judgements'. Anyone who did not go on as we do need not be simply continuing a different series (for example, 'Add 2 up to 1000, 4 up to 2000', and so forth), and in that way be 'playing a game' different from the one we happen to be playing; nor need he have misunderstood the instructions in a way that can be pointed out to him by more careful explanations. But someone like this would not be fully intelligible to us. Our relation to him would be like our relation to people who naturally reacted to the gesture of pointing by looking in the direction of the line from fingertip to wrist, or who sold wood in the way described earlier. It is not simply that they happen to have chosen to do things one way, and we happen to have chosen to do them differently, but that they would be different sorts of beings from us, beings which we could not understand and with which we could not enter into meaningful communication. They would ultimately be unfathomable to us (compare, for example, *RFM* I, 34, 61, 66, 152). In order to have a 'clear concept' of what it would be like to think and behave as they do we would have to be able to abandon many, if not all, of those 'judgements' on which our being able to think or conceive of anything at all rests.

What I have been saying will explain what would otherwise be a puzzling distinction which Wittgenstein makes in a well-known passage:

I am not saying: if such-and-such facts of nature were different people would have different concepts (in the sense of a hypothesis). But: if anyone believes that certain concepts are absolutely the correct ones, and that having different ones would mean not realizing something that we realize—then let him imagine certain very general facts of nature to be different from what we are used to, and the formation of concepts different from the usual ones will become intelligible to him. (*PI* p. 230)

The point of Wittgenstein's examples of people who do not 'play our game' is only to show that our having the concepts and practices we have is dependent upon certain facts which might not have obtained. They show only that 'the formation of concepts different from the usual ones' is intelligible to us; but it does not follow from this that those concepts themselves are intelligible to us. And since the intelligibility of alternative concepts and practices is required by the thesis of radical conventionalism which Dummett ascribes to Wittgenstein, I think that thesis is not borne out by Wittgenstein's examples.

The 'shared judgements' (for example, of sameness) upon which our being able to communicate rests, and which are responsible for our calculating, inferring, and so forth, as we do are not properly seen, then, as the results of free decisions in the manner of the logical positivists. They might have been different and, if they had been, then calculating, inferring, and so forth, would have been done differently. But this does not make them conventions in the positivists' sense. In defending the claim that we had made the correct move after '1000' in following the rule 'Add 2' we could ultimately get back to something like our 'shared judgement' that putting down '1002' is doing the same as we were doing earlier. There is nothing further we could appeal to. These 'judgements' represent the limits of our knowledge, and thus they have a role similar to the explicit conventions of the positivists.

From what has been said so far it might still look as if our 'sharing judgements' is nothing more than our all agreeing that certain propositions are true or unassailable. But the 'agreement' of which Wittgenstein speaks here is not the unanimous acceptance of a particular truth or set of truths.

'So you are saying that human agreement decides what is true and what is false?'—It is what human beings *say* that is true and false; and they agree in the *language* they use. That is not agreement in opinions but in form of life. (*PI* 241)

This 'agreement' is the universal accord of human beings in behaving in certain ways—those 'natural reactions' which we all share, or those human practices the engaging in which makes a creature human. Those are the 'facts of our natural history' which he is appealing to. The correctness of steps in calculating is not ultimately established on the basis of their agreeing with or being entailed by certain truths which we have accepted without foundation, or which are 'self-evident':

> The limits of empiricism are not assumptions unguaranteed, or intuitively known to be correct: they are ways in which we make comparisons and in which we act. (*RFM* V, 18)

This distinguishes Wittgenstein both from the Platonist and from the standard conventionalist. I shall comment on only one other aspect of this difference.

I have said that it is a 'fact of our natural history' in Wittgenstein's sense that we agree in finding certain steps in following a rule 'doing the same'. In some cases we all naturally go on in the same way from the steps which have already been taken. This is what makes it possible for us to follow any rules at all.

> And does this mean e.g. that the definition of 'same' would be this: same is what all or most human beings with one voice take for the same?—Of course not.
>
> For of course I don't make use of the agreement of human beings to affirm identity. What criterion do you use, then? None at all. (*RFM* V, 33)

But if there is no criterion for the truth of assertions of identity, how can we know they are true? Without a proof to the contrary, might not all human beings, for all their agreement, be wrong in supposing that writing '1002' is going on in the same way as writing '1000' after '998'? Wittgenstein replies that 'to use a word without a justification does not mean to use it wrongfully' (*RFM* V, 33). And in this case, at this stage, there is no 'justification' of the sort the empiricist seeks. But why not?

The correctness of particular calculations, inferences, and so forth, is decided by appeal to the rules, but can't we also ask whether those rules themselves are correct, whether our techniques of calculation, inference, and so forth, are the correct ones?

> The danger here, I believe, is one of giving a justification of our procedure when there is no such thing as a justification and we ought simply to have said: *that's how we do it*. (*RFM* II, 74)

The ultimate appeal in seeking a 'foundation' for our procedures of calculating, inferring, and so forth, can only be to 'ways in which we make comparisons and in which we act'. That is all that an account of the 'foundation' or 'source' of logical necessity can achieve. This perhaps helps to explain the point of passages like this:

> What has to be accepted, the given, is—so one could say—*forms of life*. (*PI* 226)

Because these procedures cannot be given a 'justification' it does not follow that they are shaky or unreliable, or that we are courting trouble if we decide to engage in them. We do not decide to accept or reject them at all, any more than we decide to be human beings as opposed to trees. To ask whether our human practices or forms of life themselves are 'correct' or 'justified' is to ask whether we are 'correct' or 'justified' in being the sorts of things we are.

At the end of his paper Dummett recommends interposing between the Platonist and constructivist pictures of thought and reality an intermediate picture

> of objects springing into being in response to our probing. We do not *make* the objects but must accept them as we find them (this corresponds to the proof imposing itself on us); but they were not already there for our statements to be true or false of before we carried out the investigations which brought them into being. (p. 348)

As far as I understand this, it seems to be just the picture to be derived from Wittgenstein if my interpretation is in general correct. Logical necessity, he says, is not like rails that stretch to infinity and compel us always to go in one and only one way; but neither is it the case that we are not compelled at all. Rather, there are the rails we have already travelled, and we can extend them beyond the present point only by depending on those that already exist. In order for the rails to be navigable they must be extended in smooth and natural ways; how they are to be continued is to that extent determined by the route of those rails which are already there. I have been primarily concerned to explain the sense in which we are 'responsible' for the ways in which the rails are extended, without destroying anything that could properly be called their objectivity.

2

Conventionalism and the Indeterminacy of Translation

In his early paper 'Truth by Convention' Quine asked what the thesis that the truths of logic and mathematics are true by convention comes to—what it means. His unsuccessful attempts to give it a plausible sense showed that the theory is deficient in crucial respects and that therefore the appeal to conventions cannot account for our knowledge in logic and mathematics. He concluded with the remark:

> We may wonder what one adds to the bare statement that the truths of logic and mathematics are *a priori*, or to the still barer behavioristic statement that they are firmly accepted, when he characterizes them as true by convention in such a sense.[1]

Much of Quine's subsequent philosophical effort has been to show that conventionalism adds nothing whatever to that barer behaviouristic statement.

One still hears the complaint that the most that Quine showed in 'Two Dogmas of Empiricism' was that several particular attempts to define analyticity are unsuccessful, but that he was wrong to conclude from this that analyticity cannot be defined, or that there is no distinction between analytic and synthetic statements. And it is obvious that to draw this inference would be a mistake. But it is equally obvious that Quine makes no such mistake. He says that although he has not dealt with all explanations of analyticity, what he has said can easily be extended to other possible definitions. And surely he is right in this. There is a general epistemological theory from which his arguments spring, and once one sees and understands that theory one has no difficulty in constructing objections to other accounts of analyticity. The general

This essay was first published in *Synthese*, 19 (1968–9).

[1] W. V. Quine, *The Ways of Paradox and Other Essays* (New York, 1966), 99.

theory is therefore an essential part of Quine's attack, and makes the last part of 'Two Dogmas', where that theory is outlined, extremely important, and not merely a dramatic overstatement of a brand of 'empiricism without the dogmas'.

If there were a distinction between analytic and synthetic statements, then among those statements we now accept as true there would be some which just happen to be true, which could turn out to be false tomorrow, and others which could never turn out to be false, which hold come what may. But:

> Any statement can be held true come what may, if we make drastic enough adjustments elsewhere in the system. Even a statement very close to the periphery can be held true in the face of recalcitrant experience by pleading hallucination or by amending certain statements of the kind called logical laws. Conversely, by the same token, no statement is immune to revision.[2]

If this is true then a search for a clear distinction between analytic and synthetic statements can yield nothing which has the epistemological force of the analytic–synthetic distinction as traditionally conceived.

Quine does not simply reject one or another particular theory of a priori knowledge and necessary truth; he denies the 'datum' which the appeal to analyticity was supposed to explain. If he is right the conclusion to be drawn is not that the explanation of the phenomenon of a priori knowledge along orthodox positivistic lines is deficient in some respects, but rather that *there is no such phenomenon* to be explained. We are mistaken at the outset to suppose that there is a class of statements which we could never be led to reject on the basis of sense-experience—we can decide on experiential grounds to give up any statement at all. Unlike the orthodox positivists, who described only 'necessary' truth as conventional, Quine in 'Two Dogmas' extends the realm of convention and decision to all the truths we accept; thus his attack on the conventionalist consists in outdoing him, in espousing 'a more thorough pragmatism'.[3] Because any statement can be accepted or rejected as a result of our decision, the search for a distinction between single statements that are known a priori and ones that are known a posteriori is doomed to failure. There is 'empirical

[2] W. V. Quine, *From a Logical Point of View* (Cambridge, Mass., 1953), 43.
[3] Ibid. 46.

slack' in all our beliefs, and since the whole body of our knowledge is 'underdetermined' by experience, accepting or rejecting particular items will always be a matter of decision.

Is Quine's general epistemological theory true? Is he justified in rejecting the a priori–a posteriori distinction on the grounds that no statement is immune to revision? In this paper I examine the extent to which the more recent arguments in chapter 2 of *Word and Object*[4] support his position. I think there are important consequences of those arguments that have not been clearly recognized. The aim of the chapter is to make plausible the following thesis about how much of language can be made sense of in terms of its stimulus conditions:

> the infinite totality of sentences of any given speaker's language can be so permuted, or mapped onto itself, that (a) the totality of the speaker's dispositions to verbal behavior remains invariant, and yet (b) the mapping is no mere correlation of sentences with *equivalent* sentences, in any plausible sense of equivalence however loose. Sentences without number can diverge drastically from their respective correlates, yet the divergences can systematically so offset one another that the overall pattern of associations of sentences with one another and with non-verbal stimulation is preserved. (p. 27)

Putting it interlinguistically, translation between languages is said to be 'indeterminate' in the sense that:

> manuals for translating one language into another can be set up in divergent ways, all compatible with the totality of speech dispositions, yet incompatible with one another. In countless places they will diverge in giving, as their respective translations of a sentence of the one language, sentences of the other language which stand to each other in no sort of equivalence however loose. (p. 27)

It is tempting to take the thesis of the indeterminacy of translation as a less metaphorical and more precise way of making Quine's earlier point that there is always some 'slippage' or 'empirical slack' between our full-blown language and the stimuli which give rise to our verbal behaviour. If we can produce two or more incompatible manuals for translating a foreigner's remark, all of which square with his dispositions to respond verbally to non-verbal stimuli, then the choice of one or another of those manuals is underdetermined

[4] W. V. Quine, *Word and Object* (Cambridge, Mass., 1960). Page references alone in parentheses in the text refer to this book.

by those dispositions and stimuli. Or, in the domestic case, if two non-equivalent sentences S_1 and S_2 are correlated in the mapping of the sentences, our saying S_1 rather than S_2 is not determined by sense-experience or by non-verbal stimulation alone. Since we are bound only by the need to square the totality of our utterances with experience we could decide either to say S_1 or to say S_2, as long as we made any changes required elsewhere in the system of sentences. On this suggestion, to say of a statement that it is open to revision is simply to say that its translation is indeterminate.

The thesis of the indeterminacy of translation would therefore constitute direct support for Quine's contention that *no* statement is immune to revision only if the translation of *every* statement is indeterminate. But Quine himself shows that this is not so. Both observation sentences and truth-functional logical truths can be translated without indeterminacy.

Among occasion sentences there is a spectrum of observationality running all the way from those like "Bachelor", whose utterance is due almost entirely to collateral information, to those like "Red", where collateral information makes almost no difference at all. Those nearer the "Red" extreme are observation sentences, and they are the linguist's best bet as starting-points for his radical translation. Any uncertainty affecting the translations of observation sentences is the normal inductive one, but there is no indeterminacy (pp. 42–4).

Another part of language directly accessible to radical translation is the truth-functional connectives. For every truth-function there are objective behavioural criteria in terms of assent and dissent for determining whether a particular foreign expression is to be translated as the truth-functional connective in question (pp. 57–8). Any particular hypothesis about the translation of a foreign expression as one of our familiar truth-functional connectives is of course open to falsification, but this again is characteristic of inductive hypotheses generally, and has nothing to do with indeterminacy as described by Quine. But if there are objective behavioural criteria for determining which native words correspond to our truth-functional connectives then we can also find some statements (the 'tautologies') from which the natives would not dissent under any non-inhibiting stimulatory conditions.

The translation of a foreign sentence S_1 is indeterminate if and only if there are at least two non-equivalent sentences S_2 and S_3 in the linguist's language such that no dispositions to verbal behaviour on the part of the natives are sufficient to decide between S_2 and S_3 as the translation of S_1. Or, avoiding a foreign language, the translation of a sentence S_1 is indeterminate in a given speaker's language if and only if there is at least one non-equivalent alternative to it, S_2, such that if all the sentences of that speaker's language are mapped onto themselves then S_1 is correlated with S_2 and the totality of the speaker's dispositions to verbal behaviour remains invariant. But for any observation sentence or truth-functional logical truth T_1, it is not the case that there is, in a given speaker's language, some non-equivalent alternative to it, T_2, such that if all the sentences of the speaker's language are mapped onto themselves then T_1 is correlated with T_2 and the totality of his dispositions to verbal behaviour remains invariant. If T_1 and T_2 are not equivalent, and yet can be translated on objective behavioural grounds, then the speaker's dispositions with respect to them must differ. Observation sentences and truth-functional logical truths are according to Quine's argument just those statements the differences among which *can* be determined objectively, on the basis of dispositions to verbal behaviour alone. Therefore their translation is not indeterminate, and so it is not the case that the translation of *every* sentence is indeterminate.

That Quine would approve of this conclusion is shown by his discussion of the doctrine of so-called 'pre-logical mentality'. Given the objective semantical criteria we have for the translation of logical connectives, the extreme claim that certain natives accept as true sentences translatable in the form '*p* and not-*p*' is said to be absurd. For truth-functional logic, 'fair translation preserves logical laws', and thus there is a general technique for accounting for all those cases where someone accepts 'a logic whose laws are ostensibly contrary to our own' (p. 59). Their apparent acceptance is in itself sufficient grounds for concluding that we have garbled the translation of some of the constituent logical connectives. The existence of objective behavioural criteria for the translation of logical connectives is incompatible with the indeterminacy of translation of truth-functional logical truths.

If to say of a statement that it is not immune to revision were to say only that its translation is indeterminate then Quine's arguments in *Word and Object* against the conventionalistic theory of necessary truth would be different from, and in fact incompatible with, the view outlined in 'Two Dogmas', even to the point of requiring some unavoidable or non-revisable statements. In 'Two Dogmas' *all* statements were said to be open to revision, but in *Word and Object* Quine shows that there is a class of statements whose translation is not indeterminate, and which are therefore not open to revision. But if they are not open to revision then they are unavoidable or without alternatives, and among them would be some of the statements that the positivists claimed were true solely by convention (viz., truth-functional logical truths). This, if true, would appear to be a direct refutation of the conventionalist, and so Quine would no longer be outdoing him by extending the sphere of convention and decision to all statements; on the contrary, he would be arguing that there are some statements to which there are no non-equivalent alternatives. Since those statements are not open to revision, their acceptance or rejection is not a matter of convention or decision at all. This is not a direct consequence of the indeterminacy of translation itself, but rather of the related claim that there are certain parts of a language whose translation is *not* indeterminate.

Does the argument as presently understood really refute conventionalism? Although it might well be a sufficient condition of a statement's being open to revision that its translation be indeterminate, it is not obvious that it is also a necessary condition. Quine claims that the translation of a tribe's truth-functional logical truths is not indeterminate, but the indeterminacy of which he speaks is always to be understood as indeterminacy relative to a given set of dispositions to verbal behaviour. Therefore his argument would show that there are no alternatives to our truth-functional logical truths, and hence that they are not open to revision, only if there were no relevant alternatives to our present verbal dispositions. But this is just what the conventionalist denies, since he believes that it is purely a matter of convention that we speak as we do. If our verbal dispositions determine our acceptance of a certain set of 'tautologies', then different dispositions could determine our acceptance of a different set. From the fact that we can objectively pick out a tribe's truth-functional connectives, and hence its tautologies, it does not follow that the tautologies we thereby discover will be the same as those we accept. Indeed, on Quine's view they couldn't be the same, given that the natives' dispositions differ from ours in relevant ways. So there will be alternatives to our truth-functional logical truths to the extent to which there are relevant alternatives to our present verbal dispositions. It is only because we speak as we do that we have the particular tautologies we have. Far from being a refutation, this is almost a classic statement of the conventionalist's position.

It is perhaps worth noticing that this shows our truth-functional logical truths to be true by convention in a literal sense only if we actually decided by convention to have the verbal dispositions we now have. That we did make such a decision is, to say the least, an unlikely hypothesis, and it is difficult to see what evidence there could possibly be for it. But it is too much to ask the conventionalist to prove that there actually was a time at which we explicitly decided to adopt the linguistic habits we now have, just as it is too much to ask for historical evidence concerning the date, location, and personnel of the original social contract among men. The fiction of a social contract is a way of characterizing the apparent obligations of an individual to his state, and it can be a true and illuminating description of that relation even if no such contract was ever drawn up. Similarly, the fiction of primordial linguistic conventions is a way of characterizing that alleged necessity we are under to accept certain statements as true, and it can be a true and illuminating description of that necessity even if no original conventions were ever actually made. Conventionalism amounts only to the claim that it is *just as if* we had freely adopted certain verbal dispositions. But is even that much the case?

Obviously our verbal dispositions might have been different from what they are now in all sorts of ways. We might have been disposed to utter "and" on all and only all those occasions on which we are now disposed to utter "or". We might have been disposed to utter "Rabbit" when and only when we are now disposed to utter "Tortoise", and so the stimulus meaning of "Rabbit" might have been different from what it is. But if our verbal dispositions were different in only these ways it would not follow that we accepted anything contrary to our present truth-functional logical truths. As long as there is only a class of stimulations prompting assent to "Rabbit", another prompting dissent, and perhaps a third which inhibits a verdict, then whatever those stimulations happen to be, the sentence "Rabbit and not-Rabbit" would command assent under all stimulations that would elicit a verdict to "Rabbit" at all. Verbal dispositions which differed from our present ones only in these ways would not commit their owners to different logical truths. The relevant differences in verbal dispositions must be more radical than this.

Suppose people could be conditioned to make one or the other of three or more incompatible verdicts to a queried sentence, rather than only two as they do now. There would then be a class of stimulations prompting assent to a given sentence, those prompting dissent, and those prompting some third response (and perhaps those which do not prompt any verdict at all). If there actually were some stimulations to which these people made the third response, then it would seem that we could find some compound sentences to which they would not assent under all stimulations which would elicit a verdict to the components, even though they were translations of sentences to which we *would* assent under all stimulations which would elicit from us a verdict to the components. If so, then according to Quine's argument what is a truth-functional logical truth for us would not be one for them. If there could be people with dispositions like this then there are alternatives to our truth-functional logical truths. The issue between Quine and the conventionalist therefore comes down to the question of whether relevantly different verbal dispositions of this sort are possible.

The conventionalist believes that on this point he has an airtight case, since it is a purely contingent fact that human beings respond verbally to sensory stimulation at all, and equally contingent that they respond in just the ways they now do. But a contingent fact is one that might not have obtained, so it follows that there *could* be beings with verbal dispositions of the required kind, even if there are none in fact. Quine does not deny the premisses of this argument; his opposition to it consists primarily in his rejection of the particular notion of possibility on which it depends. And this rejection in turn can be supported by the general considerations about language and meaning established in *Word and Object*.

To show that there could be three or more distinct and incompatible classes of stimulations—those commanding either assent, dissent, or some third response—or that there could be three or more 'truth-values', it is not sufficient to talk vaguely about an unspecified third response, or simply to write down matrices in which any one of three different symbols can be assigned to each component of compound sentences. One must be able to explain, or to make intelligible, what that third response is, or what the third symbol stands for. This explanation must be given in a language that we can understand, since only then will the alleged possibility have been shown to make sense within the only terms we have for making sense of anything. And thus considerations about determinacy and indeterminacy of translation are relevant.

The difficulty of specifying what this third response would be is the same as the difficulty facing a linguist who claims to have discovered a tribe which makes this third response and therefore accepts a different set of truth-functional logical truths from ours. What objectively discoverable native behaviour would provide the linguist with any warrant for concluding that they are making the third response to queried sentences? In order to support the conventionalist's conclusion the third response must be incompatible both with assent and with dissent, and yet be a genuine verdict, and not simply the expression of uncertainty, doubt, inclination to believe or to disbelieve, ignorance, or whatever. How could the linguist translate the expression for this third response into our language, and thereby come to understand it? Successful translation requires that there already exist in our language an expression for a genuine verdict incompatible both with assent and with dissent. But if there is such an expression already in our language then we too can make the third response to queried sentences, and so we would accept the same truth-functional logical truths as the hypothetical natives. If there are objective semantical criteria for translating truth-functional connectives, and hence tautologies, then our having successfully translated a tribe's language is incompatible with their accepting tautologies different from ours.

Therefore the conventionalist cannot specify how our verbal dispositions would have to differ in order for us to accept truth-functional logical truths which are genuine alternatives to our present ones. If he can make this alleged possibility intelligible, then it is not an alternative to what we can now say and understand; and if he cannot make it intelligible, then his argument fails.

A similar, but weaker, conclusion can be shown to hold even for those parts of language whose translation is indeterminate. The aim of translation into English is to correlate the various expressions of a foreign language with English ones; or, in general, to correlate expressions in a foreign language with those in the home language. Analytical hypotheses are required wherever the translation of terms is in question. They are principles to the effect that, for example, the term "gavagai" means "rabbit" rather than "rabbit stage", or that a particular foreign construction is to be translated as "are the same" rather than "are stages of the same animal". The choice among analytical hypotheses is not determined by the verbal behaviour, or dispositions to verbal behaviour, of the natives, and so there are no analytical hypotheses whose truth or falsity can be established on objective grounds (pp. 58–72).

In order to achieve the goal of correlating foreign expressions with expressions in the home language we obviously must formulate our analytical hypotheses in the home language. It would be useless to put forward analytical hypotheses associating a foreign expression with something not found in the home language at all. So the range of possible analytical hypotheses about a particular foreign expression or construction is restricted to those which can actually be formulated in the home language in such a way that their truth or falsity cannot be established on the basis of behaviour, or dispositions to behaviour, alone.

This shows, with respect to general terms for kinds of things, for example, that it is impossible for the translation of a foreign language to reveal that speakers of that language refer to or talk about types of things which we have no means of referring to or talking about in the home language, or that they do so in ways that have no analogue in the home language. Our having successfully translated a tribe's language is incompatible with their having such 'mechanisms of reference'. The hypothesis that there could be a language of this sort suffers from the same malady as the conventionalist's claim about the possibility of truth-functional logical truths different from ours. If the alleged possibility can be made intelligible then we do have means of referring to things of the type in question, and so the mechanisms of reference will not be different after all; and if it cannot be made intelligible then the possibility of mechanisms of reference different from ours will not have been demonstrated. In either case it follows that our present mechanisms of reference are not open to revision.

The point comes out more clearly in the domestic case. Because of the indeterminacy of translation the sentences of a single language can be mapped onto themselves in such a way that the totality of dispositions to verbal behaviour by speakers of the language remains invariant, and yet the mapping is not simply a correlation of sentences with equivalent sentences. If this is a necessary condition of revisability, then the alternatives among which we must choose when revising a particular statement will always have to be statements which can already be made in the language in question. There are no alternatives to saying one or the other of the various alternative things we can already say. Unlike the case of truth-functional logical truths, there will be *some* genuine alternatives here, but they will not include anything we are not now in a position to say and to understand. For observation sentences and tautologies there are no alternatives at all, and so they are not open to revision; for the rest of language there are alternatives, but they are not alternatives the adoption of which would take us beyond the language we now use and understand. This is the core of Quine's opposition to conventionalism.

For the conventionalist there are available to us an indefinitely large number of alternative 'conceptual schemes' or 'linguistic frameworks' in terms of which we can understand our experience, and we are free to choose among them purely arbitrarily, or at best on pragmatic grounds.[5] The only limitation on possible conceptual schemes is our limited ingenuity in inventing them. Each framework differs from every other in containing a different set of analytic statements or 'meaning postulates', and so in choosing one particular scheme we must accept as true all those purely 'formal' statements that are true by virtue of the meanings of the terms of that particular framework. These truths constitute the essence of the particular conceptual scheme, and so to reject them is simply to reject the scheme itself. Our acceptance of these so-called 'necessary' truths is nevertheless purely conventional, since we are always free to give up any particular conceptual scheme and adopt another from among the indefinitely many open to us.

Quine's arguments in *Word and Object* show that there is no such universe of possible alternatives open to us. Revisability is a property only of particular sentences, or restricted sets of sentences, and it cannot extend to the total system itself. It makes no sense to speak of rejecting our present language or conceptual scheme and choosing one of the alternatives to it, since we can give no content to the notion of a conceptual scheme or language which is a

[5] Cf. e.g. R. Carnap, 'Empiricism, Semantics, and Ontology', Appendix A in *Meaning and Necessity*. 2nd edn., (Chicago, 1956).

genuine alternative to our present one. No revision open to us can take us beyond the language we now use and understand—any 'alternative' is either something we already understand and can make sense of, or it is no alternative at all. Any difference between ourselves and other tribes can therefore be only partial, and will disappear when the whole language is taken into account.[6] The same holds for our own domestic case, and it is here that the indeterminacy of translation reveals the 'empirical slack' in our beliefs. The scope for the revisability of beliefs extends to all those incompatible systems of analytical hypotheses that we could adopt in attributing 'strange' views to a compatriot while still conforming to all his verbal dispositions.

> For our own views could be revised into those attributed to the compatriot . . . no conflicts with experience could ever supervene, except such as would attend our present sensible views as well. To the same degree that the radical translation of sentences is underdetermined by the totality of dispositions to verbal behavior, our own theories and beliefs in general are underdetermined by the totality of possible sensory evidence time without end. (p. 78)

If revisions can only be partial at best, and there are not a number of alternative conceptual schemes among which to choose, then clearly we must rely on the ongoing conceptual scheme we now possess. So the arguments of *Word and Object* provide the epistemological backing for Quine's repeated appeal over the years to Neurath's picture of science as a ship at sea, which, if we are to rebuild it, we must rebuild plank by plank while still staying afloat in it.

> Our boat stays afloat because at each alteration we keep the bulk of it intact as a going concern. Our words continue to make passable sense

[6] To the claim that we could discover completely disparate total schemes 'one may protest that two systems of analytical hypotheses are, as wholes, equivalent so long as no verbal behavior makes any difference between them; and, if they offer seemingly discrepant English translations, one may again argue that the apparent conflict is a conflict only of parts seen out of context. . . . When two systems of analytical hypotheses fit the totality of verbal dispositions to perfection and yet conflict in their translations of certain sentences, the conflict is precisely a conflict of parts seen without the wholes. The principle of indeterminacy of translation requires notice just because translation proceeds little by little and sentences are thought of as conveying meanings severally' (pp. 78–9).

because of continuity of change of theory; we warp usage gradually enough to avoid rupture. . . . We are limited in how we can start even if not in where we may end up. To vary Neurath's figure with Wittgenstein's, we may kick away our ladder only after we have climbed it. (p. 4)

And this in turn is behind Quine's apparently conservative attitude towards theoretical change and revision. Simplicity is a desideratum in theory construction and selection, but so also is 'familiarity of principle', which counsels 'minimum revision' and favours 'the inherited or invented conceptual scheme of one's own previous work' (p. 20). This 'taste for old things' is not just an idiosyncrasy of Quine's; it is the only course open to anyone in his attempts to fit theories to experience.

What is open to us in the way of new modes of speech and thought is controlled or determined by what we have now. Any allegedly new possibility must be capable of being fitted into, or understood in terms of, our present conceptual or linguistic apparatus. This means that what can count as possible is not as wide open as the positivists have claimed. What is a possibility for us is always a function of our actual ways of thought and speech and the state of our knowledge at the time, and so the notion of a possibility or a possible world *sub specie aeternitatis*, without connection with any actual set of verbal dispositions and beliefs, makes no sense. This is the analogue for possibility of Goodman's discovery that whether or not something confirms a particular hypothesis is always a function of the language in terms of which the 'evidence' and the hypothesis are formulated.[7] That something either does or does not confirm a particular hypothesis *sub specie aeternitatis*, completely independently of any actual language, would imply that anything confirms the hypothesis, just as the corresponding view about possibility would imply that nothing is impossible. It is useless to protest 'But surely such-and-such either is or is not *really* possible, whatever our present ways of thinking happen to be', since this assumes that we can somehow detach ourselves from our ways of thinking and confront the world directly in order to see what is possible and what is not. It is precisely because this manœuvre is impossible that we are forced to improve our conceptual scheme only by internal revision, on grounds of economy,

[7] N. Goodman, *Fact, Fiction, and Forecast* (Cambridge, Mass., 1955), esp. ch. IV.

simplicity, and convenience, and not by any 'direct' check of its correspondence with reality.[8]

It might be thought that this view is too unrealistically confining or restrictive, that it rules out all real novelty and change. Any attempt to demonstrate the possibility of forms of thought or speech not now in our repertoire has been shown to be doomed to failure. Such a demonstration could succeed only by making the alleged possibilities intelligible to us now, thereby showing, contrary to hypothesis, that they are in our linguistic repertoire after all. This is tantamount to arguing that ways of thought and speech not presently intelligible to us are not possible, and so any real novelty in human thought would be impossible after all. We would be stuck not only with the same old ship, but also with all those familiar weather-beaten planks that have always held it together. If Quine is right, how can what is unintelligible to us at one time come to be intelligible to us at another?

Quine's answer is that change is only possible against an unchanging background of theory or discourse—'we warp usage gradually enough to avoid rupture'—and so revisions can be piecemeal at best.[9] A series of small changes can cumulatively amount to a novel theory or to new linguistic forms even though each individual step is small enough not to count as a real change of meaning or as a case of something previously unintelligible becoming intelligible. The indeterminacy of translation implies that sameness of meaning is not transitive,[10] and so genuine novelty can arise after several small changes of the familiar into the still familiar.

It might be felt that this reply is less than satisfactory. As long as even gradual change is possible it will still be possible for our verbal dispositions with respect to truth-functional connectives to change, ever so slowly, into those of the imagined natives who make the third response to some queried sentences. There would then be

[8] Cf. e.g. Quine, *From a Logical Point of View*, 78–9. This theme is elaborated in Quine's Dewey Lectures, published as 'Ontological Relativity', *Journal of Philosophy*, 65 (1968), 185–212.

[9] 'Yet we must not leap to the fatalistic conclusion that we are stuck with the conceptual scheme that we grew up in. We can change it bit by bit, plank by plank, though meanwhile there is nothing to carry us along but the evolving conceptual scheme itself' (Quine, *From a Logical Point of View*, 78–9).

[10] This point is expounded and defended in more detail in Gilbert Harman, 'Quine on Meaning and Existence, I', *Review of Metaphysics*, 21 (1967), 124–51, esp. 148–50.

compound sentences to which we would not assent under all stimulations eliciting a verdict to their components, even though we now do assent to them under all such stimulations. We would then have given up some of the statements we now accept as truth-functional logical truths, thereby showing that they are revisable after all. But the translation of truth-functional logical truths was said to be determinate, so this alleged possibility appears to be incompatible with the assumption that a statement is open to revision if and only if its translation is indeterminate. If that assumption is rejected in favour of the weaker one that indeterminacy of translation is only a sufficient, but not a necessary, condition of revisability, then Quine's arguments in *Word and Object* cannot have the kind of force against conventionalism I have been suggesting, since the determinacy of translation of truth-functional logical truths would not then show that they are unrevisable and without alternatives. But the stronger assumption, along with the determinacy of translation of truth-functional logical truths, seems to imply that it is impossible for our verbal dispositions with respect to truth-functional connectives ever to change into those of the imagined natives. Novelty of that particular sort would appear to be forever precluded by Quine's argument. But surely it is possible.

I think that much of the apparent strength[11] of this objection comes from its uncritical but very natural employment of the notion of possibility Quine rejects. He shows that it is now impossible for us to revise our linguistic dispositions, and thereby our truth-functional tautologies, into those of the natives. But it does not follow from this that we can never have dispositions like theirs. To suppose that it does follow is to suppose that some things really are or are not impossible *sub specie aeternitatis*, or that what is impossible now will remain so for ever. But what is unrevisable for us now, and therefore presently without alternatives, can become revisable later. There is no metaphysically guaranteed eternal unrevisability or impossibility, even though many of our present beliefs, including the truth-functional tautologies, might never in fact be given up during the rest of the history of human life. We can agree that a particular belief is now unrevisable while

[11] I am not satisfied that the whole point of the objection is met in this way. There is a difficult and largely unexplored problem of how conceptual novelty, which seems to occur, is really possible. I suspect that this is a problem for everyone, not just for Quine.

still acknowledging that it is possible for us sometime to be led to give it up, since we can revise beliefs only when viable alternatives to them are available. Whether such alternatives are available at a given moment depends on countless complicated but still contingent facts, and we can reasonably expect many of these contingencies to change over time.[12] What cannot happen at one time often happens at another.

[12] For a good discussion of some of these factors and how they operate, see Hilary Putnam, 'The Analytic and the Synthetic', in H. Feigl and G. Maxwell (eds.), *Minnesota Studies in the Philosophy of Science*, iii (Minneapolis, 1962).

3

Inference, Belief, and Understanding

Lewis Carroll's Achilles[1] has written in his notebook:

A: Things that are equal to the same are equal to each other.
B: The two sides of this Triangle are things that are equal to the same.
Z: The two sides of this Triangle are equal to each other.

Someone might accept the hypothetical proposition that if A and B are true then Z is true without accepting either A or B (although Achilles is surely right that such a person would be wise to abandon Euclid and take to football). Both the tortoise and Achilles also agree that someone could accept A and B without accepting the conditional 'If A and B are true then Z is true.' The tortoise challenges Achilles to consider him as such a person and to 'force him, logically, to accept Z as true' (ibid.). The story suggests that he can never succeed.

The tortoise claims at the outset not to accept the conditional (call it C) that if A and B are true then Z is true,[2] but he gladly accepts it as soon as Achilles asks him to. Since he insists that every proposition he accepts should be written down, C is duly added to A, B, and Z in Achilles' notebook. When the tortoise points out, as before, that it is possible to accept A, B, and C without accepting the conditional that if A and B and C are true then Z is true, Achilles asks him to accept one more conditional. He agrees, and that conditional in turn is added to the notebook and called D. Before the same kind of interchange can be repeated the narrator, having pressing business at the bank, is obliged to leave. We are left to draw our own moral.

It seems to me that there is no sound moral to be drawn from

This essay was first published in *Mind*, 88: 350 (April 1979).

[1] Lewis Carroll, 'What the Tortoise Said to Achilles', *Mind* (1895), 278.

[2] Here I deviate slightly from Lewis Carroll's story in which the statement called C is 'If A and B are true Z must be true' (p. 279). The change does not affect any point to be made about the story. See n. 4 below.

the story about the nature of validity or logical consequence as such. Lewis Carroll does not succeed in showing that Z does not quite follow from A and B alone and that something else is therefore needed to complete the implication. The conjunction of A and B does imply Z, whatever the tortoise happens to think about it. If we agree with J. F. Thomson that 'the intention of the story is, plainly enough, to raise a difficulty about the idea of valid arguments',[3] it is difficult to see what can be learned from it. He concludes that no point legitimately raised by Lewis Carroll amounts to a difficulty about the idea of valid arguments and that a number of sound points that can be made about valid arguments are not actually made by the story. But I think there remains a significant lesson to be learned from Achilles and the tortoise. The story shows something interesting and important about inference and belief, and the lesson can be fully appreciated only if those puzzling notions are clearly distinguished from the better-understood notions of logical consequence and truth.

Thomson argues that the alleged infinite regress of the story 'is just an infinitely long red herring' (p. 105) since Achilles is wrong to suppose that if the tortoise does not accept Z although he has accepted A and B then something must be added to those premisses to force him to accept that conclusion. The tortoise thinks anyone who accepts A and B but does not accept the conditional C is not 'as yet under any logical necessity to accept Z as true' (Carroll, p. 239); Thomson says he is wrong since Z follows logically from A and B and so anyone who accepts A and B is already 'under a logical necessity' to accept Z (p. 96). There is no reason to start on the regress at all.

Achilles resorts to what he regards as a strengthening of the original argument in order to force the tortoise to the conclusion. He adds to the premisses A and B the conditional C which has those premisses as antecedent and the conclusion Z as consequent. Thomson argues that no such manœuvre can help establish the conclusion; 'strengthening' an argument in that way is always either redundant or futile.

An argument may fail to establish its conclusion on either or both of two counts; it may have one or more false premises, and, independently, the

[3] J. F. Thomson, 'What Achilles Should Have Said to the Tortoise', *Ratio* (1960), 95. The paper is full of much good sense and many helpful points that I do not discuss.

relation required to hold between the premises and the conclusion may not hold. It is clear that a strengthened argument will always be valid and so will never fail on the second count, and that if an argument fails on any count its strengthening must fail on the first of them. In particular, if an argument fails by not having enough premises its strengthening will escape that weakness but must, just because it is the strengthened form of that argument, fail by having an unacceptable premise. It follows that from the point of view of getting arguments which establish their conclusions the operation of strengthening is either redundant or futile. (pp. 97–8)

It is clear how a strengthened argument will always be valid; in fact, it will be truth-functionally valid. But it is obviously not true that if an argument fails on either of Thomson's counts then its strengthening must fail by having a false premiss. An argument that is invalid although its premisses and conclusion are true will be 'strengthened' into a valid argument all of whose then-augmented premisses will still be true, as will the conclusion. The hypothetical added in the operation of 'strengthening' such an argument will not be a logical or necessary truth[4] (if it were, the original argument would have been valid), but it will have a true antecedent and a true consequent, and so it will be true. If we are restricted to the notions of truth and validity we can say that an argument 'establishes' its conclusion if and only if it is valid and has all true premisses. But then to produce an argument that 'establishes' its conclusion in this restricted sense it will be enough simply to 'strengthen' an argument that is invalid but has all true premisses and a true conclusion. Therefore in this purely logical sense of 'establish' the operation of 'strengthening' is not always either redundant or futile in producing arguments that 'establish' their conclusion. If we took Thomson to be making a point only about the idea of valid arguments then what he says would be incorrect.

But Thomson is right to say that if an argument is invalid then it is futile simply to go in for the operation of 'strengthening' if you

[4] Thomson defines 'strengthening' as follows: 'Given an argument with premises $P_1, P_2, \ldots, P_k$ and conclusion Q let us call $(P_1 \& P_2 \& \ldots \& P_k) \rightarrow Q$ the hypothetical *associated with* that argument, and let us call the argument with the same conclusion and premises $P_1, P_2 \ldots, P_k, (P_1 \& P_2 \& \ldots \& P_k) \rightarrow Q$ the *strengthened* form of the original argument and a strengthened argument' (p. 97). It is clear that '$P_1 \& P_2 \& \ldots \& P_k \rightarrow Q$' is to be understood as a material conditional. Thomson also removes the 'must' from Lewis Carroll's conditional C. I simply follow him in doing so.

want to establish its conclusion. That, as he says, will always leave you with an 'unacceptable' premiss. But its 'unacceptability' is not equivalent to falsity, and the failure of the 'strengthened' argument to establish the conclusion is not equivalent to invalidity, so what is right in what Thomson says is not a point about valid arguments and the truth-values of their premisses, and so not a point about 'establishing' conclusions in the purely logical sense at all. 'Strengthening' alone is futile in establishing conclusions because it leaves you with a premiss that is in some way *epistemically* unacceptable even if it is true and its addition to the original premisses would yield a valid argument that 'establishes' its conclusion in the purely logical sense. So the admitted futility of 'strengthening' an argument is an epistemic matter that must be seen to be true independently of purely logical considerations.

The tortoise challenges Achilles to 'force' him to *accept* something, and if there really is a difficulty about that we should not expect it to be expressible in purely logical terms concerned only with the relations among propositions. Achilles says to the tortoise that if he refused to accept Z after accepting A and B and C and D then 'Logic would take you by the throat and *force* you to do it!' (Carroll, p. 280). But how could logic do that? Logic simply states what is the case, or that something implies something else; it does not state that people must accept certain things, or even that they must accept certain things if they already accept certain other things. As the tortoise remarks, 'Whatever *Logic* is good enough to tell me is worth *writing down*' (Carroll, p. 280), but all that gets written in the notebook is another conditional.

It is perhaps natural to say that the tortoise *must* accept Z since it follows from A and B, which he accepts. But even when the logical relations between A and B and Z are perfectly clear this 'must' is still unexplained. Certainly it is not the same as the 'must' in 'If A and B are true then Z must be true'. It is impossible for A and B to be true and Z false, but it is not impossible for 'The tortoise believes A' and 'The tortoise believes B' to be true even though 'The tortoise believes Z' is false. Or if for some reason that is in fact impossible,[5] its impossibility does not follow from the admitted impossibility of Z's being false while A and B are true, so it still needs to be explained. Someone might accept two proposi-

[5] I discuss later some reasons for thinking it might be impossible.

tions without knowing or even suspecting that they together imply some specified third proposition. He might never have heard of that third proposition at all, or if he had, he might have no opinion about it one way or the other. He might even believe it to be false, and so if he thinks of it at all he will think it does not follow from the first two. Since the tortoise accepts A and B, and Z follows from them, he might be said to be 'logically committed' to Z. But if that means only that Z follows from A and B, which he already believes, then it tells us only what we knew at the outset about the logical relations between A and B and Z. That does not help us understand how or why the tortoise in accepting A and B is 'forced' to accept Z.

Thomson tries to explain the 'must' by saying:

> anyone who accepts the premises and denies the conclusion has committed himself to at least one falsehood. This is the threat behind the 'must'. 'If you assert the premises and deny the conclusion, you will have said at least one false thing, however the facts may turn out to be.' (p. 100)

I do not think this adds anything to a description of the logical relations among the propositions in question; it does not help explain any sense in which the tortoise must accept Z. Certainly anyone who accepts the premisses and denies the conclusion of a valid argument will have accepted at least one falsehood, but that is not the position the tortoise is in. He accepts the premisses but he does not accept the conclusion; he neither accepts it nor rejects it. If he asserts everything he accepts he will not assert any falsehoods. Because there is no inconsistency among all the things he accepts, the threat of the 'must' or the sense in which he is 'forced' to accept Z is not explained by saying that we know he has accepted one false thing however the facts turn out to be. Of course we know that if he accepts A and B and has any belief one way or the other about Z then either he will accept Z or he will believe at least one falsehood. But that says no more than that Z follows from A and B, and we knew that at the outset.

It is sometimes necessary or helpful in a discussion to say to someone 'If you accept this then you *must* accept that.' It can be a way of pointing out to him that what he has already accepted gives him excellent reason for accepting something else. The remark can be made when there is a valid argument from the things he already accepts to the proposition in question or when his reasons are in some other way conclusive. Thomson rightly emphasizes that to point out that someone has good or conclusive reasons for believing something is not to state another reason he has to believe it.[6] The remark is a comment on the original premisses; it says something about them, but it does not give another part of the original argument. So when Achilles is led to remark at each point that if everything the tortoise has accepted so far is true then Z must be true he should not be seen as offering the tortoise yet another reason to believe Z. If he were doing that, he would never find enough reasons.

Thomson thinks the point is obvious and that we do not need Lewis Carroll's regress to establish it. He thinks it rests on nothing more than the truism that a conditional proposition cannot be part of its own antecedent (pp. 101–2). If someone who accepts premisses A and B is told that he must accept Z because if A and B are true then Z is true, he has not thereby been given another premiss to accept. The original argument was from A and B to Z, and the hypothetical associated with that argument has those premisses as antecedent and that conclusion as consequent. What he is told could not therefore be a premiss of the original argument since that would imply that that hypothetical (which has all the premisses of the argument in its antecedent) contains itself as part of its own antecedent. Since that is clearly absurd on the face of it Thomson concludes that we do not need Lewis Carroll's story to convince us that asserting that if A and B are true then Z is true is not giving a further reason beyond the truth of A and B for the tortoise to believe Z.

Certainly we do not need Lewis Carroll's regress to show us that a conditional cannot contain itself as part of its own antecedent. But I think there is more than that behind the insistence that a statement linking accepted premisses with a prospective conclusion—or in general a statement linking one's reasons with that for which they are reasons—cannot always be taken as a further reason one has for believing the conclusion. It is a point about inference and belief, and not simply about consequence and truth, or the logical relations among propositions. Whether or not Lewis Carroll had it in mind there is an important moral to be drawn from his story.

[6] There is a very good discussion of this point on pp. 100–2 of Thomson's paper.

What is involved in someone's believing something on the basis of something else he knows or believes? This is not simply a question about the relation between the propositions the person believes. In Lewis Carroll's story the reasons are deductively sufficient for the conclusion, but once we abandon the idea that the story is concerned with valid arguments as such we can see that it raises a quite general problem about one belief's being inferred from or based on another, whether the one belief implies the other or not. If a person knows or believes that P is true and on that basis believes that Q is true then an Epistemologist's Notebook in which the person's state is fully described would list both P and Q among his beliefs, but the relation between P and Q, and therefore the kind of reason P is will vary from one case to another.[7] It might be that P implies Q, or that if P were to be true then Q would be true, or simply that if P is true then Q is true, or even that P is reason to believe Q.[8] But in each case, when we had written P in our notebook we would have identified a reason he has for believing Q. The correct answer for him to give when asked for his reason for believing Q is 'P'.[9]

But if we who wish to represent his belief in Q as based on P are to write in our notebook everything his having that belief on that basis consists in then when we have written only P and Q we will not have written enough. Someone can believe P and believe Q and still not believe Q on the basis of P whatever the relations between the propositions P and Q happen to be. He might believe Q for some reason completely unconnected with P, or perhaps for no reason at all (if that is possible). He might never have noticed any connection between P and Q and so might never have seen that P implies Q or that if P were to be true then Q would be true or that

[7] For the idea that there is no special activity or phenomenon properly called 'deductive reasoning' see Gilbert Harman, 'Induction' in M. Swain (ed.), *Induction, Acceptance and Rational Belief* (Dordrecht, 1970). The claim does not imply that people never believe something on the basis of other things that logically imply it.

[8] For a clear demonstration that 'P is reason to believe Q' can be true even though 'If P then Q' is false, and that someone who reasons from P to Q *need* not therefore be supposed to be taking anything as strong as the conditional for granted, see Judith Jarvis Thomson, 'Reasons and Reasoning', in M. Black (ed.), *Philosophy in America* (London, 1965), 294–6.

[9] In saying this I do not imply that a person can always state his reasons for his beliefs, or that what he states when asked is always in fact his reason, or that in attributing to him one belief based on another we imply that he is able to state his reasons if asked.

if P is true then Q is true or even that P is reason to believe Q. His belief in Q could therefore fail to be based on P even though it is in fact accompanied in his mind by a belief in P. So a notebook that states only that a person believes P and believes Q would not represent that person as believing Q on the basis of P.

How are we to represent that fact in our notebook? Of course it depends on what the constraints on the proper form for notebook entries are to be. We could simply write 'He believes P, he believes Q, and the second belief is based on the first' and leave it at that. But what it is for one belief to be based on another would remain unexplained.

It is tempting to try to explain it by saying that the person must see or recognize or somehow be aware of some relation between P and Q. That was what was missing from the simple statement that he believes P and believes Q. And it does seem to capture something essential to reasonable belief.[10] It is no good believing something that actually amounts to deductively sufficient or conclusive or good or even some reason to believe something else if you never recognize or make use of that fact. The reasonable believer is one who exploits such connections and thereby comes to believe one thing on the basis of another. So whatever 'seeing some connection between P and Q' or 'drawing an inference (or reasoning) from one to the other' ultimately amounts to, it will at least involve some attitude of acceptance, recognition, awareness, or acknowledgement on the believer's part of 'P implies Q', 'If P were true then Q would be true', 'If P is true then Q is true', 'P is reason to believe Q', or some such proposition that serves to link his reason with that for which it is a reason. In going from his premiss to his conclusion he would seem to recognize or accept some such connection, and without it his belief in Q would not have been shown to be based on P. If we yield to this so far innocent-seeming temptation our notebook will show that his believing Q on the basis of P amounts to at least two things—his belief in P and his belief or recognition of something else, call it R, that expresses a relation between P and Q. If we are to write in our notebook everything involved in his believing Q on the basis of P it would seem that his acceptance of some R must be represented there.

[10] For an argument that a person who reasons from P to Q must at least be assuming or taking it for granted that P is reason to believe Q, see Thomson, 'Reasons and Reasoning', 296–8.

How is that acceptance or recognition itself to be represented? If we write R as just another thing the person believes or recognizes or takes to be true then we still will not have written everything we need to represent his belief in Q as based on P. Someone can believe P and believe 'P implies Q' or 'If P were true then Q would be true' or 'If P is true then Q is true' or even 'P is reason to believe Q' and still not believe Q on the basis of P. He might believe Q for some reason completely unconnected with P and any of those other statements, or perhaps for no reason at all (if that is possible). He might confidently believe P and confidently believe some statement R about the relation between P and Q without ever having put them together and thereby noticed a connection between two of the things he accepts and Q. His belief in Q could therefore fail to be based on P even though it is in fact accompanied in his mind by a belief in P and an acceptance of R. Since he must have 'put P and R together' and somehow have seen or acknowledged their connection with Q, then for reasons similar to those which first tempted us to write R in the notebook we would then be forced to attribute to the believer some attitude of acceptance or recognition of the relation between what is now in the notebook and Q. In going from what is now in the notebook to his conclusion he would seem to recognize or accept some connection between P and R and Q, and without it his belief in Q would not have been shown to be based on P. If we yielded to this further temptation our notebook would show that his believing Q on the basis of P amounts to at least three things—his belief in P, his acceptance of R, and his belief or recognition of something else, call it S, that expresses a relation between P and R and Q. And again, if we wrote S as just another thing the person believes or recognizes or takes to be true then we still would not have written everything we need to represent his belief in Q as based on P.

Before leaving to attend to pressing business at the bank we should pause to notice a moral to be drawn from the tale of Achilles and the tortoise.

The moral is that for every proposition or set of propositions the belief or acceptance of which is involved in someone's believing one proposition on the basis of another there must be something else, not simply a further proposition accepted, that is responsible for the one belief's being based on the other. It is perhaps unobjectionable for certain limited purposes to represent a cognitive subject in abstract terms as a set of propositions that are said to constitute his 'belief set'. But from Lewis Carroll's story we can conclude that no such fiction could ever represent any of a person's beliefs as based on other beliefs of his. A list of everything a person believes, accepts, or acknowledges must leave it indeterminate whether any of those beliefs are based on others. Given such a list we could find by simple inspection that some specified propositions P and Q are on it. Even if we know that P implies Q or that some weaker relation holds between them we will not thereby have found that the belief in Q is based on P. We could then search the list for some statement R about the relation between P and Q. If no such statement is on the list we would not have found that the belief in Q is based on P; but even if it is on the list we still would not have found that the belief in Q is based on P. We could scan the list again for a more complicated statement S about the relation between P and R and Q, but however that search turned out we would have to scan the list once again. And so on and so on. Even if God Himself looked into our heads and inspected all the members of our 'belief set' He could not thereby determine whether any of our beliefs are based on others. That is not a question that can be settled by any facts, however complex, about what we know, believe, or accept.[11]

This obviously does not imply that whenever someone believes Q on the basis of P he cannot, on pain of infinite regress, be said also to have a belief that P implies Q, or that if P were to be true then Q would be true, or that if P is true then Q is true, or that P is reason to believe that Q is true. Someone might well hold just such a belief, and it might even have occurred to him explicitly in thinking about P and Q. It often requires explicit rehearsing of such statements, or deliberately working through an argument, to bring about a belief that a certain proposition is true. The point is only that even if the person is said to believe or accept some statement R linking things he already believes with his conclusion we still must attribute to him something else in addition if we are to rep-

[11] This shows the limitations of any 'rational reconstruction' of the grounds of our beliefs which simply enumerates propositions believed and the relations holding, or believed to hold, between them. It also casts doubt on the notion of a person's 'complete' reason for a belief, and therefore indirectly on the idea that some knowledge is completely (epistemically) independent of experience in the sense that nowhere in one's complete reason for believing is there any appeal to experience.

resent his belief in that conclusion as based on those other beliefs. That additional factor cannot be identified as simply some further proposition he accepts or acknowledges. There must always exist some 'non-propositional' factor if any of his beliefs are based on others.

It might well be felt that in showing or suggesting only this Lewis Carroll has not shown very much—that it is quite obvious without his help that the propositions alone, or the relations between them, are not enough. What is important is not only which propositions are 'written' in the mind, but also that the propositions 'written' there are *believed*. Since believing something differs from wondering whether it is true, or fearing or hoping that it is, if the same proposition or sentence is involved in each case then its being believed or accepted must be represented as its being in the mind or written on the mental tablet in a certain way. That 'manner of conception'[12] is what must be understood if we are to understand what it is for one belief to be based on another. Therefore only an adequate account of the nature of belief, and not a mere list of the propositions believed, would provide an explanation of what it is for one belief to be based on another.

For example, a picture of the mind as containing a list of propositions believed, even if the list carries the title 'Things Believed', will appear ridiculous in giving no account of a person's understanding of what he believes. Believing something involves understanding it, and that in turn appears to involve seeing some of its connections with other things one understands, or at least having the capacity to see and accept those connections in appropriate circumstances. If someone could not even believe P unless he understood it, and if he could not understand P without seeing that if it is true then Q is true, then his acceptance of the conditional that if P is true then Q is true would be part of what we attribute to him in attributing to him at the outset a belief in P. Of course, one can understand and accept a proposition without thereby seeing or accepting *all* of its consequences, since many of them are remote and difficult to discern. But it seems that a person will believe at

[12] The phrase is deliberately reminiscent of Hume, who thought he was the first philosopher to see just this problem (see Hume's *A Treatise of Human Nature*, ed. Selby-Bigge (Oxford, 1958), 628). Although he lacked the full resources for a solution he made some suggestions in that direction in the appendix to his *Treatise* (625–9).

least *some* of the consequences of what he already believes if he can truly be said to have those very beliefs in the first place. The fact that belief requires understanding and understanding requires seeing connections and drawing conclusions in appropriate circumstances might therefore be thought to provide a way around Lewis Carroll's regress[13] and to explain the source of the 'must' in 'He believes this so the must believe that'.[14]

This line of thinking finds support in a closer look at Lewis Carroll's story since it must be admitted that it is difficult to see how the tortoise could understand and accept A and B without accepting Z, especially if, as seems natural to assume, he understands Z. How could anyone understand and accept 'Things that are equal to the same are equal to each other' and realize that the sides of a particular triangle are things that are equal to the same without seeing that *if* those two things are true then the sides of that triangle are equal to each other? Failure to accept that conditional is one of the best grounds we could have for concluding that the tortoise does not understand what he has 'accepted' when he has 'granted' A and B. His not accepting the conditional C tends to show that he has not seen that A is a universal generalization and that B provides an instantiation of its antecedent, but if he has not grasped even such elementary structural features of the propositions he says he believes how can he be said to understand them at all? Or perhaps he does grasp the structure of A and B but does not realize that if a universal generalization is true and its antecedent is instantiated then that instance also fulfils the consequent. But could someone who does not know even that much about what a universal generalization is be said to know that A in particular is a universal generalization? If not, it is difficult to see that he fulfils the minimum conditions for understanding, and therefore for believing, A and B.

The ease with which the tortoise 'accepts' the conditional C simply on request also makes it difficult to see that full-blooded

[13] This is perhaps the most natural and most widely adopted suggestion for avoiding the regress. For a recent example see Max Black, 'The Justification of Logical Axioms', in his *Margins of Precision* (Ithaca, 1970). He holds that 'the form of words "Understanding and accepting premises of the form *p* and *If p then q*, but not accepting the corresponding proposition of the form *q*" describes nothing at all' (p. 21).

[14] This is putting it optimistically, since the suggestion simply pushes the 'must' back one step. We would still need an explanation of why it is *impossible* for a person to understand and believe P without accepting certain other statements logically connected with it.

belief is in question. He does not ask to have the meaning or implications of that conditional explained to him more fully, or to have its connections with A and B made more explicit; he insists only that it be written in the notebook. No doubt it will always be possible for the tortoise to insist that more and more complex conditional sentences be written in the notebook, but that in itself does not give us a way of understanding how it is possible for him to believe A and B without believing C, or to believe A, B, and C without believing D. Believing something is more than having something written in a notebook.

There is no doubt that a person's understanding of what he believes is an essential ingredient in belief, and that his not responding in appropriate ways—for example, his not accepting obvious consequences or obviously reasonable conclusions from things he purports to believe or his not changing his alleged beliefs when other things he believes are obviously good reason to do so—is good evidence that he does not understand them and therefore cannot properly be said to have the relevant beliefs at all. But the attempt to locate the source of the 'must' in 'He believes this so he must believe that' in the conditions of belief-attribution seems to me to promise less than complete success with the tortoise.

It is admittedly difficult to understand exactly how the tortoise could accept A and B and not accept C if he understands what they mean, but can it be said that, given his understanding, from the fact that he accepts A and B it *follows* that he accepts C? On that view his non-acceptance of the single statement C would be conclusive falsification of our attribution to him of understanding of A and B, but that seems unduly restrictive. Understanding something is a complex matter. Certainly if someone saw *none* of the relations between a particular proposition P and others, and was not disposed to accept it even though he already believed what were obviously good reasons for it or to reject it when he believed what were obviously good reasons against it, we would at some point justifiably conclude that he did not understand it. But that shows at most that understanding something requires seeing *some* (perhaps even a great many) of its obvious connections with other things.[15] It does not immediately provide a way of showing, of some particu-

[15] The point is well illustrated in the context of a general theory of action by Donald Davidson in 'Mental Events', in Foster and Swanson (eds.), *Experience and Theory* (Amherst, Mass., 1970), and 'Psychology as Philosophy', in S. C. Brown (ed.),

lar proposition Q, that the person must see a connection between P and Q if he understands P. As long as he saw enough connections between P and other propositions he could be said to understand P even if he persisted in his non-acceptance of Q.[16] No doubt we would find this puzzling and perhaps could never satisfactorily explain what blocks his understanding at just that point, but we could not simply disregard everything that speaks in favour of his understanding P and declare that he does not understand it.

But even if the appeal to understanding is not clearly enough in itself to show that the tortoise must accept C, and therefore Z, it could still show that Lewis Carroll has not succeeded in raising a completely general problem about believing something on the basis of something else. If believing something involves understanding it,[17] and that in turn requires that one see some of its connections with other things and draw reasonable conclusions in appropriate circumstances, then even if the tortoise's situation in particular cannot be demonstrated to be impossible it does not follow that it could represent a quite general possibility with respect to *every* connection between A and B and other things. The appeal to understanding would show that a person could not be said to understand, and therefore could not believe, a proposition P if he did not see what any of its consequences were, or any of the things for which it is a good reason, or did not know what implied it or what would be good reason to believe it. If he never saw any such connections he could not be said to understand.

It is not my aim here to provide a theory of understanding along those lines and thereby to show that Lewis Carroll has not illustrated a quite general possibility. Even if the indispensability of understanding is granted and it is conceded for that reason that there is no completely general problem about believing something

Philosophy of Psychology (London, 1974). For another interesting argument to the same effect see Daniel Dennett, 'Mechanism and Responsibility', in T. Honderich (ed.), *Essays on Freedom of Action* (London, 1973).

16 For an argument that a certain minimal consistency and inferential ability is required for the possession of any beliefs, but that that does not warrant the specification of particular beliefs or inferences that *must* be accepted see Christopher Cherniak, 'Beliefs and Logical Abilities', Ph.D. thesis (University of California, Berkeley, 1977).

17 The point that believing requires understanding need not be restricted to linguistic beings for whom there is a sentence they understand that states what they believe. In what follows I concentrate on the linguistic case.

on the basis of something else we can still draw from the story a significant moral about how that all-important understanding is to be represented.

To understand a sentence is to know certain things about its structure and about the reference and meaning of its constituent terms, and thereby to know something about its relations to other sentences one understands. One aim of what is now called 'the theory of meaning' is to give a detailed and systematic description of precisely what a person knows when he knows or understands a language. Whatever the final form of such a theory might turn out to be it is natural to think of it as a specification of what a person can be said to know or believe or accept in virtue of understanding his language as he does. Therefore in attributing understanding to someone we attribute to him attitudes of the form 'He knows (or believes) that . . .' with the blanks filled by propositions about semantical and other features of his language the knowledge or acceptance of which is thought to constitute his understanding of the language. But from Lewis Carroll's story we can see that this in itself can never be a full account of what his understanding his language, and his therefore being in a position to believe one thing on the basis of another, consists in.

Even if we add to the list of a person's beliefs in our Epistemologist's Notebook a further list (call it U) of all those propositions he accepts in virtue of understanding the language in which those beliefs are expressed we still will not have written enough to show that U does in fact represent the way he understands those beliefs. If, however many propositions of whatever complexity are written in our notebook that truly describe a believer's state of mind it remains so far indeterminate whether any of his beliefs are based on others, then in particular when we have attributed to him acceptance of the members of U we will not thereby have shown that they are connected in any way with his other beliefs. For example, the truths he knows about his language are presumably general in form, and the sentences he is said to accept in accord with that understanding are particular, so it must be shown that he knows or recognizes that those particular sentences are instances of the general linguistic truths he accepts. That cannot be shown by simply adding some new, more complicated sentences to the list of things he accepts. Something else is needed to represent the fact that he understands his beliefs in the way described by U. To say that the members of U themselves must also be understood, and not just dead inscriptions on a mental tablet, does not alter the case. That is either to encourage the writing of even more propositions in our Epistemologist's Notebook or to raise once again the problem of how that understanding, and therefore his belief, is to be represented there.[18] There must be some further answer to the question of what a person's believing, and therefore, understanding, those propositions amounts to; it cannot be answered by appealing to propositions already on the list or by adding more propositions to it.[19]

This is perhaps uncontroversial and serves only to emphasize the obvious point that a person's understanding and believing things must ultimately be seen as a certain complicated disposition or competence or practical capacity. But how is that capacity to be represented in our notebook? Even if there is no objection to representing it, at least for theoretical purposes, as a matter of the person's knowing a certain set of propositions to be true,[20] a list of those propositions, even if there is added to it the further, but unexplained, statement that they are all known, will never suffice as a description of the person's state. What is needed is some explanation of what his having that alleged knowledge amounts to, as opposed to what it is knowledge of.[21] That raises ill-understood epistemological issues that must be left aside here, but the moral

[18] This holds whether those things the acceptance of which constitutes his understanding are regarded as indicative statements or as instructions, directives, imperatives (either hypothetical or categorical), rules, or other forms of 'practical' discourse.

[19] I find Daniel Dennett has made a similar point, with explicit reference to Lewis Carroll, in discussing what he calls 'the brain-writing theory of belief'. He concludes that 'writing—for instance, brain writing—is a dependent form of information-storage. The brain must store at least some of its information in a manner not capturable by a brain-writing model' ('Brain Writing and Mind Reading', in K. Gunderson (ed.), *Minnesota Studies in the Philosophy of Science*, vii (Minneapolis, 1975), 410–11).

[20] See N. Chomsky on 'competence' in e.g. *Aspects of the Theory Syntax* (Cambridge, Mass., 1965), 3–9, or *Reflections on Language* (London, 1976), 163–6. See also M. Dummett, *Frege: Philosophy of Language* (London, 1973), 461–2, and 'What is a Theory of Meaning?', in S. Guttenplan (ed.), *Mind and Language* (Oxford, 1975), 121.

[21] For an emphasis on the importance of the first half of this distinction for the theory of meaning see Dummett, 'What is a Theory of Meaning?', 106–9, 121. He uses it as a weapon against theories that would explain meaning in terms of truth-conditions alone. Chomsky on the other hand concentrates on specifying what is 'known', and not on what it is to 'know' it. He simply describes the latter as having a 'finite representation' of a 'cognitive structure' (see e.g. *Reflections on Language*, 162 ff.).

of Lewis Carroll's story does seem to impose at least some constraints on any such account of practical capacities.

If knowing or believing something to be true—whether it be some elaborate fact about the structure of one's language or some simple fact about the familiar world—involves a disposition or capacity to 'act' in certain ways then obviously that disposition or capacity itself cannot be represented as nothing more than passive assent (even assent with understanding) to some proposition. That is what gives rise to the regress. How then is an 'active' assent or acceptance to be understood? Even if 'act' is somewhat artificially extended to such things as inferring and drawing conclusions it will not do to say that believing P must be seen as a practical capacity or disposition to *act on* P in the sense that P *guides* or *directs* one's actions. Acting on a proposition in the sense of being guided by it involves understanding it, and on this picture of understanding that in turn involves accepting certain other propositions. Therefore either that further acceptance is merely passive and the regress remains, or else it in turn is a matter of being disposed to act on those other propositions as well, and so what was originally represented as a case of being disposed to act on P would involve being disposed to act on something else in addition. And that in turn would involve understanding it, and therefore being disposed to act on something else, and so on. So we cannot suppose that someone learns a first language, or originally comes to understand what he does, by applying a theory or model or set of instructions or rules that he understands. There must be some way to stop the regress that threatens any completely general search for a set of criteria or procedures for determining how something is to be understood.[22] It cannot be a condition of explaining how a person comes to understand a word or sentence in one way rather than another that there should always be something he goes by or relies on, in the sense of something he can be said to know or believe, to determine that the expression is to be applied this way rather than that. No satisfactory explanation of understanding is possible on such an overly demanding conception of a practical capacity.[23]

[22] Readers of Wittgenstein will recognize this as a central idea in the discussion of understanding in §§143–242 of his *Philosophical Investigations*, tr. G. E. M. Anscombe (Oxford, 1953). See esp. 201.

[23] It is not easy to see how Dummett's requirement (in 'What is a Theory of Meaning?') that a theory of meaning should be 'rich' or 'full-blooded' avoids this

It might be thought, on the other hand, that a person's believing and understanding things in the way he does is nothing more than his having a disposition or capacity to 'act' in relevant ways in appropriate circumstances. It is not that he acts *on*, or *in the light of*, propositions in the sense that his grasp of a set of propositions guides his actions in each case, but only that his 'actions', including his inferences, are in fact in accord with those propositions he is said to accept. Here there is no threat of a regress since there does not always have to be some further proposition the acceptance of which is needed to account for his 'acting' in the way he does. Even if the acceptance of more and more propositions can without paradox be attributed to him, they are not called for to explain why or how he understands and believes things in the way he does. But it is no accident that nothing more is called for, since on this more permissive model a person's understanding and believing what he does amounts to nothing more than his being disposed to 'act' in just the ways that are responsible for the attribution of those very beliefs to him in the first place. How he gets those dispositions and is led to activate them need not always be explained in terms of other things he knows or believes. It will at some point simply be accepted as an unexplained fact that he does, or can be brought to, respond in just those ways; or if that fact in turn can be explained it will not be in terms of further pieces of knowledge, belief, or awareness attributable to the person in question.

Therefore if it is a condition of there being such a thing as a satisfactory 'theory of understanding' that it should provide a genuine explanation in cognitive terms of how we are able to understand and believe things in the ways we do then both these extremes must somehow be avoided. An overly permissive account will be felt to leave unexplained the fact that people naturally 'see' or understand things one way rather than another, and so will be accepted, if ever, only as a last resort when the search for a more ambitious theory has been abandoned. But how could the search for an ambitious non-permissive theory that invokes cognitive attitudes to explain

difficulty. He requires that a 'theory of understanding' should 'explain' how a speaker 'derives' his understanding of a particular sentence from his knowledge of the language (p. 112), how he is 'guided' by it in grasping the content of sentences (pp. 133–4), and how he knows what 'governs the application' of a name to a thing (p. 131). For penetrating criticism of the reasons offered for Dummett's requirements see John McDowell, 'On the Sense and Reference of a Proper Name', *Mind* (1977).

the sources of a person's understanding and beliefs be anything but a search for an overly demanding, and therefore necessarily unavailable, theory? It is one of the many merits of Lewis Carroll's engaging story that it can be seen as presenting us with just that problem. It might seem that the solution is obvious and that we must inevitably fall back on a more permissive and therefore less 'explanatory' conception at some point; but it will be time to proclaim the obviousness of that fact when philosophers no longer pursue theories of knowledge and understanding that could succeed only by denying it.

4

Evolution and the Necessities of Thought

Homo sapiens is an evolved species, and so the existence of its members with the general characteristics they have is itself a product of the evolutionary process. That process continues at present, and so there must be true evolutionary explanations of why human beings in general are the ways they are. Many will be inclined to accept this generalization with respect to straightforwardly physical characteristics of human beings, but the same point of view can be applied to complex human cultural and intellectual products as well. In particular, the theory of evolution itself can be seen as an elaborate evolutionary product with high 'adaptive value'; it enables us to adapt more easily to an environment that continually thwarted our efforts to understand it without such a theory.

Thomas Goudge discusses this idea in *The Ascent of Life*. Whether or not we agree with him that man is 'psychically immature,' that he is still in his 'racial adolescence,' and that his present knowledge is 'undoubtedly inchoate,' we must surely admit that, seen in evolutionary perspective, 'he has hardly made more than a start in the cognitive enterprise' and that, if human evolution con-

This essay was first published in L. W. Sumner, J. Slater, and F. Wilson (eds.), *Pragmatism and Purpose: Essays Presented to T. A. Goudge* (University of Toronto Press, Toronto, 1981). It was my good fortune to be a student of Thomas A. Goudge as an undergraduate at the University of Toronto. Whether he was explaining Moore on 'Existence is not a predicate' or Fichte on 'Das Ich setzt sich,' criticizing Quine's attack on analyticity, or inviting us to criticize Hegel's attack on formal logic, the clarity and order, and the refreshing sense that in each case there was something definite and specifiable there to engage the mind, served to dispel that feeling of disorientation, even incipient asphyxiation, some of us had been suffering from, however inarticulately, in our earlier ruminations on Plotinus, or T. H. Green, or whatever it had happened to be. But it was not simply a matter of ventilation. The fresh, clean air increased, or in my case actually generated, the conviction that there were things to be done in philosophy, and that gaining a thorough, sympathetic knowledge and keeping one's wits about one could just possibly lead somewhere. It was an important experience for me, and I will always be grateful for it.

tinues for another twenty thousand years or so, 'the frontiers of knowledge will almost certainly be far beyond those of the present day'.[1] From all this Goudge concludes that it is absurd to suppose that 'man can establish now, once for all, the limits of possible knowledge'.[2]

In this paper I want to raise very briefly and at a regrettably high level of generality one of the many puzzling questions that arise quite naturally when we try to think of human beings and the development of human knowledge from an evolutionary point of view. I will not try to resolve the issue. It will be enough if I can indicate in one particular way how difficult it is to adopt the evolutionary point of view completely, or to restrict ourselves to it consistently. I think the attempt to do so has implications for our understanding of ourselves and our knowledge that are not always explicitly recognized and squarely faced.

It is undoubtedly true, as Goudge says, that we cannot set boundaries to the future scope or extent of human knowledge, but talk of 'the limits of possible knowledge' also carries with it the more Kantian idea of conditions that must be fulfilled by any possible knowledge. If there are any such conditions, and we know them to be fulfilled, then at least some of the things we now know express 'limits' or 'constraints' that no future knowledge can overstep.

In particular, if we now know some things to be not just true, but necessarily true, then since what is necessarily true could not possibly be false, it would seem that some of the things we now know do, in a sense, express 'limits' or 'constraints' on any possible future knowledge. I want to ask whether it is possible to think of human knowledge as a flexible, constantly changing product of the evolutionary process, one that might well be unrecognizably different in twenty thousand years, while continuing to believe that many of the things we now know are known to be necessarily true.

I think most philosophers would be inclined to answer, 'Yes'. In *The Thought of C. S. Peirce* Goudge himself gives an affirmative answer, at least in the case of logic. He points out that, on Peirce's conception of rational human thought as itself a product of the evolutionary process, it would be 'theoretically possible to write a natural history of knowledge, one chapter of which would embrace

[1] Thomas A. Goudge, *The Ascent of Life* (Toronto, 1961), 210.
[2] Ibid.

logic as a type of human activity'.[3] We might then come to understand how certain ways of thinking proved themselves efficacious in the struggle for existence and thus became fixed habits and were 'eventually formulated by the logician as the principles of inference'.[4] Such a naturalistic, genetic account of our coming to accept or acknowledge certain principles of logic is not to be thought of as an explanation of the special 'validity' of the principles themselves. We do not regard inferences as valid simply because they proceed in accordance with principles that have survived in the struggle for existence. We have an independent notion of validity, and Goudge tentatively suggests that any adequate account of logical validity must appeal to the *necessity* of certain principles or truths.[5] But our having knowledge of such necessities, he holds, is not 'necessarily incompatible with a naturalistic conception of logic'.[6]

Goudge himself does not develop the suggestion, but I think many who endorse it would do so on the basis of a certain widespread conception of the nature of necessary truth—a conception that is thought to point the way, perhaps the only way, to a successful account of the compatibility between a sophisticated evolutionary naturalism and the necessity of many of the things we know. But it seems to me that what has come to be the more or less standard way of thinking about necessary truth and its source in fact makes it much more difficult to explain the alleged compatibility than it might look at first sight.

Certainly there is no straightforward logical incompatibility between there being a true naturalistic explanation of our believing that p, on the one hand, and its being true that p, or even its being necessarily true that p, on the other. Simply from the fact that there is a true explanation of the origin of a belief, either in an individual or in a group of individuals, nothing at all follows one way or another about the truth-value, or the modality, of what is believed. This holds even if the kind of explanation offered is one that we normally take as showing that the belief in question is false. For example, to say that someone believes that the bed before him is covered with leaves because he has just taken a hallucinatory drug certainly suggests that the bed is not covered with leaves, that he is simply hallucinating that it is, and that his belief is false. But

[3] Thomas A. Goudge, *The Thought of C. S. Peirce* (Toronto, 1950), 128.
[4] Ibid. [5] Ibid. 134. [6] Ibid. 135.

however unlikely it is that a perfectly normal bed in perfectly ordinary circumstances should be covered with leaves, its not being covered with leaves does not follow logically from the admitted truth that someone is hallucinating that it is covered with leaves. It is at least possible for it to be covered with leaves and for someone simultaneously to hallucinate that it is. And, to take another example, if we know that it came to someone in a dream, and he subsequently believed, that Goldbach's conjecture is necessarily true, it does not follow from those facts alone that it is not the case that Goldbach's conjecture is necessarily true. Its being necessarily true and his dreaming and subsequently believing that it is is a possible state of affairs.

Similarly, if we admit in an evolutionary spirit that human beings believe what they do, or even that they believe some things to be necessarily true, because having such beliefs has great 'adaptive value' for the species and facilitates its adjustment to the world in which it lives, it does not follow from that alone that those beliefs are not true, or that none of them are necessarily true. It is at least possible for a proposition to be true, or to be necessarily true, even though people's believing it, or believing it to be necessary, is of considerable value in their efforts to survive.

But although the mere logical consistency between the truth, or the necessary truth, of a belief and a true naturalistic explanation of its origin must be admitted, to appeal only to that consistency seems to me a relatively superficial and unsatisfactory response to the challenge posed by an evolutionary theory of human knowledge.

For one thing, some explanations of the origin or retention of a belief are such that once we accept them we can no longer hold the belief in question or see it as defensible. Someone who hallucinates a bed covered with leaves and on that basis believes that the bed before him is covered with leaves does not thereby know that the bed is covered with leaves, even if it is. Someone who dreams, and thereby comes to believe, that Goldbach's conjecture is necessarily true does not on that basis know that it is necessarily true, even if it is. Therefore, even if the truth of such explanations does not logically imply the falsity of what is believed, a person accepting such explanations as an account of his own beliefs is no longer entitled to continue to hold those beliefs. His believing what he does has been to that extent discredited, even if what he believes should happen to be true, even necessarily true. The mere logical compatibility between a true naturalistic explanation of someone's believing something and the truth, or necessary truth, of what he believes is therefore not enough to show that one who accepts the explanation can reasonably continue to attribute truth, for example, to the proposition that the bed before him is covered with leaves, or necessary truth to Goldbach's conjecture. Accepting the explanations in those cases has radical implications for the way he sees his own beliefs.

A belief that is shown to be solely the result of a hallucination or a dream is thereby discredited because the truth or probable truth of what is believed plays no role in the explanation of the fact that it is believed.[7] Given the facts described, the man would have believed that the bed is covered with leaves even if it had not been so covered; its actual state had no effect on what he believed about it. And the necessary truth of Goldbach's conjecture was not in any way responsible for the man's dreaming and coming to believe that that conjecture is necessarily true. However, when the truth or probable truth of what is believed does play an essential role in the explanation of the origin or retention of that very belief, one can accept such an explanation of one's beliefs without seeing them as in any way brought into question. In fact, many would argue that that is precisely what it is to have a reasonable or justified belief.[8]

This leaves it open to the evolutionary epistemologist to argue that in explaining the origin and retention of the beliefs of human beings solely in terms of their usefulness or 'adaptive value', he is not necessarily thereby discrediting those beliefs. His account could be accepted with impunity if the mode of explanation he envisages, unlike the appeal to hallucination or dreams, makes essential use of the truth or probable truth of the beliefs whose origin is being explained. It might well be argued, for example, that the survival in a species of a set of beliefs about its environment is some reason in itself to conclude that those beliefs are probably true, or approximately true, since they were acquired and retained as a result of interaction with the very environment they are about. If survival is

[7] For discussion of some of the problems involved in explaining one's own beliefs in a way that does not render them true, probable, or reasonable see e.g. S. Hampshire, *Freedom of Mind and Other Essays* (Princeton, 1971) and B. Williams, 'Deciding to Believe', in his *Problems of the Self* (Cambridge, 1973).

[8] See e.g. Gilbert Harman, *Thought* (Princeton, 1973), esp. ch. 8.

thought to be more likely with true than with false beliefs then we might even think of ourselves as getting closer and closer to the whole truth as time goes on by getting a more and more accurate 'map' of the world we live in. On this view, appeal to the 'adaptive value' of our beliefs, far from discrediting those beliefs, actually provides positive support for them; it is argued in effect that the world would probably not have tolerated complete falsity for such a long time.

Whether an argument along these lines could be made at all plausible is a complicated question that I shall not pursue. My concern here is only with the general condition that must be fulfilled by an evolutionary explanation of our beliefs that does not detach us from those beliefs and represent them as no more likely to be true and therefore no more worthy of our assent than the products of comfortable hallucinations or congenial dreams. It will employ a notion of the truth of what is believed independently of its being believed, and it will somehow show that the truth of what is believed is implied or rendered probable by the evolutionary explanation of our acceptance and retention of the beliefs in question.

Whether evolutionary explanations fulfil the specified condition in the case of our accepting some things as true and rejecting others is perhaps an open question, but it does not even seem possible to fulfil that condition in explaining our ascribing *necessary* truth to some of the things we believe. There an appeal to the independent necessary truth of what is believed seems to no avail. An evolutionary explanation of our thought about necessity will explain how and why we have a notion of necessary truth as something objective and independent of its being believed, and why we ascribe it to some things and withhold it from others. But the facts appealed to by any naturalistic explanation of our thinking in those ways will be contingent facts about the world and its inhabitants that are held to be responsible for human beings' thinking and believing what they do. The explanation would not, and, it will be felt, could not, introduce the independent necessary truth of what is believed into the explanation of its being believed to be necessarily true.

The impossibility of any such appeal will be felt especially strongly if we think of necessary truth and its source along more or less standard lines. According to that conception, the nature of necessary truth is not to be understood by reflecting on its alleged relation to some independent domain, but only by understanding its relation to, or its source in, the ways we think and speak about the world. Necessary truths are not taken to describe or reflect any features holding necessarily of the world independently of our thought. They do not straightforwardly describe our contingent ways of thinking and speaking either, nor are they merely directives or injunctions to think or speak in certain ways; they are genuine truths, and they hold necessarily, but they are thought to owe their special status only to our thinking or speaking in certain ways, and not to the way things necessarily are independently of us. In short, necessary truths are in some sense our own 'creation'—they are true by 'convention' or 'decision', and not by virtue of any 'facts'.

Any such conventionalist view can be made credible only if there is some way to distinguish it from the apparently rival view that necessary truths are true in virtue of the way things necessarily are. There must be something that shows that in coming to know necessary truths we are simply acknowledging and accepting the consequences of our own ways of thinking and speaking, and not discovering independent, objective, necessary features of the world. What is taken to show this is the existence of possible alternatives to our present ways of thinking and speaking which are such that, if we had thought or spoken in those ways, or if we came to do so in the future, we would solely thereby accept a set of necessary truths different from our present ones even though everything else about the world remained exactly the same. Hence our present ways of thinking and speaking, and no objective features of the world, are thought somehow to be responsible for the truth of what we now believe to be necessarily true. Not only does conventionalism about necessity imply the existence of alternatives to our present ways of thinking and speaking—alternative 'conventions' we could have 'chosen' instead—but the appeal to such relevant alternatives must be an essential part of any attempt to establish the truth of conventionalism against its rivals.[9]

[9] C. I. Lewis has stressed perhaps more than anyone else the need to appeal to possible alternatives to our present ways of thinking in any attempt to support conventionalism, or indeed any view according to which the necessary or the a priori are shown to be the 'contribution of the mind'. See esp. C. I. Lewis, *Mind and the World Order* (New York, 1929), chs. 7, 8.

There is in fact some question whether an argument for conventionalism could amount to anything more than that. Certainly there was no actual convening, and no actual agreement made, any more than an actual social contract was drawn up by our forefathers. The most that can be said is that it is *as if* there had been an explicit agreement; and even that must rest on an appeal to the existence of alternative ways of thinking and speaking.

An evolutionary view of the development of human knowledge appears most congenial if we think of necessity in this way. It appeals perforce only to contingent facts about us and the world in order to explain our believing some things to be necessarily true, and it stresses the contingency of our ways of thinking and speaking, and therefore, in that sense at least, the existence of alternatives to them. Necessary truth is therefore thought to pose no problem for an evolutionary view precisely because necessary truth, unlike truth itself, is thought to be in some sense a 'creation' of ours—a by-product of our cognitive interaction with the world that is not a representation of any objective states of affairs holding independently of our thinking in certain ways.

But whether this apparently attractive accommodation of necessity to evolutionary theory is possible depends on a question that seems to me never to have been squarely faced or adequately resolved by defenders of this standard conception of necessary truth. Precisely what relation is supposed to hold between our thinking or speaking in certain ways and the necessary truth of any of those things we now regard as necessarily true? If our thinking or speaking in those ways is in some sense 'responsible' for the necessary truth of the things we now accept as necessary, exactly how is that notion of 'responsibility' to be understood?

Consider something that we believe to be necessarily true, for example 'If all men are mortal and Socrates is a man then Socrates is mortal.' Does conventionalism, or indeed any view according to which necessary truth is in some sense our own 'creation', imply that the truth of that statement is due solely to our present ways of thinking or speaking in the sense that if we had thought or spoken in certain other ways, or had adopted relevantly different 'conventions', then it would not have been true that if all men are mortal and Socrates is a man then Socrates is mortal? If that is an implication of conventionalism, then to accept conventionalism would be to concede that under certain (vaguely specified but nevertheless possible) circumstances it would not have been true that if all men are mortal and Socrates is a man then Socrates is mortal. That claim in itself is difficult to understand, but it seems at least to carry the implication that there are possible circumstances in which it would not have been true that if all men are mortal and Socrates is a man then Socrates is mortal. But we take that familiar conditional to be necessarily true, and so we cannot allow that there are such circumstances—that there are in that sense alternatives to its truth. Acknowledging possible alternatives to the truth of *p* is incompatible with regarding it as necessarily true that *p*. Therefore we cannot accept what appears to be an implication of conventionalism while continuing to believe that it is necessarily true that if all men are mortal and Socrates is a man then Socrates is mortal.

There is another difficulty in the view that all necessary truths are true by convention. Even among logical truths alone there are an infinite number we now accept, and so we could not have conventionally endowed each of them singly with the truth we now attribute to them. Our explicit conventions would have to have been general ones, from which the truth of individual logical truths follows. But if one truth follows logically from another then the conditional with the latter as antecedent and the former as consequent is itself a logical truth, and so in attempting to render true by general convention some individual logical truth we make essential use of some other logical truth whose truth is so far unaccounted for. If that truth in turn had already been derived from some general convention of its own there would still be some other conditional whose truth had not been explicitly secured by convention. Any attempt to represent all necessary truths as true by convention makes use of at least one necessary truth whose truth is not accounted for by that very representation, so not all necessary truths could be shown to be true by convention.[10]

This shows that the attractive idea that in coming to know necessary truths we are simply acknowledging and accepting the consequences of our own conventional ways of thinking and speaking does not avoid all appeal to necessary truths holding independently

[10] This argument was first directed against conventionalism by Quine in 'Truth by Convention' in his *The Ways of Paradox and Other Essays* (New York, 1966). He there expresses his own indebtedness to Lewis Carroll's classic 'What the Tortoise Said to Achilles', *Mind* (1895).

of our having 'adopted' certain 'conventions'. That our 'conventions' have the consequences they do will not itself have been shown to be true simply by convention. But conventionalism is attractive only in so far as it purports to explain all necessary truth without appeal to any non-conventional necessities. I am inclined to think that the satisfaction provided by conventionalism is therefore illusory.

Conventionalism tries to do too much. It is supposed to explain both our acknowledging or accepting certain things as necessarily true and the very 'nature' or 'source' of the truth of the necessary truths we accept. In the latter task it fails, either by not showing the truths in question to be true in all possible circumstances, or by not showing all of them to be true by convention. But we can abandon the hope of explaining the very nature of necessary truth, and thereby abandon conventionalism, without abandoning the problem of explaining our believing or accepting some things as necessarily true. We do attribute necessary truth to some things and withhold it from others, and, I think, we regard necessary truth as something holding objectively, independently of our contingent ways of thinking. How and why we do so ought to be discoverable and understandable in the same general way that any other complex contingent fact about human behaviour is to be understood. That is precisely what an evolutionary explanation tries to do.

There is no need to expect an evolutionary explanation also to provide what we could regard as a fully adequate analysis or definition of the puzzling notion of necessary truth. It might well make our possession and employment of that notion intelligible in illuminating ways without thereby yielding a helpful, non-circular explanation of the very nature of necessary truth. It is probably misguided to expect to find such an equivalence, anyway. Certainly there is not much genuine illumination to be gained from familiar explanations of necessity in terms of possibility and negation. If we find necessity and our thought of it puzzling we are not likely to get the kind of understanding we seek by tracing fairly obvious equivalences between it and other notions we find equally puzzling for the same reasons.

But the lack of a helpful analysis or definition of necessity does not leave the notion completely mysterious or obscure. We could understand a lot more than we do about our possession and employment of the notion of necessity without ever being able to define it in a way that could serve to introduce the idea to someone who lacks it. Taking our possession of the idea for granted, we can still ask why we ascribe it and withhold it in just the ways we do, what function the idea has for us, what we can do in virtue of possessing it that we could not do without it, and even, perhaps, why we have an idea of necessity at all. These are undoubtedly difficult questions, and very general ones, but they do not obviously require for their answer a non-circular definition or analysis, in the strict sense, of 'necessary' or 'possible'. They are questions to be answered, if at all, by the naturalistic study of human beings.

There is a close parallel in the case of truth itself.[11] To explain the point or function of the notion of truth, and how and why we ascribe truth to some things and not to others, or why we believe what we do and not something else, is not necessarily to provide an analysis or definition of the notion of truth.[12] Explanations of many of our beliefs will take into account what we perceive, and what we believe or take ourselves to know already, and will explain the connection believed to hold between our perceptions or the prior set of beliefs and the belief in question. But a full and accurate statement of these 'epistemic' conditions under which we unhestitatingly ascribe truth to a particular proposition does not necessarily amount to a statement of what it is for that proposition to be true. Our notion of truth could still be a notion of something holding fully objectively and independently of what we know or believe, even though 'epistemic' considerations play an essential role in explaining why we have a notion of truth and how and why we employ it as we do.

Similarly, it might well be that 'epistemic' considerations help explain our possession and employment of the notion of necessity. Explanations of why we regard some things as necessary can be expected to take into account the special place or role of those

[11] For the idea that we must understand the *point* of the notion of truth for us, and not just discover some set of conditions that serves to distinguish the true from the false, see M. Dummett, 'Truth', *Proceedings of the Aristotelian Society*, 59 (1958–9), and *Frege: Philosophy of Language* (London, 1973), ch. 13.

[12] For an outline of an explanation of the origin of the concept of truth, and with it the concept of belief, without attempting to analyse or define either notion, see D. Davidson, 'Thought and Talk' in S. Guttenplan (ed.), *Mind and Language* (Oxford, 1975).

things among all our beliefs, or the special connection believed to hold between them and certain specially placed beliefs.[13] The details of such an account would be extremely complex, and are not available at present. But a full and accurate statement of the 'epistemic' conditions under which we unhesitatingly ascribe necessity to a particular proposition does not necessarily amount to a statement of what it is for the proposition to be necessary. Our notion of necessity could still be a notion of something holding fully objectively and independently of what we know or believe even though 'epistemic' considerations play an essential role in explaining why we have a notion of necessity and how and why we employ it as we do. It is to these questions of explanation, and not to the search for a definition of truth or of necessity, that evolutionary theory might be expected to make a contribution.

But now it will appear that we are thrown back on the original difficulty about necessity. It will still be felt that, since the considerations appealed to by an evolutionary explanation of our believing some things to be necessarily true are themselves contingent, the independent necessary truth of what is believed could play no essential role in a correct naturalistic explanation of its being believed to be necessarily true. In that sense, the true explanation of our thinking about necessity would not require that thinking itself to be 'veridical'; in contrast with the notion of truth, in this case there would need to be nothing objectively answering to our notion of necessity in order for us fully to understand our possession and employment of it. And that can be seen as a repudiation of the notion of necessity as a will-o'-the-wisp or at best a confusion.

[13] Quine is one who has especially emphasized the different degrees of 'centrality' or 'revisability' among all our beliefs, and has suggested that this difference in epistemic status is perhaps all that necessity really amounts to: 'Our system of statements has such a thick cushion of indeterminacy, in relation to experience, that vast domains of law can easily be held immune to revision on principle. We can always turn to other quarters of the system when revisions are called for by unexpected experiences. Mathematics and logic, central as they are to the conceptual scheme, tend to be accorded such immunity, in view of our conservative preference for revisions which disturb the system least; and herein, perhaps, lies the "necessity" which the laws of mathematics and logic are felt to enjoy' (W. V. Quine, *Methods of Logic* (New York, 1950), p. xiii). This might well be the right place to look for an explanation of our ascriptions of necessity without yielding a *definition* of necessity in such 'epistemic' terms as 'centrality' or 'degrees of likelihood of revision in the face of recalcitrant experience'.

The problem is reminiscent of the case of Hume and the idea of necessary or causal connection. He held that there is nothing to be found in the world or in our experience that answers to the idea of necessary connection. Only after the repeated observation of resembling pairs of phenomena do we arrive at the 'fiction' of an objective causal connection between phenomena of those two kinds, but there is nothing more 'in' the phenomena in question than their spatial and temporal relations and their membership in classes some of whose members have been constantly conjoined in our experience. For Hume this is a genetic, naturalistic (although not evolutionary) explanation of our thinking about necessary connection, but it explains our thinking in those ways without ever supposing that such thinking is correct or 'veridical'. It is a 'fiction' or 'projection' we cannot help indulging in, but nothing more.

It is easy to see Hume's view as a sceptical argument for rejecting the idea of necessary or causal connection altogether, and making do with the regularities we find in our experience and the expectations they give rise to.[14] The genetic explanation is thought to expose the idea of necessity as superfluous, or as a confusion to be jettisoned in the name of clarity. But that was not Hume's own reaction, and to suppose that it was is to misconstrue the relation between his philosophical theory of causality and the behaviour of human beings in their ordinary and scientific pursuits. Despite his philosophical 'discoveries' Hume did not abandon the idea of causality or necessary connection when he thought about the world as a plain man, or indeed as a general theorist of human nature. He sought causal explanations of why human beings think, feel, and act in the ways they do, and in particular he thought he had found a causal explanation of our thought about causality.[15] According to that explanation, it is inevitable that human beings with certain kinds of experience will come to think in causal terms, and Hume himself was no exception to the 'principles of human nature' he discovered. It was inevitable, then, that he too would continue to think in causal terms despite his philosophical 'discoveries'.

It might well be that if we understood the source of the idea of necessity that we attribute to some propositions and not others, and

[14] See e.g. R. Braithwaite, *Scientific Explanation* (Cambridge, 1953), ch. 9; E. Nagel, *The Structure of Science* (New York, 1961); ch. 4, and many others.

[15] I have elaborated this intepretation in my *Hume* (London, 1977).

could explain the point or function that idea has for us, and what we can do in virtue of possessing it that we could not do without it, the question of whether or not to jettison the idea would be as idle as it was for Hume with the idea of causality. Kant strengthened the case by showing the indispensability of the idea of causality for even so much as the thought of an objective occurrence. If our idea of necessity were found to play an equally central role in our thought, then although when we try to detach ourselves philosophically from our ways of thinking about necessity and seek their foundations in something objective and independent of our thought we inevitably fail, we would still not be able simply to give up those ways of thinking while retaining enough of the rest of our thought to make our experience intelligible to us. We might see from a naturalistic study of human beings that there are compelling reasons why we do, and must, ascribe necessity to some of the things we believe even though our best philosophical reflection can find no objective foundations for that necessity, or finds the very possibility of them obscure. This might make us at least as sceptical of the process of philosophical reflection that seems to have such devastating results as of the notion of necessity itself, especially if we had some understanding of its efficacy or indispensability in our thought.

In any case, we find ourselves in an unstable position. Taking an evolutionary perspective, we must acknowledge the contingency and explicability of our present ways of thinking, and in particular our present ascriptions of necessity. But if we do regard some things as necessarily true we thereby deny their contingency and cannot countenance the possibility of alternatives to them. We must simultaneously appreciate the contingency of the fact that the limits of our thought lie just where they do while remaining unable to think beyond those limits.[16] It is not easy to hold consistently to both

[16] Quine seems to be alluding to some such distinction when he acknowledges the possibility of a physical theory 'of radically different form from ours', but 'empirically equivalent' to it: 'Once this is recognized, the scientific achievement of our culture becomes in a way more impressive than ever. For, in the midst of all this formless freedom for variation, our science has developed in such a way as to maintain always a manageably narrow spectrum of visible alternatives among which to choose when need arises to revise a theory. It is this narrowing of sights, or tunnel vision, that has made for the continuity of science, through the vicissitudes of refutation and correction. And it is this also that has fostered the illusion of there being only one solution to the riddle of the universe' (W. V. Quine, 'The Nature of Natural Knowledge', in Guttenplan (ed.), *Mind and Language*, 81). (*cont. overleaf*)

points of view simultaneously, and we inevitably find ourselves moving back and forth somewhat unsurely between them. That is perhaps inevitable when we try to stand outside the evolutionary process and see it as a whole, *sub specie aeternitatis*, while the terms we use to try to understand that process and our place in it are themselves products of the very process we are trying vainly to transcend.

For an expression of Wittgenstein's endorsement of a similar distinction, see e.g.: 'I am not saying: if such-and-such facts of nature were different people would have different concepts (in the sense of a hypothesis). But: if anyone believes that certain concepts are absolutely the correct ones, and that having different ones would mean not realizing something that we realize—then let him imagine certain very general facts of nature to be different from what we are used to, and the formation of concepts different from the usual ones will become intelligible to him' (*Philosophical Investigations*, p. 230). I tried to elaborate on the implications of this distinction for conventionalism in my 'Wittgenstein and Logical Necessity', Ch. 1 above.

5

Wittgenstein's 'Treatment' of the Quest for 'a language which describes my inner experiences and which only I myself can understand'

At §243 of *Philosophical Investigations*[1] Wittgenstein begins to consider the question of whether a person could write down or give vocal expression to his 'inner experiences' 'for his private use'. Of course, it seems we can already do that in our common language. Obviously we can keep private diaries or keep the details of our inner lives to ourselves if we want to. But that is not what Wittgenstein means. For him, 'The individual words of this [imagined] language are to refer to what can only be known to the person speaking; to his immediate private sensations. So another person cannot understand the language' (*PI* §243). Why does he ask about such a language, why does he ask the question just here, and what is his answer? Does he even try to answer it, and if so how? I want to say as much as I can as clearly as I can in the time available to suggest how these questions of mine should be answered.[2]

First, I think Wittgenstein considers the possibility of such a language because he wants to bring out the importance of what he has already been calling 'customs', 'habits', 'regularities', 'uses', or

This essay was first published in P. Weingartner and H. Czermak (eds.), *Epistemology and Philosophy of Science: Proceedings of the Seventh International Wittgenstein Symposium, Kirchberg, 1982* (Vienna, 1983).

[1] Tr. G. E. M. Anscombe (Oxford, 1953). References to '*PI*' in parentheses in the text refer to this book.

[2] Many, perhaps all, of the particular points I touch on here have also been made by others elsewhere, some of them in print. In putting them together in the way I do I am perhaps only giving expression to what seems to be a growing consensus about how Wittgenstein is to be read. I have in mind in particular the work of Rogers Albritton, Paul Bassen, Stanley Cavell, Robert Fogelin, Bruce Goldberg, James Hopkins and Saul Kripke. I think there is nothing in what I say that all of them would disagree with, but no doubt none of them would agree with all of it.

'institutions' for the possibility of meaning something. The discussion of understanding and of grasping or following a rule in earlier pages of *PI* reached the apparent 'paradox' that every action can be interpreted so that it accords with some particular rule, but if everything can be made out to accord with a particular rule it can also be made out to conflict with it, and so there would be neither accord nor conflict (*PI* §201). The way out of this so-called 'paradox' was to recognize that grasping or following a rule must be understood, not as a matter of having before one's mind some interpreting *expression* or *formula*, but rather as something that is exhibited in what the person actually does, in his conforming to an existing custom or institution of behaving in a certain way.[3] Obeying a rule is, or on a particular occasion requires, a general practice (cf. e.g. *PI* §199).

If that is so, if that 'solution' to the 'paradox' of *PI* §201 is correct, how could a person talk about his immediate private sensations in a language only he can understand? A language only he can understand would be a language not embodied in a generally shared practice. It would at best depend only on a practice which the 'private' speaker alone engaged in. And that would seem to cause difficulty for Wittgenstein's stress on the need for a general practice or institution. Since doesn't it seem, at least at first sight, that a person *could* refer to his immediate private sensations in a language only he can understand? Isn't that possibility at least conceivable? If it is, so much the worse, it would seem, for the idea that meaning or language or rules require a generally shared practice.

Wittgenstein begins to consider this apparent challenge at precisely paragraph §243, I think, because he has just summed up the earlier discussion in fairly sweeping terms—and not altogether clearly, it seems to me. He realizes that it might sound as if what he is saying is that human accord or agreement is what determines what is true and what is false, and he replies:

> It is what human beings *say* that is true and false; and they agree [are in accord] in the *language* they use. That is not agreement [accord] in opinions but in form of life. (*PI* §241)

[3] The significance of this 'paradox' and its implications has been stressed by Fogelin, *Wittgenstein* (Henley and Boston, 1976) and by Kripke, *Wittgenstein on Rules and Private Language* (Cambridge, Mass., 1982).

If language is to be a means of communication there must be agreement [accord] not only in definitions but also (queer as this may sound) in judgements. (*PI* §242)

These rather obscure and sweeping remarks are immediately followed by the question of the possibility of the 'private' language Wittgenstein considers. For what agreement or accord in judgements with his fellow human beings would be enjoyed by a man who speaks a language only he can understand? It would seem that he need not even speak of things known to his fellow human beings at all; he speaks only of his 'immediate private sensations'.[4]

There is very widespread agreement that what Wittgenstein does with the idea of such a language is to *refute* it—that he simply proves that a 'private language' is impossible.[5] And from that proof many powerful philosophical conclusions about the relation between body and mind, about our knowledge of other minds, and about the nature of psychological concepts—and no doubt about other things as well—are thought to follow and thereby to constitute Wittgenstein's philosophy of mind. Now I believe that no such conclusions or theories—and especially those widely discussed semantic theses we have heard so much about which would link 'behavioural criteria' to 'mental concepts'—are to be found in Wittgenstein's text. In fact, I think it was an important part of Wittgenstein's own conception of what he was doing and of what needed to be done that no such philosophical doctrines or conclusions should be found there. I can hardly prove those large negative claims here, let alone establish the general line of interpretation they rest on. I will content myself with considering some of the remarks that have been thought to be central for the more-or-less orthodox way of interpreting Wittgenstein on these matters and trying to show that they do not give us reason to attribute to him any kind of impossibility proof with respect to a so-called 'private language'. Most of the proofs his interpreters have claimed to find have turned out to be pretty weak, or sometimes even

[4] An explanation along these lines of the transition to questions of 'privacy' in §243 is to be found in Fogelin, *Wittgenstein*, 154–6. A related account, with more emphasis on the notion of meaning, can be found in Hopkins, 'Wittgenstein and Physicalism', *Proceedings of the Aristotelian Society*, 75 (1974–5), 131.

[5] See, e.g. David Pears, *Ludwig Wittgenstein* (New York, 1970) and Anthony Kenny, *Wittgenstein* (London, 1973). This line of interpretation is so widespread as perhaps not to require further and more specific documentation.

downright fallacious, anyway, as most of the interpreters themselves have pointed out.

I concentrate primarily on *PI* §258 where Wittgenstein invites us to imagine keeping a diary to record the recurrence of a certain sensation by means of the new language we are trying to imagine. I associate or connect a sign "*S*" with the sensation in question by concentrating my attention on the sensation while uttering or writing down the sign. That is how I am supposed to impress on myself the connection between the sign and the sensation.

> But 'I impress it on myself' can only mean: this process brings it about that I remember that connection *right* in the future. But in the present case I have no criterion of correctness. One would like to say: whatever is going to seem right to me is right. And that only means that here we can't talk about 'right'. (*PI* §258)

These four sentences have come in for a great deal of interpretation—I would say above all over-interpretation—and have been found to contain the heart of Wittgenstein's alleged impossibility proof (and much else besides).

It is widely agreed that Wittgenstein is arguing here that after the first occasion on which I have concentrated my attention on the sensation and associated the name with it I would still be left with no way of telling whether my saying or writing the sign "*S*" on a new occasion is correct. The interpretation usually given to his saying 'I have no criterion of correctness' is that I have no test or no way of telling whether the new application is correct, and without a test or criterion of correctness in that sense I simply could not tell. *Why* do I lack a criterion of correctness in that sense? It has been supposed that the answer is given in the next sentence: I would not be in a position to distinguish what only seems to me to be correct from what is in fact correct ('whatever is going to seem right to me is right'). And, so the attributed argument runs, without any way of drawing the distinction in a particular case between what seems to me to be right and what is right, 'we can't talk about "right"' or correctness at all. Or, what is often taken to be the same thing, since we can't even talk about "right", there is no such *thing* as being right or correct. But if there is no such thing as a correct employment of the sign "*S*", then obviously the sign "*S*" has not been given any employment at all by the initial ceremony, and therefore it has not been given any meaning at all and therefore meaningful talk of one's inner experiences in a language only oneself can understand is impossible. *Quod erat demonstrandum*.

All this is, by now, quite a familiar story. And there are quite familiar difficulties in it. In the step which goes from my having no way of telling on a particular occasion whether my application of an expression is correct to the conclusion that therefore there can be no such thing as correctness or incorrectness at all Wittgenstein would be relying on and therefore committed to a fairly crude and strict form of verificationism or reductionism. He would be implying that a state of affairs could obtain or not obtain—it would be an intelligible or possible state of affairs—only if it is ascertainable by means of a particular test or criterion on each occasion that it does obtain or that it does not. Such a crude thesis is sufficiently implausible that we should perhaps be wary of attributing it to anyone who does not explicitly state it. But if Wittgenstein were indeed arguing in the familiar way I have outlined here he would seem to be committed to even more implausible conclusions (if anything can be more implausible than that form of verificationism or reductionism). He would be in danger of having proved the impossibility of any language at all.

The argument as I presented it gives as the only reason for saying that I could never tell on any particular occasion whether my application of the sign "*S*" is correct the fact that a distinction can always be drawn between the way things seem to me and the way they are, and that I would lack a reliable test or criterion of actual, as opposed to seeming, correctness. But why is that same general point not applicable to any language whatever? A distinction *can* be drawn, after all, between something's being so and its seeming to be so. Even in those cases in which the two coincide—when the way things seem is the way they in fact are—it does not *follow* from the fact that things seem a certain way that they are that way. Therefore even from the fact that it seems to a whole group or community of people that they are using an expression in a certain way and that they are using it correctly it does not immediately follow that in fact they are—even if they are. Once the possibility of its seeming a certain way to them is admitted, something more will be needed, something more than a test it could simply *seem* to all of them that they were performing, to get them to the stronger conclusion that what they are doing is in fact as it seems and is in fact correct. If Wittgenstein were saying that some test of actual as opposed to seeming correctness must always be available if an expression is to be given a meaningful employment, and if I am right that there *is* no test that could do that job, Wittgenstein would be committed to saying that no expression can be given any meaning, not even those in a so-called 'public language'.[6]

That disastrous conclusion might be avoided by denying the possibility or intelligibility of a quite general distinction between seeming correctness and actual correctness in the case of a whole group or community of speakers. Such a denial would itself have to be established, of course—no simple task, in my opinion—and that would also mean that some further reason would now have to be found for Wittgenstein's alleged dependence on the distinction between "seems" and "is" in the particular case he considers. Many have found that further reason in the fallibility of memory and the absence in this so-called 'private' case of any independent check on its reliability.[7] But is the general fallibility of memory really a good reason for denying that the 'private' speaker we are trying to imagine can remember what sensation he had a few minutes ago, or even yesterday? Suppose he is known, and knows himself, to have a good memory in other areas in which we all can check up on him. Why then could we not give him the benefit of the doubt in this case and concede that here too he is probably remembering the sensation correctly even though we outsiders cannot directly tell whether he is correct or not?[8] It would seem that only another appeal to an implausibly strict form of verificationism or reductionism could save the original argument against this very sensible-sounding objection.

But I want to drop this recapitulation of how various epistemological and metaphysical theses get attributed to Wittgenstein. Let me instead go back to those sentences in *PI* §258 that have generated such interpretations and try to suggest a simpler reading, one that is more in line with other important but less-noticed things Wittgenstein says and does.

First, it is rarely noticed, or stressed, that after raising his question about the conceivability of the kind of language he has in

[6] This form of objection to the argument as presented has been deployed to good effect in Fogelin, *Wittgenstein*, 162–3, 165–9.

[7] See Pears, *Ludwig Wittgenstein*, and Kenny, *Wittgenstein*.

[8] This form of reply is made by Pears, *Ludwig Wittgenstein*.

mind, and before coming to the concrete example he imagines in *PI* §258, Wittgenstein first ruminates about some difficult questions of philosophical method or procedure, in particular about imaginability or conceivability. Or, more precisely, about what we are inclined to *say* about imaginability or conceivability when philosophizing. He also mentions in passing what the mathematician is inclined to say about the objectivity and reality of mathematical facts. That inclination, he says, is not itself a philosophy of mathematics, any more than what we are inclined to say about our sensations is a philosophy of mind. It is something, rather, for what he calls 'philosophical *treatment*' (*PI* §254). And he follows that immediately with the general remark: 'The philosopher treats a question; as an illness (is treated)' (*PI* §255). (Here I deviate slightly from Anscombe's translation which says: 'The philosopher's treatment of a question is like the treatment of an illness.' To my ear that carries the no doubt unintended suggestion that the philosopher deals with a question *in the same way* as a doctor deals with an illness, and perhaps even that the questions the philosopher deals with themselves are, or are expressions of, illnesses. I hope I am right that no such suggestions are carried by the German 'Der Philosoph behandelt eine Frage; wie eine Krankheit.') In any case, I want to emphasize the first part—that the philosopher *treats* (*behandelt*) a question—because I think that for Wittgenstein that is meant to be something different from simply answering it.

Having made that general methodological remark, Wittgenstein immediately gets back to the subject at hand. 'Now, what about the language which describes my inner experiences and which only I myself can understand?' (*PI* §256), he asks, suggesting that that idea itself is what is now to be subjected to philosophical 'treatment'. First, the idea of naming or referring to our sensations is scrutinized, and an important point from the early sections of *Philosophical Investigations* is repeated. We are reminded that 'a great deal of stage-setting in the language is presupposed if the mere act of naming is to make sense' and 'when we speak of someone's having given a name to "pain", for example, 'what is presupposed is the existence of the grammar of the word "pain"; it shows the post where the new word is stationed' (*PI* §257). This point—even the very metaphor of 'the post where the word is stationed'—takes us back to §§28–38 of the *Investigations*. There too, after the discussion of ostensive teaching, it was said that 'the ostensive definition explains the use—the meaning—of the word when the overall role of the word in the language is clear' (*PI* §30). So there is nothing new in Wittgenstein's later concentration here in *PI* §258 on the attempt to 'associate' a name and a thing by pointing to or fixing one's attention on the thing. We are simply being reminded, in a more concrete and graphic way, of the real force of that earlier point. What is new here is the idea that the naming of the sensation is supposed to take place in a language only the speaker can understand.

Obviously, then, it is not simply a question of whether someone can name his sensations, even for his private use. We can already do that in our ordinary language, as Wittgenstein says (*PI* §243). Nor would the question be settled by imagining someone who refers to or talks about his sensations as we already do in the language we've got. In our familiar language my words for sensations are tied up with my natural expressions of sensation, so other people can understand them as well as I. They already do. So the special 'language' we are enquiring into must somehow connect words with sensations, but *not* with the natural expressions of sensation. Already the task becomes a bit more puzzling. How does a speaker of that special language name his pain? The idea of 'naming a pain' or 'naming a sensation' in that special way is what now comes in for philosophical 'treatment'.

In *PI* §258 the 'treatment' amounts, more or less, to trying to do it. Wittgenstein tries to imagine a good case of the attempt's being made and then brings out what stands in the way of success, and why. The 'treatment' consists in trying to realize the idea, to make it apply to something. That is a characteristic procedure of Wittgenstein's. He follows it right from the very beginning of the *Investigations*, and later even refers to his procedure as what he calls 'the method of §2' (*PI* §48). It is the simple expedient of trying to describe or imagine a situation to which the philosophical idea in question truly applies.[9] What happens when we try to make the idea real in that way in this case?

The idea to be made real in *PI* §258 is the idea of naming a pain

[9] The similarity between the procedure used here and that used, and even described, elsewhere, has been observed by Bassen, 'The Private Language Argument of *PI* Paragraph 258', PhD thesis (University of California, Berkeley, 1971) and by Hopkins, 'Wittgenstein and Physicalism'.

or a sensation, but without the familiar 'grammar' or 'stage-setting', or the connection with natural expressions of sensation, that are all present in our ordinary talk of our sensations. If all of that *were* presupposed I would not be talking about my sensations in a language only I can understand and so would not be fulfilling the idea we are interested in. But how is the sensation to be named when all that 'stage-setting' is dropped? Concentrating one's attention on it or inwardly pointing to it would not be enough. Why not? We know that for Wittgenstein it is because, as he puts it, 'I have no criterion of correctness' for the application of the expression '*S*' that I am trying to introduce. But why not? I suggest that it is *not* because I would have no infallible or even reliable test for recognizing the same thing again—that whole line of argument seemed dubious on other grounds anyway. Rather it is because once all the normal 'stage-setting' or 'grammar' of sensation-words is excluded from the situation, as it must be in order to 'name the sensation' in the required special way, the original naked ceremony of pointing or concentrating one's attention does not manage to determine *anything* as the correct use of the sign "*S*". There is no 'criterion' of correctness in the sense that there is nothing in what happens in the ceremony so far that brings it about that some particular application of the term is correct and that some other is not. That is what I thank Wittgenstein means here by saying there is no 'criterion of correctness'. Before trying to say more about why I think that is what he means, it is worth pointing out, parenthetically, that *if* that is what he means, *if* that were the point he is making, it would be very natural to say what he does say in the rest of *PI* §258. If there is so far not even any such thing as 'the correct application', perhaps one would then want to say, as Wittgenstein suggests, that in that situation whatever is going to seem right to me is right, and that that only means that here we cannot even talk about "right" at all.

Now why do I say that so far there is no such thing as the correct, or even the incorrect, application of the sign "*S*"? Not because there is no test or way of telling whether a particular application is correct, or because my memory might be failing me, but rather because there is so far nothing that even an infallible memory could remember.[10] Let me try to explain.

[10] This way of putting the point is to be found in Bruce Goldberg's excellent 'The Linguistic Expression of Feeling', *American Philosophical Quarterly*, 8 (1971), 89.

Suppose the person trying to name his sensation in the way we are imagining does indeed have a sensation and suppose he does concentrate his attention on it while writing down "*S*", and suppose he even undertakes to write down "*S*" whenever he has the same thing again. Has he given a name to his sensation in a language only he can understand? Has he determined what is the correct application of "*S*" in the future? It is tempting to answer 'Yes', I think, because we suppose that it will be correct for him to write "*S*" whenever he has something similar to what he is having and concentrating his attention on in the original ceremony. But every two things, or every two situations, are similar to each other in some respects; there will always be some predicates true of both of them, so in those respects they will be the same or similar.[11] So in what particular respects does the future thing or future occasion have to be similar to the original one to make it correct to write "*S*" on that future occasion? Has that been determined by the original ceremony?

It is tempting to say, I think, that the relevant respects will be whatever respects the speaker himself has in mind, whatever he is concentrating on and intending to take as relevant to the question of whether the new occasion is similar to the original one, whatever those respects are in which he intends to classify future occasions as similar. But what respects could those be in this case? The thing he is concentrating on was described as a sensation, perhaps a pain, but if he undertook to use the sign "*S*" as the word "pain" or the word "sensation" is used, if he meant to name the thing *as a* pain or *as a* sensation, the new word "*S*" would have to have the same 'grammar' as the word "pain" or the word "sensation".[12] And we all already understand those words in the common language we all speak and understand. So he cannot choose as relevant those respects which determine that a future occasion contains the same *pain* or the same *sensation* as the original ceremony, since then he would no longer be naming or referring to his inner experiences in a language only he can understand. We could all understand it. What then is he to do? How—i.e. under what aspects—is he to concentrate on his inner experience in order to fulfil that condition?

[11] This is the point stressed and exploited by Goldberg (ibid.).

[12] The importance of this point is clearly developed in Bassen, 'The Private Language Argument'.

Here we come to the important point. It is here, I think, that we naturally try to vault ourselves out of our language as it is and aspire to something we find it easy to think must be possible. Of course we don't want to make the sign "*S*" into a name for a sensation if that means giving it the same meaning as the word "sensation" already has in English. Nor do we want to make it into a sensation-word if that means giving it the kind of use or 'grammar' that sensation-words like "pain" already have. So let us try to drop talk of sensations and say the man is simply going to record the presence of *something* whenever he has it or whenever it appears—something 'inner' if you like, but something he needn't think of as a sensation in order to have. He just has it, concentrates on it, and names it. Isn't that enough to avoid this apparently rather trivial difficulty of being too closely tied to our common language? Wittgenstein suggests not. 'It would not help', he says, 'to say that it need not be a *sensation*; that when he writes "*S*" he has *something*—and that is all that can be said. "Has" and "something" also belong to our common language' (*PI* §261). They too have a 'grammar'; there are 'posts' at which those words are 'stationed', just as there are 'posts' for the words "pain" and "sensation". So for the very same reason that we had to drop the words "pain" and "sensation" from our description of the totally 'private' speaker's original ceremony we now must drop the words "has" and "something" as well. 'So in the end', as Wittgenstein remarks, 'when one is doing philosophy one gets to the point where one would like just to emit an inarticulate sound' (*PI* §261). Inarticulate, presumably, because it would have to be a sound without the kind of 'grammar' or use that any of the familiar words of our common language already have. Its role would have to be something completely new, something not already pre-empted by any of the expressions we have already got and all understand. But then, as Wittgenstein points out in a devastating parting shot, even a totally new, hitherto inarticulate sound 'is an expression only as it occurs in a particular language-game, which should now be described' (*PI* §261). So still, the original naked ceremony alone is not enough. But how can the language-game or practice with the new word be described so that word can be understood only to the speaker himself? As Wittgenstein asks in the next section, 'Is it to be assumed that you invent the technique of using the word; or that you found it ready-made?' (*PI* §262).

The important point for the interpretation of *PI* §258 is that it does not matter what is in fact before your mind, or what the thing is that you are concentrating on when you utter or write a certain expression you are trying to give meaning to. That alone is not enough to give that expression a particular meaning or kind of meaning. But not because you are concentrating on something 'inner'. The same is true of an object you might actually hold in your hand, or something you might physically point to while uttering some expression.[13] The expression in question could still be a colour-word or a numeral or a name for a kind of thing or a proper name—in fact, given the right surroundings, it could be any kind of word at all. And what kind of word it is, what kind of meaning, if any, it is to have, is not determined one way or the other by the ostensive ceremony alone. That is a point, one might say *the* point about a word's having to have a use, or the need for a general practice, that goes right back to the beginning of the *Investigations*. Nothing is settled by one's simply saying or thinking 'This word is to name or to refer to THIS, or to things like THIS.' An ostensive definition can explain the meaning, the use, of an expression only when the overall use of the expression, or of expressions of that kind, is already clear.

It will no doubt be disappointing to many people to find that this familiar, some might even say mundane, point is what lies behind the famous paragraph §258. Certainly it is a far cry from the heady epistemological and metaphysical theses that have been found there in the past. It will be disappointing to many too, I think, because it no longer amounts to a conclusive proof, or even to an argument which purports to be conclusive. What I called Wittgenstein's parting shot seems simply to be a request or a demand for a description of a language-game or institution which could give some kind of meaning to the hitherto inarticulate sound introduced by the 'private' speaker. But a challenge or a rhetorical question does not amount to a proof that no such description could possibly be given. So isn't that a disappointing resolution of the question? Is Wittgenstein saying it is impossible or not?

Whether we find what Wittgenstein says disappointing or not will depend on what we want and expect from reading his works. I think

[13] That the same conclusion holds for 'public' objects as well is emphasized by both Bassen (ibid.) and Goldberg, 'The Linguistic Expression of Feeling'.

we gain most by taking none of his questions as rhetorical, by trying to answer all of them as realistically and concretely as we can. That is what he himself tries to do in *PI* §258 with the question of how someone could give a name to his sensation in a language only he can understand. It was the very attempt to do it that seemed to take us further and further away from the workings of our language as it actually is and towards something that would have to lie outside the general practices in which that language is embodied. Perhaps that is the best, or the only, way fully to appreciate the depth and importance of those practices—or at least of some general practices. And trying to meet the later challenge (trying to describe a practice for the hitherto inarticulate sound) might be expected to bring the significance of our general practices home to us even more strongly if we have not already seen the force of the point. But for those who demand philosophical results in the form of statable philosophical propositions or theories this will no doubt remain disappointing or worse. I think all that can be said in Wittgenstein's defence at this point is—so be it. Those who seek 'results' in that way *should* remain disappointed with Wittgenstein. That is still better, I think, than inventing a set of definite doctrines and then claiming to find them, perhaps evasively suggested or only rhetorically expressed, in his unsystematic text. Wittgenstein from the very beginning of his work in the *Tractatus* was suspicious of, and later explicitly set against, the whole idea of a philosophical theory or a philosophical proposition. That alone does not mean that he managed to avoid them completely, of course. It is not that easy to avoid being in the grip of a philosophical theory. But it does mean that we will come closer to understanding Wittgenstein's thought if we try to see the *Philosophical Investigations* for what he says it is: philosophical remarks which cover 'a wide field of thought criss-cross in every direction' and in which 'the same points were always being approached afresh from different directions' (*PI* p. ix). Given our normal expectations of philosophical writing we might naturally find such an 'album' (as Wittgenstein calls it) disappointing. But then it is perhaps always disappointing to find, on picking up a book on philosophy, that we are going to have to do most of the work ourselves if we are going to get what it has to offer.

6

Wittgenstein on Meaning, Understanding, and Community

Wittgenstein began dictating what became *The Blue Book* by asking 'What is the meaning of a word?' (*BB* 1). But he immediately backed away from the question and recommended asking 'What is an explanation of the meaning of a word?'[1] instead. He thought questions as blunt as 'What is meaning?', 'What is length?', and 'What is the number one?' produce in us a 'mental cramp'. 'We feel we can't point to anything in reply to them and yet ought to point to something' (*BB* 1). Asking what it is to explain the meaning, or to understand the meaning, or for someone to mean one thing rather than another, he said, would 'cure you of the temptation to look about you for something which you might call the meaning' (*BB* 1).

The trouble with looking about you in that way is not that you will never find anything and so will be forever frustrated. What is worse is that you probably will find something. Wittgenstein thought it was almost inevitable that you would find something mental or psychological—something you take to be 'in the mind'. I think he was right about that. Images, feelings, or ideas have been the stock in trade of philosophical accounts of the workings of language. And more recent appeals to encoded 'information' or to a 'language of thought' or to mental 'grasp' of instructions or rules are no real improvement.

Once we ask what is meaning there seems to be nowhere but 'the mind' to look. An inscription there on the page, or a burst of sound

This essay was first published in R. Haller and J. Brandl (eds.), *Wittgenstein—Towards a Re-evaluation: Proceedings of the Fourteenth International Wittgenstein Symposium* (Vienna, 1990). I am grateful to Hannah Ginsborg and Hans Sluga for helpful discussions of an earlier version.

[1] L. Wittgenstein, *The Blue and Brown Books* (Oxford, 1958), 1. References to '*BB*' in parentheses in the text refer to this book.

from a human mouth, do not in themselves give us anything we can call the meaning. On their own, the signs of our language seem 'dead', as Wittgenstein puts it. 'Without a sense, or without the thought, a proposition would be an utterly dead and trivial thing' (*BB* 4). So what must be added to the 'dead' signs to give them the kind of 'life' they have for us is understanding and meaning.

It is hard to see how moving 'dead' signs around, or simply adding more 'dead' signs to those already there, could ever give those signs 'life'. So it seems that the thinking or meaning or understanding that are needed must be something immaterial, something 'with properties different from all mere signs' (*BB* 4). And so we come to think that the essential mental processes have to take place in 'a queer kind of medium', the mind; and that 'the mechanism of the mind, the nature of which, it seems, we don't quite understand, can bring about effects which no material mechanism could' (*BB* 5). Now a material mechanism could systematically produce inscriptions or sounds. It could also react to inscriptions or sounds presented to it. But how could it produce a sign with meaning or respond with understanding to signs it was presented with? Only some kind of mental mechanism would seem capable of effects like that.

Wittgenstein resists this natural conception of the workings of language. Despite his initial warning about the question 'What is the meaning of a word?' he allows himself what looks like an answer to it. In *The Blue Book* he offers:

> But if we had to name anything which is the life of the sign we should have to say that it was its use. (*BB* 4)

In *Philosophical Investigations*[2] this is put less reticently but with more qualifications as:

> For a *large* class of cases—though not for all—in which we employ the word 'meaning' it can be explained thus: the meaning of a word is its use in the language. (*PI* §43)

Signs do not get their meanings from processes accompanying or producing the utterance of them or the response to them.

> The sign (the sentence) gets its significance from the system of signs, from the language to which it belongs. Roughly: understanding a sentence means understanding a language. (*BB* 5)

[2] L. Wittgenstein, *Philosophical Investigations*, tr. G. E. M. Anscombe (Oxford, 1953). References to '*PI*' in parentheses in the text refer to this book.

Wittgenstein stresses that to understand a language 'means to be master of a technique' (*PI* §199). He says that when the concepts of understanding, meaning, and thinking are better understood it will become clear what leads us—and, he says, did lead him—to think 'that if anyone utters a sentence and *means* or *understands* it he is operating a calculus according to definite rules' (*PI* §81).

The point is not to suggest to the contrary that a person who means or understands something is operating a calculus according to indefinite or vague or open-ended rules—whatever that would be like. Nor is the complaint that the person would have to operate the calculus in a 'queer' immaterial medium. The point is that a person who means or understands a sentence he utters or hears is not operating a calculus at all. Speaking or understanding is not exhibiting the effects of the operation of a mechanism which somehow gives those signs their meaning or determines one's understanding of them. The technique mastered by someone who speaks and understands a language is nothing more than the person's capacity to produce the correct signs of the language in the right way on the appropriate occasions and to respond appropriately to the utterances of others.

To say that what gives a sign its 'life' or meaning is its use, or to say that its meaning *is* its use, is to give only a very special kind of answer to the question 'What is the meaning of a word?' Or perhaps it is a very special kind of question. The answer does not tell us what the meaning of any particular word is, or how the meaning of one word differs from the meaning of another. Someone without a dictionary handy who asks 'What is the meaning of the English word "otiose"?' will not be pleased to be told that its meaning is its use. The appeal to use in general explains only what it is for an expression to have some meaning or other, or what distinguishes meaningful inscriptions and sounds from other things that have no meaning. The same holds for understanding. To say that understanding the expression "otiose" involves understanding a language and having mastered the technique of using that word correctly in that language is not to say what understanding that word in particular amounts to, or precisely what understanding people have of it.

But even at this general level we can say that if a person is to use a certain sign correctly, or to understand what a certain sign means, there must be such a thing as the correct use of that sign, or what that sign means. There must be something that he can do correctly, and something for him to understand. We could say that someone who uses an expression correctly is following or obeying the rule for the use of that expression. Wittgenstein would not object to that way of putting it. But if that is what the person is doing, there obviously must be something that *is* the rule for the use of that expression. I do not mean that there must be some inscription or sound which states or expresses the rule. That would be just one more 'dead' sign, and could not by itself determine the correctness of anything. I mean that there must in fact be a correct way to use and to respond to the sign in question, some way of performing that amounts to following the rule for the use of that sign. Only then will there be something that amounts to using and responding to the expression correctly.

For there to be such correctness and incorrectness of performance there must be some practice or pattern of behaviour which an individual's actions either do or do not conform to. Wittgenstein puts this by saying:

> It is not possible that there should have been only one occasion on which someone obeyed a rule. It is not possible that there should have been only one occasion on which a report was made, an order given or understood; and so on.—To obey a rule, to make a report, to give an order, to play a game of chess, are *customs* (uses, institutions). (*PI* §99)

It is at this point that he adds the important thought that to understand a language is to be master of a technique. That is to stress the fact that to be master of a technique there must *be* some technique for one to be master of. There must be something that one's doing it correctly—that is to say, one's doing it—amounts to. In the case of speaking and understanding a language, there must at the very least be some regularity, some general pattern of activity, for one's performance to conform to. Otherwise there would be no such thing as correctness or incorrectness, no following a rule or failing to follow it. Of course, not every regularity is a case of rule-following, so more than simple regularity is involved in someone's doing something correctly. But at least a regularity, a practice, or some pattern of behaviour is required.

Languages are spoken in communities, and over long periods of time. Members of linguistic communities on the whole use the expressions of their language in more or less the same ways. That is a truism. It is only because there are such regularities in behaviour that there is anything for an individual speaker to conform to, and only then can a person be speaking correctly or incorrectly. But if meaning is only use, and no helpful appeal can be made to ideas in people's minds, or to their grasp of a rule, or to any other mental mechanism, it might seem that in talking about meaning there could be nothing other than consensus within the community to talk about, and nothing other than a speaker's conformity to that consensus to refer to in talking about understanding. If an expression's having a meaning is just a matter of its having a certain use in the community, then saying what its meaning is involves nothing more than saying how things are done in that community. And in the community there will be consensus in the use of the sign. So it might seem that saying how someone means or understands a particular expression—specifying the way he means or understands it—could amount to nothing more than saying that what he does with that expression is the same as what the community at large does with it.

But that is not so. It is important to see that the 'community' or 'practices' view of meaning does not restrict us to speaking only of consensus and conformity in speaking about meaning and understanding. Even if the only thing that determines what an expression means is the general practice in the use of that expression in the community it does not follow that to say what it means is to say only that it has a use in the community, or that everyone uses it in the same way. Nor does it follow that to say what a person means by his application of an expression on a particular occasion, or to say how he understands it, is to say only that his use of the expression conforms to that of his community. I think this is crucial for the proper understanding of Wittgenstein's conception of meaning or language. I want to try to bring out why.

Wittgenstein often draws attention to the human agreement or accord (*Übereinstimmung*) that must be present among members of a community for there to be consensus in their employment of their expressions. He does not mean simply beliefs or opinions as to what is so that fellow-speakers will almost certainly share. He speaks also of 'ways in which we make comparisons and in which we act'[3]—natural ways of responding on which the possibility of

[3] L. Wittgenstein, *Remarks on the Foundation of Mathematics*, tr. G. E. M. Anscombe (Oxford, 1956), VII, 21.

human language rests. If each of us were not endowed with certain natural similarities of reaction from occasion to occasion there would be no learning of language (and not much learning of anything else). And if human beings did not share their natural ways of responding with one another there would not be enough similarity or regularity throughout a community for there to be such a thing as a shared language at all.

Someone who says something in a particular language makes use of the resources of that language. But in saying what he says he is not mentioning or referring to those resources or saying anything about what they are. Nor is he stating any of the facts which make possible the acquisition and deployment of those resources. The shared reactions, affinities, or 'judgements' of members of a linguistic community are what Wittgenstein calls 'pre-conditions of the language-game'.[4] But they are not affirmed by the typical affirmations made by speakers. They could be said to be presupposed by the language or language-game, but that does not mean that affirmations made in that language state or describe or mention those agreements or shared reactions.

Of course, it is possible, if we want to, to state some facts of the kind that make the learning and therefore the sharing of a language possible. That we all respond to the gesture of pointing by looking in the direction of the line from wrist to fingertip, for example, is the kind of shared reaction which Wittgenstein thinks makes our language and other general practices possible. It is a fact that we all respond in that way. To state such 'facts of our natural history' is of course to state in language some of the facts on which the possibility of language, and hence the possibility of stating them, depends. But we are not typically, and certainly not exclusively, concerned with the conditions of our language. We usually speak of other things.

Similarly, we do not state any such facts or 'pre-conditions' when we say what a certain expression means, or when we say of someone that he means such-and-such by a particular expression he uses, or that he understands it in such-and-such a way. If the expression means something there must be a consensus in its use, and so members of the community must share those reactions or 'judgements' which make the general practice possible. But that the

[4] Ibid. V, 7.

community shares those reactions or 'judgements' is not something I state to be so when I say what some expression means in that community—for example, when I say that "otiose" in English means functionless.[5] And if an individual person did not share enough reactions or 'judgements' with his community he could never come to understand or mean things as he does. But that he shares those reactions or 'judgements' is not something I state to be so when I say that he means such-and-such by an expression he uses—for example, that he means plus by the sign he writes between the numerals "68" and "57". The 'pre-conditions' of there being something for someone to mean or understand will of course be fulfilled if what I say about him is true. But I am not saying that those conditions are fulfilled when I say what an expression means or that someone means or understands the expression in a certain way.

What holds for the shared 'judgements' or reactions in this respect holds for the general practice as well. There must be a general practice or custom in effect for there to be such a thing as a correct or an incorrect move, or a rule that is followed or broken. Such consensus could also therefore be called a 'pre-condition of the language-game'. But this consensus or uniformity of practice in the employment of our words is typically not asserted when we say things in the language. I say or imply nothing about my or anyone else's linguistic community when I say that it is raining, or when I say that 68 plus 57 equals 125.

Similarly, I do not state that there is a community-wide consensus or uniformity of practice when I say that "otiose" in English means functionless, or when I say of someone that he means plus by the sign he writes between two numerals. To say what the word "otiose" means in English is not to say simply that that expression has a standard use among the community of English speakers. Every meaningful expression of English has a standard use among the community of English speakers; that tells us nothing about what any particular expressions mean or how they differ from one another. To identify the meaning of an expression I have to say precisely *what* use it has. I cannot do that if I am restricted merely to equating its

[5] Throughout this paper I use this strictly ungrammatical way of saying what a word means in order to emphasize that it does not say that two expressions have the same meaning. The only expression mentioned is the one between the quotation marks.

use with that of some other mentioned expression. It will not be enough for me to say that the word "otiose" has the same use in the English-speaking community as the word "functionless" does. Even if that is true, it does not tell us what either "otiose" or "functionless" mean. It says only that they have the same use, and therefore the same meaning, whatever that meaning might be. I must go beyond the mere mention of expressions and use some language of my own to specify the use of the expression. But once I can do that I can say, for example, that "otiose" means functionless, or that something is rightly called "otiose" when it is without a function. In saying that I do not refer to the community at all. I make use of the resources that are provided by my community's general practice, if you like, but I do not describe or refer to that practice when I make use of those resources. I say, simply, that something is rightly called "otiose" when it is without a function.

The same is true of my saying what a particular person means by a certain expression, or what he understands by it. For example, to say only that a person uses the sign he now writes between two numerals in the same way as the rest of the community uses that sign is not to say what he means by that sign, or how he understands it. It says at most that he is part of the general consensus in that community; it says nothing about what that use specifically is.

I get no closer to saying what he means or how he understands the sign if I leave out the community and say only that he uses the sign in the same way as I do, or that he would respond to questions involving that sign with the same answers as I would give. Even if that is true, it does not specify how either of us uses that sign, or which particular answers he or I would give to those questions. I must go beyond the fact that his use of the sign agrees with that of the community, or agrees with my own use of it, and specify more directly what that use is. I can say that in the community the sign means plus, or that it is used as the sign for addition, and that he uses it in the same way. Or I can say that the answers I would give to questions involving that sign would be the sums of the numbers flanking it, and his would too. That does specify what he means or understands by it. But once I am using the language in this way to identify the function or the meaning in question, as I must, I have no need to refer to the general practices of the community, or to my own practices. I can say straight off that he means plus by the plus sign, or that he uses it and understands it as the sign for addition.

So the statement 'Members of the community all use the word "otiose" in the same way' is not equivalent to '"Otiose" means functionless in that community.' Nor is the statement 'Members of the community all use the word "otiose" in the same way as they use the word "functionless".' Similarly, the statement 'He uses the sign he writes between those two numerals in the same way as the rest of the community uses it' is not equivalent to 'He means or understand plus by that sign' or 'He means or understands that sign as the sign for addition.' That he uses it as everyone else does is one thing; that they all use it as the sign for addition is something more.

It would not be wrong to put this by saying that the fact that the community means functionless cannot be simply the fact that they all use the word "otiose" in the same way. Nor would it be wrong to say that a person's meaning plus cannot be simply the fact of his using the sign in the same way as the rest of the community uses it. It would not be wrong, but perhaps it would be dangerous. Someone might then be tempted to ask what the fact of the community's meaning functionless could possibly amount to beyond the consensus in its use, or what the fact of the person's meaning plus could possibly be, beyond his conformity to his community's general practice. If an appeal to something 'in the mind' has already been rejected, so the fact of their meaning what they do cannot be the fact of their having an idea in mind or a grasp of a rule or the operation of any other such 'mental mechanism', it might look as if there could be no such fact at all as the fact that "otiose" means functionless, and no such fact as the fact that the person means plus. The fact of anyone's meaning anything by anything might seem to have vanished into thin air.

That is the paradox presented by Kripke's Wittgenstein.[6] I think that if it is arrived at in the way I have just suggested it is an over-reaction. It *can* be said what the fact of something's meaning what it does amounts to. If that does not solve the paradox (as I think it doesn't) it is because it is really an expression of an unsatisfiable demand. (I return to this at the end.)

[6] Saul A. Kripke, *Wittgenstein on Rules and Private Language* (Cambridge, Mass., 1982).

In any case, I think it would be no solution to the alleged paradox simply to abandon the idea of there being such a thing as what a word means, or how a person understands it, and try to explain our ascriptions of meaning and understanding without supposing that they have 'truth-conditions' at all.[7] For one thing, even restricting ourselves to the conditions under which such ascriptions are justifiably asserted, the mere facts of general consensus in the community or of the conformity of individual speakers could not give us what we want. Knowing only that all members of a community use the word "otiose" in the same way does not even justify us in asserting that what "otiose" means is functionless. And knowing only that someone uses a certain sign he puts between two numerals in the same way as everyone else in the community uses that sign does not in itself justify us in asserting that what he means or understands by that sign is plus. Nor is that justified by my knowing only that he uses or responds to that sign in the same way as I do. We are never justified in making such specific ascriptions on such general and indiscriminate grounds.

Secondly, the suggestion that 'assertability conditions' for ascriptions of meaning and understanding are all we can find or even hope for can make no sense of *what* we are said to be justified in asserting when the 'assertability conditions' are fulfilled. The apparent paradox was that there is no such fact as the fact of the community's meaning plus by a certain sign, or of a certain person's meaning plus by it on a particular occasion. There is only something we are justified in asserting. But if that is so, *what* are we said to be justified in asserting? We are presumably justified in asserting that the community means plus by that sign, or that the person means plus by it. But if there really are no such facts, if what is to be asserted has no 'truth-conditions', there would seem to be nothing for us to assert. Perhaps the most we could say is that we are justified in asserting that we are justified in asserting that they mean plus. But that just moves the difficulty on to the next step. *What* are we justified in asserting that we are justified in asserting? It might be thought that we can avoid that question—that it would be enough simply to say that there is an expression we would be justified in using assertively in certain circumstances, without our having to identify anything that could be called the content of that

[7] See e.g. ibid. 73 ff.

expression, or saying what it means. The suggestion would be that when we know that a person's use of the sign conforms to the use of it in the community at large we are justified in using assertively the complex expression 'He means plus by that sign'. No 'truth-conditions' for that expression would need to be given or understood.

The suggestion fails, for two reasons, First, mere conformity to community practice does not justify us in uttering 'He means plus by that sign' rather than, say, 'He means times by it' or 'He means larger than', as long as his use of the signs for those other functions also conforms to the community's use of them. That is the first difficulty mentioned earlier. There is conformity in each case. If conformity to community practice is the only evidence, nothing in the evidence shows why we could use only the one expression assertively and not the others.

But the suggestion also fails because using assertively the expression 'He means plus by that sign' is not the same thing as asserting that the person means plus by that sign. What assertion you are making in using a certain expression assertively depends in part on what the expression you are using means. If you use a particular expression in order to ascribe a specific, determinate meaning or understanding to a community or a person, the expression you use must itself have a determinate meaning. But the notion of 'assertability conditions' and the suggestion which speaks only of the assertive use of certain mentioned expressions were introduced precisely because it was held that there is no such fact as the fact of an expression's having a determinate meaning, or someone's meaning some particular thing by an expression he uses. So that suggestion cannot make sense of our specific ascriptions of meaning and understanding at all.

The paradoxical thought that seemed to lead off in this direction was the thought that there is no such fact as the fact that "otiose" means functionless, or the fact that the person means plus by a certain sign. But all that lay behind that thought as I presented it was the uncontroversial point that the statement 'Members of the community all use the word "otiose" in the same way' is not equivalent to '"Otiose" means functionless in that community', and the statement 'He uses that sign in the same way as it is used in the community at large' is not equivalent to 'He means plus by that sign.' They clearly are not equivalent. But it obviously would be an extreme over-reaction to conclude that therefore there is no such fact as the community's meaning functionless by "otiose" or the person's meaning plus. All we can conclude is that the fact of their meaning what they do is not simply the fact that they all use certain signs in the same way.

But that just as obviously does not imply that there must be something more to the word "otiose's" meaning functionless than the community's using that word as it does, or something more to the person's meaning plus by the use of a certain sign than his using it in the same way the community uses it. What matters in each case is *how* they use the expressions in question—not simply whether they all use them in the same way, but what particular role the expressions actually play in what the people are doing when they use them. Those uses can be described. They are observable matters of fact. I do not mean to suggest that it is easy to describe them accurately. But I think there is no hope of describing or identifying those uses uniquely if we are restricted to saying only whether the use of two mentioned expressions is the same or not. And there is no hope of saying what a person means or understands by a particular expression if we are restricted to saying only whether his use of that mentioned expression conforms to his community's use of it. In neither case would we be in a position to say what the particular use in question is.

The point is perhaps obvious. But it should be equally obvious that the idea that meaning is use, and that sameness of use implies sameness of meaning, does not imply that we are or must be restricted in this way when we say what something or somebody means. There is nothing in the 'community' or 'practices' view of meaning that limits us to speaking only about sameness or difference of use of certain mentioned expressions. Nothing prevents us from making free use of any words we have at our disposal which we already understand to say as explicitly as we can exactly what something or somebody means. Again, I do not say it is always easy. But it is not impossible, as it would be if we were restricted to speaking only of sameness or difference of use of merely mentioned expressions. Using words I already understand I can say, for example, that in the English-speaking community the word "otiose" means functionless, and those of you who know what it is for something to be functionless will know exactly what "otiose" means. Or I can say of a particular person that he means plus or addition by a certain sign, and those of you who know what addition is will know exactly what he means by it. None of that is incompatible with the idea that an expression's having a meaning is just a matter of its having a certain use in some community, and that saying what its meaning is involves nothing more than saying how things are done in that community.

One charge brought against the idea that meaning is use, or that the correctness of a person's application of an expression can be measured only by its conformity to the general practice of the community, is that there then could be no such thing as incorrectness for the community as a whole. And that leads to the thought that the community can do no wrong. Whatever it calls "otiose", it seems, will be otiose, for example, or whatever it calls "plus" or "addition" will be plus or addition. This is the implication Wittgenstein is repudiating when he writes:

> 'So you are saying that human agreement decides what is true and what is false?'—It is what human beings *say* that is true and false; and they agree in the *language* they use. That is not agreement in opinions but in form of life. (*PI* §241)

He is right to repudiate it. Even if whether the word "otiose" means functionless or not depends only on how that word is used in the community, it does not follow that whatever way a community happened to use that word would make it mean functionless. It's not even true that any way the community used the word "otiose" would make it mean otiose. That word's meaning what it now does depends on how it has been and is now used. It might have been used differently, and then it would have meant something else. Human consensus in the use of the word "otiose" is not what determines whether something is otiose or not, although the particular use we give to the word does determine what it means.

Similarly, it cannot be said that plus or addition is whatever a community uses the plus-sign or the word "plus" to stand for. That we all use it as we do is what gives that sign its particular meaning. But it could have had a quite different use. Just as I could easily recognize that another community use that same sign differently, so I could even recognize that my own community had changed its use of it. If I woke up to find that my fellow-speakers no longer gave the sum when asked for the number equal to two numbers flanking a plus sign I might think they had all mysteriously forgotten how to add. More likely I would conclude, if it persisted, that they no longer meant plus by that sign. I certainly could not conclude that the sum was now something different from what it used to be. The sum is not the result of whatever the community calls "plus" or "addition". The sum is not even whatever the community calls "the sum". And the view that nothing determines what a word means except the use the community makes of it does not imply that it is.

But this will not be felt to go to the heart of the complaint that if meaning is nothing but use the community can do no wrong. I think this is partly the feeling that nothing *tells* the community how to use its words. Each individual person is instructed and made to conform to the consensus, but the practice at large floats free, without guidance from anyone or anything. The community doesn't follow any instructions, it doesn't have anything in mind.

One short answer to this complaint is to say that only particular applications can be said to be correct or incorrect, and that there must be some standard or practice or pattern of behaviour for there to be such a thing as correctness or incorrectness at all. But that answer will be found unsatisfying, since conformity to an incorrect standard does not make one's performance correct. We know that in general to do something the same way everyone else does it is not necessarily to do it right.

But at least in the case of language, if there were no shared general practice in the use of expressions there would be no such thing as what those expressions mean. You are using the word "otiose" correctly when you use it as others use it, i.e., to mean functionless. Any other use of that word by you would be incorrect. But that is not true of the community at large. If the word was used in some other way the community would not be using it incorrectly; it would simply be giving it a different use, and hence a different meaning. And someone's use of the word would then be correct only if it conformed to the use it then had in that community. That is the sense in which individual applications of words can be correct or incorrect in a way that general practices in the use of words cannot.

But I think the real source of the complaint is the feeling that what holds for the community when it means something by the words it uses must be the same (except for being more general) as what holds for an individual when he means something by the words he uses. It is felt that in each case there must be something that tells speakers what words to use, or guides them in applying their words as they do. That is why the rejection of an idea 'in the mind' or an internal grasp of a rule or the operation of any other such mental mechanism can seem to lead to the paradoxical conclusion that there is no such fact as the fact that "otiose" means functionless or that a person means plus. Of course, we can say what those facts would be if we are allowed to make use of words we already understand. Once we know what it is for something to be functionless we can tell whether a certain word means that or not; and once we know what a sum is we can tell whether a particular sign means plus. But that does not give us a way of stating the facts of meaning which could be understood by someone who did not already understand those words, who did not already know what it is to be functionless or what the operation of addition is.

That, I believe, is the real source of dissatisfaction. The facts we can discover and state about the meanings of expressions could not be appealed to in the kind of explanation of meaning and language that we aspire to in philosophy. We think we must find some facts, the recognition of which would not require that we already speak and understand a language, and some rules which would tell us what, given those facts, it was correct to say. Familiar, everyday statements of what a particular expression means cannot serve. They make essential use of words that are already 'alive', that already have a meaning, so they seem incapable of explaining in the right way how any words come to have any meaning or come to be understood at all. Nothing we say within the language about the meaning or understanding of expressions could serve to get us into language in the first place. So something 'in the mind', something that could lead us from what we can recognize to what it would be correct to say, continues to seem the only alternative.

7

Quine's Physicalism

Quine's philosophical interest in the nature of the world has been predominantly ontological. The question has been: what is there? What objects exist? And how do we tell? To this last meta-metaphysical question his answer is well known and by now apparently accepted almost everywhere ontology is practised. We tell what there is by rewriting systematically in canonical quantificational form the totality of our current science, or all the sentences we can in good conscience accept, and then looking to see what objects must fall within the range of the variables of quantification to make those sentences true. To be is to be the value of a bound variable.

There are two separate ingredients in this view of ontology: the question of the criterion of commitment—what determines which objects a set of sentences is committed to—and the question of what objects we are in fact committed to by a certain stretch of discourse or, putting it strategically, what objects we should commit ourselves to in schematizing our views in canonical quantificational form. Answers to that second question can differ widely even though the same criterion of commitment is accepted by all.

Quine's official advice for answering the substantive question is—or at least used to be—'tolerance and an experimental spirit'.[1] We seek the simplest scheme, but simplicity alone, even if we understood it better, would not necessarily yield a unique solution. A 'physicalistic' ontology of external physical bodies, for example, is not easily said to be simpler than a 'phenomenalistic' ontology of 'individual subjective events of sensation or reflection'.[2] Each scheme has its advantages, and one cannot be reduced to or

This essay was first published in R. Barrett and R. Gibson (eds.), *Perspectives on Quine* (Blackwell, Oxford, 1990).

[1] W. V. Quine, 'On What There Is', in his *From a Logical Point of View* (Cambridge, Mass., 1953), 19.

[2] Ibid., 17.

translated into the other. In the 1950s Quine was still recommending that each scheme should be developed on its own and the relations between them explored.

By the time of *Word and Object* in 1960 the purely phenomenalistic ontology had been pretty firmly rejected in favour of the physicalistic scheme, and on just the kinds of grounds we would expect—its lack of utility for a general theory of the world. Subjective sensory objects could never suffice to the exclusion of physical objects, so we have to acknowledge physical objects anyway, and sensory objects are not needed in addition to physical objects, either to account for the truth of perceptual statements or to account for the truth of what we say about physical objects themselves. Physical objects, on the other hand, are indispensable. Quine held in 1960 that 'in a contest for sheer systematic utility to science, the notion of physical object still leads the field'.[3] We must accept physical objects, so in that sense we must be physicalists.

In this ontological form physicalism makes no claim of exclusiveness. Quine's physicalism has always been accompanied by an explicit acknowledgment of other, non-physical objects as well—abstract objects such as classes. There is simply no making sense of the truths of mathematics without quantifying over such things. They suffice for that purpose, he is happy to find, but there is no eliminating them. True to his criterion, Quine accepts the consequences and, even if somewhat reluctantly, admits the existence of those abstract entities needed to serve as the objects of mathematics and hence as objects essential to the totality of the science of the world.

What there is, for Quine, is physical objects and classes. Those are the objects that make up the world. At least that is how things were up to and including *Word and Object*. It would be better now to say that what there *was* for Quine was physical objects and classes. Today it is different. Today, for Quine, there are only classes. But despite that purely ontological economy, he still holds firmly to something he calls physicalism.

The change in view is the result of developments both in physics and in philosophy. The philosophical developments are largely Quine's own—in particular, his thesis of the inscrutability of reference. That is the view that it is indeterminate what objects the sin-

[3] W. V. Quine, *Word and Object* (Cambridge, Mass., 1960), 238.

gular terms, pronouns and bound variables of our true sentences refer to. All possible evidence from the use of such sentences is compatible with assignments of objects of any one of several different kinds as referents for a given sentence. This important idea was not explicit in *Word and Object*. It finds its source, I believe, in Quine's absolutely crucial insistence on the primacy of the sentence over the term—one of the central ideas of his philosophy. And it has as one of its consequences a certain indeterminacy of translation. Another consequence, although more remote, is the ultimate withering away of ontology as the key to the philosophical study of the way the world is.

The inscrutability of reference might seem at first sight to serve the interests of physicalism, since it gives us a way of holding to a purely physical ontology even in a world first described as containing non-physical minds attached to some of the physical objects. Dualism is in that respect an unstable ontological view. As long as the minds in question are never disembodied, there will always be an associated physical state of a body for every state of each non-physical mind. It will be that particular state of the associated body, whatever it happens to be, which at that moment accompanies the state of mind in question. To specify the relation between mind and body in this way is to specify a function which assigns to each state of a mind in that world a particular physical state of the body that has that mind attached to it. This is what Quine calls a proxy function, in this case from minds to bodies, and it effects a reduction of the one domain of objects to the other. In interpreting what looked like mental sentences we can then bypass all quantification over mental states or entities and move directly to physical states or bodies as the only objects involved. What seemed to be mental predications would then come to be true of physical states of the body without affecting the truth value of any of the original, apparently mental, sentences.

This is a way of avoiding an ontology of non-physical, mental entities. And since there are plenty of physical objects and states which lack accompanying mental states, there is no prospect of eliminating the physical ontology by working a proxy function in the opposite direction. The domain of the physical is in that sense wider than that of the mental, and every mental thing has its purely physical proxy, so the mental can be ontologically reduced to, or collapsed into, the physical.

The threat to physical objects comes not from mentalism, but from physics itself. It was already clear that familiar physical bodies like chairs and apples were not to serve as the values of the variables of the truths of physics. Aside from the vagueness of the boundaries of such bodies, there was also a need to accommodate physical masses or stuff like salt and water, and physical events or processes, none of which are bodies at all. Quine has therefore long pressed for the generic notion of a *physical object*—not just a body but, roughly speaking, the material content of any portion of space-time, contiguous and continuous or not.

This view of material content or stuff might have sufficed for a world of small, well-behaved particles like atoms in the classical sense, or even electrons if they had identity-conditions. But Quine finds he must now adapt his physicalism to the realization that the notion of matter itself is problematic at the level of electrons and lower. Particles will no longer serve as entities; what counts are states, and since bodies themselves have gone by the board, not states of bodies but states of regions. In his somewhat wistful essay 'Whither physical objects?' Quine observes that 'the physicists' age-old attachment to matter has relaxed. Matter is quitting the field, and field theory is the order of the day.'[4] The notion of physical object now no longer leads the field in the contest for systematic utility to science.

Field theory for Quine speaks only of the distribution of various states over space-time regions. With talk of the material content of those space-time regions eliminated, that is all we are left with. What then is there? What objects exist? What entities do such theories commit us to? If not physical objects even in Quine's extended sense, what becomes of physicalism?

The problem is serious if physicalism is still meant to be an ontological thesis. The device of the proxy function can now serve to eliminate the physicalist ontology completely, just as it banished minds from a world containing associated physical objects. The first step is to quantify only over space-time regions themselves. They are then the only things that exist, and each of them is in some physical state or other. If only a limited number of such states were possible we could have a different predicate denoting each of them and thus restrict our ontological commitments to nothing more

[4] W. V. Quine, 'Whither Physical Objects?', *Boston Studies in Philosophy of Science* (1976), 499.

than the space-time regions alone. But if we must allow for an infinity of different possible states—to specify points along continua of variation in intensity of different magnitudes, for example—we will need ways of quantifying over such states. And here the proxy function comes into play. All we need to quantify over to make sense of the predication to a space-time region of a certain degree of intensity of a property is the space-time region itself and the number that measures the intensity. Rather than say that there is such a thing as the temperature of a certain region *r* we can say simply that there is a number *n* of which a certain predicate 'F' is true. The 'F' in question will be something like 'is the number of temperature-degrees-Celsius of the region *r*'. We are left, then, with only numbers and space-time regions among the values of the variables.

Once numbers have been admitted for any purpose they might as well be used for any other ontological purpose for which they serve. So the space-time regions can now be eliminated in favour of sets of the ordered quadruples of real numbers that pick each one of them out. A system of coordinates must be fixed for that purpose, but with any arbitrary starting-point in place, reference to each of the regions will be secured by a set of quadruples of real numbers alone. To attribute a state of a certain degree of intensity to a space-time region is therefore to be committed at most only to numbers—to those real numbers that are the region and those that measure the intensity. This is ultimately only an ontology of classes. The rest is predication, and so irrelevant to ontology.

Pythagoras lives. All there is is numbers, or classes. And there are no classes of elements that are not classes. Without bodies, without physical objects, without space–time regions, without any other objects, it is just classes all the way down. The only ground element is the null set; all the rest of the vast abstract ontology is perched on that.

Physics and philosophy appear to have converged to yield this startling result, but it was actually implicit in the idea of ontological reduction alone, or what we might call in a Quinian spirit 'deferred ontology'.[5] Recent developments in physics might have encouraged the change, but they were not essential. Physical

[5] For Quine's idea of 'deferred ostension' see 'Ontological Relativity' in his *Ontological Relativity and Other Essays* (New York, 1969), 39–41.

objects themselves, if they were still around, could simply be identified by proxy function with their spatiotemporal coordinates, and those coordinates themselves could be reduced to the numbers that identify them. And so, eventually, to classes. The predicates we attribute to objects could then be rewritten or reconstrued as true rather of the numbers or the classes in question. So the 'airy' abstract ontology Quine is now left with was available all along. Deferred ontology, or the inscrutability of reference, was enough.

You might think that a physicalist without physical objects would not have much to believe in. That would be true if physicalism remained an ontological thesis. Quine did think of physicalism that way in the past. He would then have found unattractive the ontological economy we now know he could have achieved by going only for abstract objects right from the beginning. He reminisces about the old days of physicalism and speaks of his 'robust sense of the reality of physical objects'[6] as a reason he then had to resist the ontological economy he has now accepted. It was presumably that same robust sense that led him to proclaim with Nelson Goodman forty years ago: 'We do not believe in abstract objects . . . We renounce them altogether.'[7]

I must say that I find such native or intuitive ontological predilections puzzling, and for what I think are good Quinian reasons. Quine says he wanted his ontology to do justice to his 'robust sense of the reality of physical objects', but what could that 'robust sense' be? It could presumably amount to nothing more than a robust disposition to assert or to assent to whole sentences which eventually get parsed as containing what come to be called physical object terms. That robust disposition is not a 'sense' of anything ontological. It couldn't be. It is prior to ontology. It is something that could be expressed only in sentences we understand and accept before we start any systematization of the language, when there is still no question of ontology at all. At that point we have equally robust dispositions to assert sentences apparently about abstract objects, and about mental objects, and about many other things, but that presumably does not amount to a reason for favouring an abstract, or a mentalistic, or any other particular ontology.

6 'Whither Physical Objects?', 502.

7 N. Goodman and W. V. Quine, 'Steps toward a Constructive Nominalism', *Journal of Symbolic Logic* (1947), 105.

Of course, anyone who thought that we are directly and indubitably acquainted with physical objects would know they exist and so would know that any acceptable ontology simply has to admit them. The only question would then be whether it is also best to quantify over physical objects at the higher 'theoretical' levels of discourse, further removed from what is directly observed. But Quine rejects that whole idea. For him, all objects are in the relevant sense 'theoretical'. That is again a consequence of his stress on the primacy of the sentence. Observation *sentences* are direct responses to present sensory stimuli, but what objects, if any, those sentences refer to is itself a 'theoretical' question to be answered only by the smoothest and most economical rewriting of all the sentences with which they are systematically connected—ultimately the whole of science. Ontology is in that sense a wholly 'theoretical' matter. So Quine's views appear to leave no room for invidious ontological distinctions felt beforehand among kinds of objects, or among our attitudes towards them. Physicalism as an ontology should be at the outset no more or no less attractive than any other ontology. There is, after all, no first philosophy, nothing antecedent to all our beliefs about the world which could somehow give us an inside tip about what there really is, or what we should really want our best theories to commit us to. I confess that I have never felt I understood ontology very well. I could never see how a 'robust sense of the reality' of certain objects could be the *source* of one particular ontological view rather than others. It is reassuring to find that such a 'sense' plays no role in Quine's most recent ontologizing.

In any case, for whatever reasons, he and his fellow physicalists in the old days, Quine says, 'welcomed bodies with open arms. Ungrudgingly we opened the way to other physical objects too, however ill shaped and loosely knit, for at worst they were kinfolk.'[8] But not all species of object were so warmly greeted at that ontological haven, even if they were smooth and symmetrical and free of all blemish. Mathematical objects, Quine says, 'attained the ontological scene only begrudgedly for services rendered. A way of dispensing with them and making do with a strictly physical ontology would have been exceedingly welcome, whereas the opposite reduction did not appeal to us.'[9] And just think what the world has

[8] 'Whither Physical Objects?', 502. [9] Ibid.

now come to. Those things that were let in only at the service entrance, and only on sufferance because pure principle demanded it, have now taken over everywhere!

Quine thought it would have been best to find some principle to exclude such objects. Alas, it has turned out not to be possible, but what warms his physicalist heart about this whole débâcle is that it shows that physics, or the physical, still dominates after all. It was only to better serve physics that physical objects had to be introduced over simple bodies. It was again for the development of physics that those physical objects had to give way in turn to space-time regions. And then there was no need to stop simplifying even further the ontology of physics. Classes had to be there for the mathematics needed for physics anyway, so that space-time regions themselves could be collapsed into those very classes. But the driving force, the 'bias' as Quine puts it, was physical first and last. That is the consolation, even though among all the objects that now make up the world there is not to be found a single physical object.

That consolation—the primacy of physics—is what keeps alive Quine's hopes for a significant physicalism in a world populated exclusively by abstract objects. But one conclusion seems to be—and Quine draws it—that 'ontology is not what mainly matters'.[10] Ontology deals only with objects, but it is what we say about the objects that exist that counts for our theory of the world, especially now given the inscrutability of reference. We must specify something or other to serve as objects of reference of what we say. What has been found to serve best for all cases all at once are the purely abstract objects of set theory. But that concerns only the references of our sentences. And for Quine 'sentences, in their truth or falsity, are what run deep; ontology is by the way.'[11] Physicalism, in order to survive, must now be understood not as a thesis about the objects referred to by the referring parts of a sentence, but rather about something distinctive in the rest of the sentence, in what is said about those objects, in the predicates involved. Questions of reference and ontology have become incidental to what the world is like, and now, as Quine puts it, 'the lexicon of natural science, not the ontology, is where the metaphysical action is.'[12]

[10] W. V. Quine, 'Facts of the Matter', in R. Shahan and C. Swoyer (eds.), *Essays on the Philosophy of W. V. Quine*, (Norman, Okla., 1979), 164–5.

[11] Ibid. 165.

[12] 'Whither Physical Objects?', 504.

The lexicon of *physics* in particular is where the action is for Quine. It plays an essential role in expressing the metaphysical idea that, roughly speaking, the world is fundamentally physical and only physical. This makes it difficult to give some fixed, determinate content to the doctrine of physicalism, since no one can say once and for all what any lexicon which would count as physical must be. There is no telling in advance what vocabulary will be most useful to physicists in devising their theories. Any predicates we choose today could be jettisoned tomorrow while physics marches on with a new lexicon.

Quine thinks this leaves his formulation of physicalism 'incomplete'.[13] But it seems to me worse than that. The gap in formulation can never be filled in, so the thesis contains nothing to make it a version of *physicalism* in particular. To say only that there is or will be some single, unified science capable of expressing everything that is fundamentally true of the world is not to attribute any specific character to the world. It is to say only that there is a body of truth, and some science is capable of discovering it. To express the idea that the world is a purely physical world you at least have to add that the science in question is physics, or a purely physical science. And for that you need a determinate notion of the physical. So what exactly does the doctrine of physicalism say about the world? What character does it attribute to it? I think this is a more serious problem than it has seemed.

Assuming a physical vocabulary fixed somehow, the metaphysical pay-off of physicalism for Quine is largely to be found in its bearing on the nature of the mental. If the world is through and through physical, then there is no distinctively mental realm. It was easy enough to see how this would go when it was a question of objects, of ontology: there are only physical objects in the world, and no minds or mental objects, But now even physical objects are out of the way, and the thesis must be formulated in terms of predicates or lexicon alone. It can scarcely be the thesis that the physical predicates are the only predicates we have. It is rather the idea that the physical lexicon is 'fundamental' in some way, or more 'fundamental' than others. The physical sentences must somehow be the only sentences that are determinately true, or the only ones that are 'fundamentally' true, so that strictly speaking there are

[13] 'Facts of the Matter', 166.

only physical facts. The physical lexicon alone must somehow be sufficient to express everything that is the case.

That is the idea behind Quine's thesis of the indeterminacy of translation and his corresponding rejection of meaning, the mental, the intentional, or the propositional attitudes as fit subjects for serious scientific study. There is simply no 'fact of the matter', for Quine, whether a certain expression as used on a particular occasion, or in general, means such-and-such or is to be translated one way rather than another. It is not just that we can come to conflicting opinions about it on the basis of the available evidence; that is presumably true of all hypotheses that go beyond the evidence. It is not mere inductive, epistemic underdetermination. It is rather that there simply is no truth of the matter beyond the physical facts. We might not know what those physical facts are, but given what they are, whatever they are, there is nothing in the world for our opinions about translation or meaning to conflict about.

The same holds for most attributions of so-called propositional attitudes, involving as they do the indirect quotation of the person's actual or potential words. The 'true and ultimate structure of reality' for Quine includes 'no quotation but direct quotation and no propositional attitudes but only the physical constitution and behavior of organisms'.[14] In reality, it is not true that the word 'rabbit' means rabbit or that there are people who think it is raining. In declaring the unreality of all such specially intentional or mental phenomena Quine is speaking only from the standpoint of his physicalism. That doctrine is therefore crucial to the defence of his views on mind and meaning.

Of course, we all speak in intentional or apparently mentalistic terms, and Quine the physicalist does not recommend that we stop. Nor is there any hope of strictly reducing the intentional or mental vocabulary to some purely physical idiom. He stresses only what he calls the extreme looseness of fit between all such mentalistic language and the true character of reality. One way to try to express the fundamentally physical character of reality is to say that there is no difference in the world without there being a physical difference. More precisely, 'there is no difference in matters of fact without a difference in the fulfilment of the physical-state predicates by space-time regions.'[15] Applied to the mind, this means for Quine that:

[14] *Word and Object*, 221.

[15] 'Facts of the Matter', 166.

> If a man were twice in the same physical state, then, the physicalist holds, he would believe the same things both times, he would have the same thoughts, and he would have all the same unactualized dispositions to thought and action. Where positions and states of bodies do not matter, there is no fact of the matter.[16]

The lingering reference here to bodies is accidental. We can say simply 'where the physical states of space-time regions do not matter, there is no fact of the matter.'

The implications of this thesis will vary depending on how widely or narrowly we take the notion of 'the same physical state'. Must a person have the same thoughts, feelings, or mental life whenever the region exactly enclosing his body is in the same physical state? On one reading the person is not in the same physical state if different purely physical relational predicates are true of him. Being next to, or being exactly 3,000 miles due east of, a certain place or thing is something that might or might not be true of someone without being discernible in the region exactly enclosing his body. All it takes to make a difference in what is true of him is a different thing in a distant location, or a different physical state in another region. My neighbour's location affects what is true of me without any effort on my part, but I am in a different physical state if he is in Hawaii from what I am in if he is in Haiti. Or perhaps I should say the world is in a different state—a different physical state. So even to allow for different relational but purely physical truths the thesis must presumably be read as saying only that where the physical states of no space-time regions at all matter, there is no fact of the matter. Otherwise, some purely physical differences could not be accommodated. So the physicalist thesis is at most that if the whole universe were twice in the very same physical state the same thoughts, feelings, or mental life would be present each time. The states need not be identifiable by looking only within what we loosely call the person's own body.

When the expression 'the same physical state' is taken maximally broadly in this way we might begin to wonder whether the universe ever could get into exactly the same physical state twice. Any two temporally distinct physical states will each occur at a different temporal distance from something else that occurs, so there will always be something true of each interval that is not true of the other, even if they are otherwise very similar. They are in that broad

[16] Ibid. 162.

sense different physical states, just as I am put into different physical states by my neighbour's wanderings even though everything looks pretty much the same here at home. But if no two temporally distinct physical states of the universe could be the same physical state, perhaps we do not concede very much to the physicalist when we agree that *if* the whole universe were to be twice in the very same physical state the same thoughts, feelings, or mental life would be present as well.

But now there is a difficulty for physicalism from another direction. It says there is no difference in the world without a physical difference, or no difference in matters of fact without a difference in physical states of space-time regions. But what is this 'world' of which it speaks, or these 'matters of fact' which it appeals to? To say that the *physical* world or *physical* matters of fact are what are at stake would reduce physicalism to a truism. That there is no difference in the *physical* world without a physical difference, or that there is no difference in *physical* matters of fact without a difference in truths about the physical states of space-time regions, is hardly controversial. The most adamant dualist, even spiritualist, could accept it.

It would seem then that it must be the world in general, or all matters of fact, that physical matters of fact somehow exhaust or underlie. To give physicalism some bite, the world in question must be understood as, to coin a phrase, everything that is the case. But Quine cannot say that every matter of fact is a physical matter of fact, or that the purely physical lexicon is adequate to express everything that is the case. Nor can he say that there is no difference in truths or in matters of fact without a physical difference. The whole domain of mathematical truth stands as an impressive counter-example. To go no further than arithmetic, the fact that 7 plus 5 is 12 is not the same fact as the fact that 9 times 8 is 72. They are different mathematical truths. Here, then, is a difference in the world or in what is the case with no physical difference. We cannot say simply 'Where the physical states of space-time regions do not matter, there is no fact of the matter.'

Someone who thought that mathematical statements do not really state how things are, or that they are not really truths about the world, might try to defend an exclusive physicalism that way (although he would still have to explain his idea of 'the world' without simply identifying it with the physical world). But what could support the idea that mathematical statements are not about the world, except the idea that mathematical statements are not true or false? And what could possibly support that? Certainly nothing that would appeal to Quine. For him, and rightly I believe, 'sentences, in their truth and falsity, are what run deep.'[17] If the world is everything that is the case, or everything that is said to be so by whatever is true, then it is part of the way the world is that 7 plus 5 is 12.

Quine therefore tries to restrict his physicalism by speaking not of difference but of change: there is no change without a change in physical states of space-time regions.[18] This version is meant to avoid the difficulty about mathematics since 'mathematical objects ... [Quine says] are changeless.'[19] One sees the point of this manoeuvre—to restrict physicalism to the changeable world—but is it strictly true, on Quine's view, that mathematical objects are changeless? A space-time region, ontologically speaking, just *is* a set of ordered quadruples of real numbers—a mathematical object. But if a region could change from being in one physical state to being in another, then what was once true of that abstract mathematical object would no longer be true of it. It would have changed. Simpler examples are at hand. Forty-eight used to number the united states of America. Now it doesn't. So the number 48 has changed in that respect. When we say, as we do, that the country is what has changed, and that the number 48 has remained unchanged throughout, we are not speaking ontologically. It presumably takes some sort of *object* if there is going to be such a thing as change, so in a world whose only objects are abstract mathematical objects those objects will have to be what changes if anything does.

It therefore might seem better to put the point in terms not of mathematical objects but of mathematical truth. There can presumably be no change of mathematical truth, even if mathematical objects could be said in that odd way to change some of their non-mathematical properties. Anything that is mathematically true of mathematical objects is non-temporally or eternally true of them. That is something that cannot change. So the purely mathematical world—understood as a domain of truth—is changeless after all.

The trouble is that this holds for all truth, and therefore for the

[17] 'Facts of the Matter', 165. [18] Ibid. 166. [19] Ibid. 166.

entire world as Quine understands it. There can be no change in the truth-value of anything that is true, once all spatial and temporal and other indices are fully specified. If it is true that feature *F* is present at a certain place and time, it is (and was) eternally true. Likewise, if it is false. Quine has always endorsed this idea of the eternal sentence. But then, it appears, no truth about a space-time region could strictly speaking change. What happens when what we loosely call change occurs is that a certain complex predicate is true of an entire space-time region, and a different predicate is true of another region. But that is difference, not change, even if the two regions are very close, even contiguous, temporally. It is still just a difference in two matters of fact, and there is no thing that has changed. On this view what we call change is really just difference.

But appealing only to differences in matters of fact is not enough to express physicalism in an acceptable way, as we saw. To say that with no differences in physical truths or matters of fact there are no differences in any truths or matters of fact would run up against the original problem of accommodating mathematical truth. There we have difference, but with no physical difference. How then is the doctrine of physicalism to be stated, and what exactly is it meant to imply about the mind or intentional phenomena?

Suppose we continue to speak loosely, as we do, of a changing or a changeable world, and of physicalism as the thesis that there is no change without physical change. This is still not satisfactory, since we lack an independent characterization of the physical, but even without it perhaps we can assess some of its implications for the mental or the intentional. Physicalism as now understood is not the thesis that there is no mental difference without a physical difference, so it does not directly imply that someone who is twice in the same physical state would have the same thoughts, feelings or mental life on each occasion. It implies at most that someone who changes from being in one mental state to being in another also changes from being in one physical state to being in another. Even if a person undergoes the same mental change on two different occasions—for example, he twice stops believing that it is raining and starts believing that it isn't—it does not follow from this thesis that he undergoes the same physical change on each occasion. We can conclude only that he does not change his mind either time without undergoing some physical change or other. He starts out in the same mental state each time, but he need not start out in the same physical state each time, or end up in the same physical state either. So on this thesis the mental state of believing that it is raining, or believing that it is not raining, need not always be associated with one and the same physical state.

Nor does physicalism as now understood imply that a person undergoing physical change when a change in his mental life occurs always undergoes a change in state that could be identified by inspecting only the space-time region exactly enclosing his body. All that follows is that he changes in respect of some physical state or other. But strictly speaking a person changes his physical state every time any physical change occurs anywhere in the universe. So the most we can conclude is that there is no mental change without some physical change somewhere in the universe.

Anyone who believes in a constantly changing physical world might well accept that thesis, even if he also believes that there are mental or intentional facts—that "rabbit" means rabbit, for example, or that people sometimes believe that it is raining. If we think that change is a constant and ubiquitous feature of the world—at least at the submicroscopic level of fundamental states of space-time regions—then everything else we believe about the world will obviously have to be consistent with that fact and accommodate itself to it. That seems to present no difficulty in the case of mathematics. It puts no constraints on what mathematical beliefs we can hold. What constraints, if any, does it impose on what psychological or mental or intentional statements could be true?

It does imply that there is no completely disembodied psychology, or at least that there is no psychological or mental change in a world in which there is no physical change. But anyone who already believes in constant physical change will not be reluctant to admit that mental or intentional sentences are true in a world in which there is constant physical change. The same holds of all sentences that are true. If the world is everything that is the case, and one thing that is the case is that 9 times 8 is 72, and another thing that is the case is that there is constant and ubiquitous physical change, then 9 times 8 is 72 in a world in which there is constant and ubiquitous physical change. Of course that does not mean that the one statement is true *because* the other one is. And neither statement can be reduced to or translated into the other. Neither statement implies the other. It is just that they are both true. That, we take it, is just the way the world is.

But if another thing that is the case is that, for example, someone just came to believe that it is not raining, and it is also the case that there is constant and ubiquitous physical change, then when the person started believing that it is not raining there was some physical change occurring in the world. The person did not get that belief without some physical change occurring. Of course that does not mean that the psychological statement is true *because* the physical statement is true. And neither statement can be reduced to or translated into the other. Neither statement implies the other. It is just that they are both true. That, we take it, is just the way the world is. If we believe that the person did not get that belief without some physical change occurring, or if we believe in general that no psychological or mental event occurs without some physical change occurring, have we thereby accepted Quine's physicalism? No one who believes in constant physical change could deny it, whatever else he believes as well.

It seems to me that any view of the world that would accord truth to psychological or mental or intentional statements has to find room for such phenomena in a constantly changing physical world. But that demand is not imposed by a metaphysical thesis called physicalism. It is no more than any reasonable believer in psychological or mental or intentional facts has ever had to do. A misplaced emphasis on objects or ontology has muddied the waters here. It was thought that our mental life could be secured in a physical world only by finding some non-physical entity for it to occur in, or to—something that can think and feel and act, and yet could exist apart, on its own. And no such entities were forthcoming. But ontology was the wrong thing to be looking at, as Quine's more recent reflections remind us. Dualism was always a non-starter as an ontology.

Once we get away from concentrating on the object and focus instead on the fact, or stop thinking of the term and look instead to the whole sentence, we find that what needs to be understood is the nature or structure of psychological or mental or intentional facts—the conditions under which full sentences of those kinds are true. And since we also know sentences of many other kinds to be true as well, our understanding must be consistent with, and somehow fitted in with, all those other truths. It is not an easy job.

Psychological or mental or intentional sentences have many special features that make it hard to see how they work and how they are related to the physical or mathematical or other non-intentional truths or falsehoods which typically form part of their content. But to say it is difficult, even extremely difficult, or even that we still have no idea how to do it, is a far cry from saying that such sentences are simply not true, or not really true, or that psychological or intentional phenomena are simply not part of the world.

Quine holds that psychological or intentional or attitude-attributing sentences are not determinately or objectively true or false. They do not state anything that is so, or not so, in reality. They belong to that indeterminate realm of sentences we all persist in uttering most of the time even though their truth or falsity is not fixed by anything in the world—by any matters of fact at all. But the facts he thinks they float free of are all and only the physical facts (with perhaps the mathematical facts thrown in as well). I agree that they float free of all those facts. No psychological or intentional or attitude-attributing sentences follow from all the physical (and all the mathematical) truths alone. In that sense they are underdetermined by the physical (and mathematical) facts. But that will show that such sentences are not determinately true of the world only if it can be shown that the world is really nothing more than the physical (or the physical and the mathematical) facts. That is what Quine's physicalism says, and it is therefore an essential ingredient in his thesis of indeterminacy. The mere fact of one set of sentences being underdetermined by another does not imply that the truth or falsity of those underdetermined sentences is indeterminate, or that there is no fact of the matter as to whether they are true or false. The sentences of physics are underdetermined relative to the truths of mathematics, for example, but that does not imply that there is no determinate physical truth, or that there is no fact of the matter as to whether the sentences of physics are true.

A defence of Quine's physicalism is therefore essential to establishing the indeterminacy of the mental or intentional, and hence to the exclusion of psychological or mental or intentional sentences from the class of sentences which state the way the world is. We still have no independent specification of the domain of the physical, so we still do not know even how to state that thesis. That is one unsolved problem. But even if we could state the thesis of physicalism we would need some reason for thinking it is true—for thinking that mental or intentional sentences are indeed incapable of stating the way the world is. That is the doctrine of indeterminacy, or 'no fact of the matter'. Physicalism, then, cannot be brought in to establish that doctrine in the first place. It is part of it.

So what reasons can we find for accepting such a physicalism? What do we start with, and what do we have to go on in trying to decide whether it is true? Of course, we think many physical sentences are true. No one wants to deny that. But that is not enough. We have to believe somehow that they are the *only* sentences that are true. But we also think many mental or intentional sentences are true as well. And as long as we think some mental or intentional sentences are true we will have good reason to reject Quine's purely physicalistic picture of the world, just as we have reason to reject it if we think anything is mathematically true.

8

Meaning, Understanding, and Translation

I

When I hear someone speaking and understand what is said, do I translate the words I hear into words of my own? I think the answer in general is 'No'. Of course, I might sometimes have to translate what I hear if I am not very good in the language the other person is speaking. But if I speak that language well, and the other person is speaking clearly and intelligibly enough, I simply understand. There is no question of translating what I hear into words of my own. If I speak the language, the words I hear *are* words of my own. I don't need any others.

If I don't always translate, do I nevertheless always *interpret* the words I hear and understand? It might seem that of course I do, since understanding what you hear is just the same thing as interpreting it. If that really is what interpreting is, and if I am right about translation, it follows that interpreting something you hear cannot be the same thing as translating it into words of your own. Translation involves the substitution of one expression for another, but in understanding or interpreting something said in a language I already speak well, the only expressions involved are those I hear.

But there is also such a thing as giving an interpretation of what was said. Like translation, it is a matter of producing another expression which you believe stands in a certain relation to the original. If I am right that understanding does not require translation, it does not require giving an interpretation in this sense either. That is not to say that I cannot offer an interpretation of what I hear if I want to. But I could not even search for such an interpretation if I did not understand what I heard in the first place. And I

This essay was first published in the *Canadian Journal of Philosophy: Supplementary Volume*, 16 (1990).

could never know that I had come up with a proper interpretation if I did not also understand the new expression I offer in place of the original.

This takes us to the reason why understanding an expression could not in general involve translating it into some other expression or giving an interpretation of it. If it did, we would never manage to understand anything. Translating (or giving an interpretation of) an expression involves producing another expression which you know means the same as (or is an interpretation of) the original. But that is not sufficient for understanding that expression. It is possible to know that two expressions mean the same without knowing what either one of them means. If your knowledge that two expressions mean the same is going to amount to understanding one of those expressions it must also be true that you understand the expression known to be its translation or interpretation. But if understanding an expression always required a translation or interpretation into another expression, understanding the second expression would involve knowing that it means the same as still another expression. And that knowledge again would not be sufficient, since you would have to understand that further expression in turn. And that would require knowing that it means the same as yet another expression, and so on. You would never satisfy conditions sufficient for understanding the original expression. Since we do understand expressions we see and hear, understanding cannot in general involve translation or interpretation into another expression.

This familiar regress argument seems to me conclusive. It shows that there must at some point be such a thing as understanding an expression which does not amount to translating it into another expression. That tells us only what understanding an expression or a language is *not*; it does not tell us what it is. But it imposes constraints which seem easy to forget or even to overstep in trying to give a positive account of understanding and meaning. Here I offer some thoughts on the consequences of keeping the negative conclusion clearly in mind.

II

One thing it shows is that little is to be gained, except obscurity, by following what seems to be a very natural line of thinking about understanding an expression or saying something with a particular meaning. It has admittedly proved very difficult to account for meaning and understanding simply in terms of what is apparently to be observed right on the surface, in our ordinary handling of the overt sings we see and hear and use every day. Saying something with a particular meaning is more than simply the production of sounds or marks; and responding with understanding to a meaningful expression is not simply an effect of someone's hearing a noise or seeing an inscription. It is only because thinking, meaning, and understanding are present that the production of and response to sounds and marks amount to human communication. Those essential ingredients of communication therefore seem to be something added to observable acts of uttering and responding to overt sounds or marks. So we find it almost irresistible to appeal to something somehow 'behind' our observable utterances and responses, something we must understand to be mental or inner.

The move inwards begins in earnest when we think of those essential ingredients as involving entities or items other than the overt expressions of English or French or Japanese which we produce and respond to. The simplest version of this line of thought is the traditional view that the words we see and hear and use stand for or are associated with ideas or images or items in the mind. Words written or spoken thereby serve to make the contents of our minds accessible to others. Understanding those public words is then a matter of knowing what mental things they are connected with. Another version is the more recent idea that observable expressions of English and other languages stand in a certain relation to something written or somehow embodied in an inner 'language of thought'.[1] Natural languages thereby provide the world's people with different local means of making public what they all think in a universal human language. Understanding overt expressions is then a matter of knowing their relation to expressions in that inner language.

The appeal to entities other than expressions of English or other natural languages is essential to these and other mentalistic hypotheses. If that were not so, they would be saying no more than that we do understand and mean something by our public words. But these accounts attempt to say something positive about what meaning or understanding those words amounts to. They say it

[1] See e.g. Jerry Fodor, *The Language of Thought* (New York, 1975).

involves knowledge of the relation between public expressions and something else—ideas in 'the mind' or words or sentences in a 'language of thought'. But even if that is so, we know from the regress argument that such knowledge alone would not be sufficient for knowing what the public expressions mean. We must also understand the expressions or items in the mind or in thought which we know they express. And that understanding cannot be understood simply as knowledge that the inner item in turn bears a certain relation to yet another item or expression. Or if it does, it cannot go on that way forever.

That is of course the whole point of the appeal to entities 'in the mind' or in 'thought'. It takes us beyond mere public marks and sounds, and so seems capable of explaining our use of and response to them, but it incurs no threat of regress. Those items are where the buck stops. Could we really be said to have something 'in the mind' if we did not understand it? And how could items which were not understood be said to belong to a language of *thought*? Being understood would seem to be just what being 'in the mind' or 'in thought' amounts to. So the understanding which speakers possess of items 'in the mind' or of tokens in a 'language of thought' is not to be thought of simply as knowledge of a relation between those mental items and something else.

But that still tells us only what that understanding is *not*; it does not tell us what it is. The problem of saying what it is to understand observable expressions of a natural language has been moved one step inwards and raised about certain hypothesized mental items instead. It is the same problem, with the added difficulty that now we are less sure what sorts of items or expressions we are talking about. The regress argument shows that a form of understanding that is not simply knowledge of a relation between expressions must be present at some point. The question is what that form of understanding amounts to, wherever it happens to be present.

The move away from public expressions to inner items takes us no nearer an answer to the question. Just as an act of responding with understanding to a public sound is more than simply an effect of that sound, so it is more than simply an effect of that sound in conjunction with some inner items as well. And just as saying something with a particular meaning is more than simply the production of a sound, so it is more than the production of a sound by some inner item. What is left out in each case is the idea that it is someone's *knowingly or intentionally* producing or responding to sounds and marks in certain ways that makes it human communication. Saying something with a particular meaning, or understanding the meaning of what is said, cannot be described in purely extensional causal terms. The mere presence and causal efficacy of an expression or item is not enough, whether the item in question be inner or outer, mental or physical. The understanding or the intention or the meaning must still be accounted for.

It is true that inner mental items were the sort of thing that would stop a regress. But another way to avoid a regress would be to refuse to take even one step inwards and try to account for our understanding and meaning something by natural-language expressions without appeal to knowledge of their relations to other expressions or items at all. That would not require that everything that is observable in the overt handling of familiar expressions must be described only in neutral causal terms. It would not be to deny that thinking, meaning, and understanding must be present if producing and responding to sounds and marks is to amount to human communication. It would mean only that those essential aspects of communication must themselves be understood without taking an unhelpful step inwards.

III

To speak and understand a natural language is to possess a certain distinctive ability or capacity. Someone who speaks and understands English can do a great many things that those who do not understand it cannot do. Uttering English words with a particular meaning, or recognizing what is said in English on a particular occasion, are individual exercises of that general ability or capacity. Someone who lacks the capacity might happen to respond to an English utterance on a particular occasion in the same way as an English speaker does, but he would not be understanding the expression or recognizing what was said. And someone who cannot speak English but happens to utter some English words does not mean by them what an English speaker who utters them means.

What are abilities? What is it that someone who has got a certain ability has got? The whole idea has been found problematic in philosophy. That is one reason it has not seemed promising to try to account for understanding and meaning solely in terms of our ability to use and respond to marks and sounds we see and hear. I can offer no general philosophical account of abilities or capacities, or of human linguistic ability in particular. I am not sure what sort of thing such an account would be. There certainly seems little hope of explaining what an ability is in terms which make no reference to any abilities or capacities at all. I confine myself to certain negative lessons to be learned from the regress argument.

Abilities can be described by describing what someone who has the ability can do. What those who can swim can do is to progress at or below the surface of water by working the arms and legs. Those who can speak and understand English can communicate smoothly with many other English speakers. But that does not tell us much. What exactly is it that someone who speaks and understands English can do? A full description of the ability would include a full description of the English language. This problem of description would arise even if we were concerned with inner mental items instead. The presence of items in the mind or tokens in a language of thought amounts to understanding something only if those who possess them are able to do things which those who lack them cannot do. The ability in question must be described.

Linguistic ability can be described as the possession of a certain kind of knowledge. That is not just knowing how to do something—knowing how to speak English, or knowing how to use a particular English word, as the swimmer can be said to know how to swim, or to know how to flutter kick. I think it can also be described as knowledge which is propositional in its content. Perhaps the same is true of the swimmer; he knows, for example, that he must inhale with his nose or mouth out of the water. An English speaker knows a great deal about what English expressions mean, or about what is true of the things to which they are truly applied. He need not be able to offer explicit definitions if asked; he exhibits his knowledge in his use of those forms of expression of which he is master. Nor need the swimmer be able to *say* that he must inhale with his nose or mouth out of the water; he shows in what he does that he knows that. But to say that a speaker's knowledge is exhibited in his use of the words he understands—in what he does with those words—is not to imply that the relevant use can be described in neutral, non-intensional or non-semantical terms.

Many English speakers know that the English word "otiose", for example, means without a function,[2] or that if that word is true of something then the thing is without a function. Someone who hears English speakers utter expressions on particular occasions and understands them often knows what is being said. If she hears an English speaker utter "It's raining" in certain circumstances she can know that the speaker said that it is raining. That is knowledge that someone who does not understand English does not typically get, or does not get in the same way, in those circumstances. What exactly is that knowledge, and what does it take to get it?

The regress argument reminds us that it cannot be simply knowledge of the relation between certain mentioned expressions. The English speaker knows that "otiose" means without a function; or a hearer knows that on that occasion the speaker said that it is raining. That is not simply knowledge that the word "otiose" means the same as the expression "without a function", or that the words the speaker uttered mean the same as the expression "It's raining". Someone who understood no English or who had no idea what the speaker said could know such things as those. Someone who knows what "otiose" means could even be said to know that "otiose" means otiose, or that if the word "otiose" is true of something then the thing is otiose. Such knowledge is not trivial; it is a real achievement. It is knowledge of a contingent fact which could have been otherwise. The word "otiose" could have meant something different, or nothing at all. Knowing that it means otiose is not simply the unremarkable knowledge that the word "otiose" means the same as the word "otiose", or that if the word "otiose" is true of something then the word "otiose" is true of it.

The same holds for the translation or translatability of one expression into another, even if we accept the idea of a 'homophonic' translation of an expression into another expression which

[2] This way of stating what a competent speaker knows is not, strictly speaking, always grammatical. When it is, it can fail to state what is intended (e.g. "Nothing" means nothing). I choose to put it this way in order to emphasize that what the speaker knows is not the sameness of meaning of two expressions. The only expression mentioned is the one between the quotation marks. I think the grammatical "true of" locution could replace the vernacular "means" throughout without affecting the import of anything I want to say here.

sounds or looks exactly like it.[3] Someone who knows that "otiose" means without a function knows what "otiose" means, but someone who knows only that the word "otiose" can be translated by the expression "without a function" might not know what it means. The same is true of someone who knows (unsurprisingly) that "otiose" can be ('homophonically') translated by "otiose". And someone who knows that the speaker said that it is raining knows more than that the speaker's utterance "It's raining" can be ('homophonically') translated by the expression "It's raining".

So speakers know something when they know the meanings of words, or know what was said. And it is not just knowledge of a relation between expressions. Of course, if a person who understands the word "otiose" were to try to *say* what he knows he would have to use some expressions to say it. He might say 'I know that "otiose" means without a function' or 'I know that if the word "otiose" is true of something then it is without a function.' Although he uses those words to express what he knows, the knowledge he expresses is not knowledge of some relation between the words he is using and the word he is talking about. He knows what "otiose" means, not just something about the relation between some words. Similarly, someone who *says* what she knows when she knows what the speaker said might say 'I know that the speaker who uttered "It's raining" said that it is raining.' But that is not to state knowledge of a relation between the words she is using and the words the speaker uttered. If it were, it would not amount to the knowledge she possesses in understanding or knowing what the speaker said. She knows what was said, not just something about the relations between the speaker's words and some other words. That is true even if the relation in question is translation or translatability.

Someone might misunderstand the word "otiose" and think it means hateful. He does not know what "otiose" means. He is probably confusing "otiose" with "odious". If he tries to express what

[3] The idea of 'homophonic translation' is introduced by W. V. Quine in *Word and Object* (Cambridge, Mass., 1960). In speaking of it as the 'normal tacit method' that is 'so fundamental to the very acquisition and use of one's mother tongue' (p. 59) he strongly suggests that he thinks that that is how we come to understand one another. The point that a 'translation manual' alone is not sufficient for understanding is central to Donald Davidson's theory of 'radical interpretation'. See 'Radical Interpretation' and other essays in his *Inquiries into Truth and Interpretation* (Oxford, 1984).

he thinks he knows and says 'I know that the word "otiose" means the same as the word "hateful"', we could easily detect his error. Those two words do not mean the same in English. We also would know he had got things wrong if he talked not about the relation between two expressions but said 'I know that "otiose" means hateful'. As long as we know what he means by the word "hateful" we know what mistake he is making about "otiose". But just to be on the safe side he might say simply 'I know that "otiose" means otiose'. He would then be using the very words that someone who really does know what the word means could use. And such a person would be expressing knowledge of what "otiose" means. Knowledge that "otiose" means otiose is a real achievement; not even all English speakers have it. But every speaker who uses the word "otiose" at all could use that same sentence to try to express what he takes to be his knowledge of what it means. So the misinformed speaker who intentionally utters that sentence is not saying that he knows that "otiose" means otiose. What he is saying depends not only on what sentence he utters, but on what he thinks his words mean. In the case in question, he probably means that he knows that the word "otiose" means hateful. But of course he knows no such thing, since it is not true.

Similarly, suppose someone thought that the word "raining" meant snowing. When she hears a speaker utter "It's raining" and thinks she knows what is being said she could express what she thinks she knows by saying 'I know that he said that it is raining.' But she, in uttering those words, would not be expressing knowledge that the speaker said that it is raining, even though someone else who does know what "raining" means could use those same words to express that knowledge. Whether speakers know what something means, or what somebody said, is not the same question as whether they would use a certain sentence to express what they think they know.

Understanding is a matter of knowing what something means, or knowing what somebody said on a particular occasion, not simply a matter of using or being disposed to use a certain sentence. Even someone who intentionally utters the sentence '"Otiose" means without a function' will not be stating that "otiose" means without a function if in saying it he does not know what the word "function" means. If we suspect that he does not know what the words he is using mean, so we do not know what he is saying, we can try to find out. One thing we could do is ask him what he thinks "function" means, or what he means by it. That is not our only, or perhaps our best, alternative, but it is often in fact enough. But if some 'bizarre skeptic'[4] were to question the speaker's knowledge of the meanings of his expressions and were to insist that he also must state what he takes himself to know about the meanings of the expressions he uses in giving those explanations of what he knows, and the meanings of those further expressions, and so on, the speaker could never tell the 'skeptic' anything he knows about the meanings of words.

If, for *every* word a person utters, he cannot say what he means by it unless he also states what he means by the words he uses in giving the explanation, it would be impossible for him to say what he means. Each putative 'statement' of his meaning would involve the utterance of a certain sentence, and if what he meant by that sentence in turn could be fixed only by his making a further, so far unfixed, statement, there would be no fixed statement he would be making, no determinate fact he would be stating. This is just another application of the familiar regress argument. Understanding (and in this case stating what you know the meaning to be) would be impossible if it always required the production of some expression, and for every expression produced, another expression had to be produced to fix its meaning.

The fact that, under these conditions, no one could say what he means by a certain word might lead one to conclude that there is simply no such fact as his meaning something by that word, no fact of knowing what it means, and perhaps no such fact as its meaning one thing rather than another. That paradoxical conclusion would indeed follow if it is true that all facts can be stated, and no fact of what words mean, or of speakers' knowing what they mean, could be stated unless it had also been stated what the words used in that very statement mean, and the words used in that further statement, and so on.[5] But that requirement is so strong as

[4] See e.g. Saul A. Kripke, *Wittgenstein on Rules and Private Language* (Cambridge, Mass., 1982), 8 ff.

[5] Kripke's 'skeptic' sometimes seems to be invoking this demand. See e.g. pp. 13–14, 16. Each candidate answer to the question 'What do you mean by "+"?' is found wanting on the grounds that the meanings of the words used in that answer are open to the same kinds of doubts as the meaning of '+' was. The 'skeptic' does not appear to accept the consequences of insisting on this requirement in general.

to rule out the posibility of stating any fact whatever, not just facts of meaning. If my saying that roses are red required that I say what "roses" means, and what "are" means, and what "red" means, and saying that in turn required that I say what "means" means, and "flowers", and so on, I would never manage to state that roses are red at all.

The paradoxical conclusion would also follow if it were true in general that knowing what an expression means requires that there be some expression or item which tells you what it means.[6] The helpful expression or item could do its job only if you knew what it meant, but the general requirement would imply that there must also be some expression which tells you that, and then something else that tells you what that means, and so on. Under those conditions, you could never know what an expression means. This is perhaps the most familiar application of the regress argument.[7]

You can state what you take to be a fact by intentionally uttering a certain sentence, knowing what it means. If what you say is true, you will have stated a fact. Someone who utters the sentence '"Otiose" means hateful' and knowingly uses those words correctly says that "otiose" means hateful. His knowledge of the meanings of the words he is using in that sentence is what enables him to say it. But what he thereby says about the word he is mentioning is not true, so it is not something he knows. His ignorance might eventually show up in his (wrong) use of the word "otiose". But someone who does know that "otiose" means without a function and uses his words correctly to say what it means speaks the truth. In this case he expresses his knowledge by stating what he knows, but it need never be expressed in that way. His knowledge of its meaning could also be expected to show up in his (correct) use of the word "otiose". He might possess the knowledge without ever saying that he's got it or ever saying what he knows. That is true of all of us with respect to most of the words we understand and use correctly. That is why our best way to find out what people know or think their words mean is to listen to them when they speak of

[6] This seems to be the demand that Kripke's 'skeptic' most often insists on. It appears to be behind the second of the two conditions he says any successful answer to the 'skeptical' challenge must meet (p. 11). See also e.g. pp. 13, 19.

[7] The regress involved in the appeal to a rule or schema which guides or instructs us in the interpretation of a given sign is a major theme of Wittgenstein's *Philosophical* (Oxford, 1953).

things other than the meanings of their words, to see what capacity or knowledge they exhibit in saying things and responding to others.

What an expression means is determined by its use in the linguistic community. Only if there is some general consensus in its use does it have any meaning at all. Someone who shows in his correct use of an expression that he knows what it means uses it in accordance with that consensus; he uses it as others use it. That is something we can observe to be true of a particular speaker. But his knowledge of what his expression means is not simply knowledge that he uses it as others use it. Nor is it even knowledge that his expression is properly used as others use it—that its correct use is in accordance with the consensus in the commuity. That is true of every word; its correct use is in accordance with the community's use of it. So it is possible to know that fact about the correct use of a particular word without knowing what the word means. Knowledge that someone (even oneself) uses a certain word in the same way as others use it is still only knowledge of a relation between mentioned expressions. But that is not sufficient for knowledge of what the word means.

This does not imply that there must be something more to a word's meaning what it does than its having a certain use in the linguistic community, or something more to a person's using a word correctly than his using it in accordance with the community's use of it. What matters to its meaning is *how* the word is used. That is what someone who knows what it means knows. That use can be described; it is an observable matter of fact. But there seems no hope of describing it or identifying it uniquely for any particular word by saying only that its use is the same as or different from that of some other mentioned expression. We must speak of the things the word applies to, or state what it can be used to say about them, not just mention some expressions and the relations between them. That is what someone who knows what a word means can do.

Knowledge of what words mean and of what was said on a particular occasion is exhibited in successful communication. When someone who knows English hears a speaker utter "It's raining" and knows that the speaker said that it is raining she takes the speaker to know what his words mean and to be uttering them intentionally. Not only does she herself possess the ability to speak and understand English, she also ascribes that same ability, or something like it, to the speaker she hears. She at least supposes him to be speaking some language, or to be using his expressions intentionally with knowledge or at least belief that they mean such-and-such. She ascribes to him a certain linguistic competence or ability. Without some such attribution of intention and knowledge to the speaker she probably could not know whether anything was being said, or what in particular it is.

This is perhaps another reason why it has seemed difficult to account for understanding and meaning solely in terms of our ability to use and respond to the marks and sounds we see and hear. The ability or knowledge in question is not only something speakers possess; it is also something they ascribe to each other in communication. Asking what is required in order to know what a word means or to recognize what a speaker said on a particular occasion is therefore in itself unlikely to yield a philosophically satisfying explication. The knowledge deployed in particular exercises of the ability includes knowledge or belief to the effect that others have the very kind of knowledge or ability which was to be analysed. We rely on others' ability to speak their language and on their knowing what their words mean in our coming to know what is said on particular occasions, and hence in our coming to know the meanings of those words ourselves, and so being able to speak the language.

IV

General doubts can be raised about the presence of a specific ability or capacity, and therefore about whether anyone can really know what an expression means, or what someone said on a particular occasion. The only evidence there could ever be for what an expression means is the way it is used now and the way it has been used in the past. The only evidence there could ever be for the possession of a certain ability is a person's behaviour in exercising or failing to exercise the ability. If there is no way of knowing that the word "otiose" is being used here and now to mean without a function there would be no way of knowing that that is what it means. And if there is no way of knowing that someone has said that it is raining on a particular occasion there would be no way of knowing that someone has the ability to use English words to say that it is raining. There would then be no such thing as knowing the meanings of words or knowing that anyone has the ability to speak a particular language like English.

It cannot be denied that all evidence is confined to the past and the present. But that in itself has no sceptical consequences for claims about what expressions mean or about what was said on a particular occasion. It is true that the past use of an expression can be described in a way that does not logically imply anything about what it means now, and a person's past exercise of an ability or capacity does not logically imply that he is exercising that same capacity now, whatever he is doing. But that does not prevent us from knowing, for example, that "otiose" is now used in English to mean without a function, or that an English speaker who just uttered "It's raining" said that it is raining. If we know that "otiose" has meant without a function in the past we can know that that is what it means on this present occasion. If we know that a speaker has used "It's raining" and many other English sentences knowingly in the past to say things in English we can know that in the past he has had the ability to speak English. And when we hear him now utter "It's raining" we can know that he has retained the ability he has shown so often in the past. Of course, what we know about the past does not logically imply what we claim to know about the present. But if that alone prevented us from knowing anything about meaning or about speakers' abilities, then for that same reason we could never know that the laws of nature that have held up till now will hold a minute from now either. Any doubts generated in this way would be completely general.

If the 'evidence' allowed to be available is past uses of the word "otiose" to mean without a function, or past exercises of a person's ability to say and mean things in English, then, there is nothing in the idea that we are restricted to such evidence to suggest in particular that we cannot know what expressions mean or what abilities speakers possess. It would be an ordinary inductive inference. But what can seem problematic about talk of meaning or talk of abilities or capacities is that it apparently goes well beyond even what is available in the evidence in any particular case. If it is to be known that a word now has or is used with a certain meaning, it must be because it has been used with that meaning many times in the past. But it can be argued that all the evidence available in each of those past applications of the word is compatible with many conflicting but equally well-confirmed hypotheses as to the meaning with which it was then used. And the evidence from each of a speaker's past uses of his words is compatible with his not having the ability to use those words to mean what they mean in English, and therefore with his never having exercised the ability to speak English at all.

For example, all applications of the word "otiose" which have come into anyone's, or even all of mankind's, ken have been limited to things in a certain geographical area. Suppose the word has never in fact been applied to anything in China. Then it could be said that all the evidence so far as to what "otiose" means is compatible with its not meaning without a function, or with its not being true of all and only the things that are without a function. The evidence from actual applications, even assuming that all of them have been correct, equally supports the hypothesis that "otiose" is true of things without a function if they are not in China and otherwise things that are hateful. Since that is all the evidence there could now be for what the word means, it could be argued that there is nothing in the evidence to favour the hypothesis that "otiose" means without a function over its meaning without-a-function-if-not-in-China-and-otherwise-hateful. How then could anyone ever come to know that it means without a function?

Similarly, someone who hears an English speaker utter "It's raining" in certain circumstances and concludes that he said that it is raining typically attributes to the speaker the ability to use that expression to mean that it is raining. But all the evidence available at any time for the attribution of that ability to the speaker must come from his past uses of that expression. And each of those past uses' having been what they were is compatible with the speaker's possessing any one of a great many different abilities in the exercise of which he would not then have been saying that it is raining. Suppose he had never used "It's raining" in China, and that that is where he now utters it. Then it could be argued that each of his past performances is compatible with his having exercised the ability to use the expression "It's raining" to say that it is raining if it is not in China but is snowing if it is. If there is nothing in the evidence that favours the hypothesis that he has the one ability rather than the other, how could anyone ever come to know on a particular occasion that he is exercising the ability to use that expression to mean that it is raining? How then could it be known that the speaker knows or has the ability to speak English rather than some other ability?

These arguments have a certain undeniable force. I am not one to dismiss them simply because of their paradoxical or unacceptable conclusion. There is a great deal to be learned from understanding how they are to be avoided. But I think they do not raise a special problem about meaning or understanding or linguistic ability in particular. Even the ability to swim could be shown to be equally problematic on the same grounds. The only evidence for anyone's now having the ability to swim must come from past performances of swimming. But all the swimming anyone, or even all of mankind, has observed has occurred before AD 2100. And there is nothing in all that evidence that favours the hypothesis that a given person has the ability to swim over the hypothesis that he has the ability to swim-if-observed-before-AD 2100-or-otherwise-glide-smoothly-through-the-air-a-foot-above-the-water. Let us call that "swiding". How then could anyone ever come to know now that people have the ability to swim? How could it be known that the ability someone is exhibiting right there in the water is the ability to swim rather than the ability to swide?

Nor do sceptical arguments of this form raise a special problem even about human abilities or capacites in general. They are instances of a sweeping philosophical problem about non-demonstrative inference. All the emeralds anyone, or even all of mankind, has observed have been found to be green. But they have also all been first observed before AD 2100. So there could be said to be nothing in all that evidence that favours the hypothesis that all emeralds are green over the hypothesis that they are all green-if-observed-before-AD 2100-and-otherwise-blue (i.e. grue).[8] If we are willing to say on grounds like these that no one can ever know that "otiose" means without a function, or that no one can ever know that a given speaker has the ability to speak English, we must also be willing to say that no one can ever know anything at all about what has not yet been observed. The same pattern of sceptical argument is applied in each case.

That pattern of argument does not even require reference to par-

[8] See Nelson Goodman, *Fact, Fiction, and Forecast* (Cambridge, Mass., 1955), 72–83—the (still unanswered) prototype of all sceptical arguments of this general form.

ticular times and places such as AD 2100 or China. All the emeralds anyone has observed or ever will observe will be observed emeralds, so all the 'evidence' there will ever be from observation is compatible with the hypothesis that all emeralds are green-if-observed-and-otherwise-blue. And all the things that are ever referred to as "otiose" will be things that are referred to, so there is nothing in all the 'evidence' there will ever be from actual applications to favour the hypothesis that "otiose" means without a function over its meaning without-a-function-if-referred-to-and-otherwise-hateful. If we conclude on grounds like these that no one can know that "otiose" means without a function we must also conclude that no one can know that unobserved emeralds are green—or, in general, that no one can know anything about what is not observed. Nothing special about our knowledge of the meanings of our words or our knowledge of speakers' abilities will have been revealed.

To apply this kind of general sceptical doubt to the case of meaning and understanding would have an even more devastating result. The traditional problem of non-demonstrative inference is how someone goes from his current observation of a green emerald and the knowledge that all emeralds observed so far have been green to the conclusion that all emeralds are green (or that the next one observed will be). But doubts can be raised along these same lines about the person's knowledge or belief that all observed emeralds have been green, or even his observation that an emerald right before him now is green. It could be argued that all the 'evidence' there could ever be for a person's being in that state is compatible with his now observing, not that his emerald is green, but that it is green-if-first-observed-before-AD 2100-and-otherwise-blue. And of course it is equally compatible with his now observing any one of a thousand other quite different facts involving that emerald right before him. The same is true of the person doing laps in the swimming pool; he could be exhibiting an ability to swim, or equally an ability to swide, or any one of a thousand other quite different abilities. It would be equally problematic on the same grounds whether the person can even observe that the thing before him is an emerald. So the alleged fact that he is observing that there is a green emerald before him goes well beyond all possible 'evidence' available at the time. It even goes well beyond all the 'evidence' there will ever be. Can we conclude that there could be no such fact as a person's observing that there is a green emerald before him, and therefore no such fact at all as someone's knowing or believing or observing something? If so, the problem of non-demonstrative inference vanishes.

The complete generality of doubts of this kind shows that a certain indeterminacy will always be discoverable in all ascriptions of meaning to words or linguistic ability and understanding to speakers and hearers. But it is indeterminacy or non-factuality only relative to descriptions of what people do when they say something or understand what is said which do not use any intensional or semantical terms. A mark is made on paper in the presence of a bird. A rabbit scurries by and a sound comes from a human mouth. One person emits a cry and another picks up a slab of stone and carries it towards him. From such 'evidence' alone it would probably be impossible ever to support any determinate hypothesis as to what those marks or sounds mean. It therefore could not be determined on that basis whether the people know what they mean, whether they recognize what was said on a particular occasion, or whether they possess this or that specific linguistic ability or competence. If making the phenomena of meaning, understanding, and linguistic ability philosophically intelligible to ourselves requires explaining them exclusively in terms of such neutral extensional 'evidence' it is almost certainly impossible. But that does not prevent those of us who can speak from knowing what our words mean, or, since we have intensional or semantical terms available to us, even from saying what they mean if we have to. Nor does it prevent us from knowing what somebody said on a particular occasion. Even if that involves our attibuting to the speaker knowledge of and ability to speak a particular language, so be it. It is our own linguistic capacity which enables us to do that, and so to make sense of what people say and of the words they use.

9

The Background of Thought

There is a simple and, to me, conclusive demonstration that thinking, or intentional phenomena generally, cannot be accounted for or even fully described by speaking exclusively of 'representations' or 'intentional contents' or 'objects' present to the mind. The metaphor of presence before the mind is not the real source of the difficulty. Even if 'representations' were little plastic flash-cards and 'the mind' was a special little pocket they fit into, and an 'object's' being 'present to the mind' was defined as a card's being in that pocket, we still could not explain someone's thinking that *p* as just a matter of there being a card with '*p*' on it in that person's special pocket.

I think everyone after a moment's thought would agree with this. It seems obvious that 'representations' alone are not enough because, at the very least, the person also has to understand what is on his card, he has to 'grasp' the 'content' that is represented there. That suggests that thinking involves both 'representations' or 'contents' and a grasp or an understanding of them. But then those graspings or understandings are themselves presumably psychological phenomena, so it would seem that a complete theory of the mind ought to account for them as well. To say that they too consist of nothing more than the presence before the mind of 'objects' or 'representations' would lead eventually to a regress. Either nothing but 'representations' or 'contents' would be mentioned, and so still no account of what a person's thinking something amounts to would be forthcoming, or psychological phenomena would have to be appealed to which were not themselves explained as merely the presence before the mind of certain 'representations' or 'intentional contents'. Or if they were, there would be still others which were not. The point is not that there are some particular kinds of

This essay was first published in E. LePore and R. Van Gulick (eds.), *Searle and his Critics* (Blackwell, Oxford, 1991).

psychological phenomena that simply cannot be described that way; it is rather that not all psychological phenomena can be described that way. The theory of 'representations' or 'intentional contents' alone is by itself inadequate, however far it is taken.

The strategy of deflating the theory of mental objects in this way is prominent throughout Part I of Wittgenstein's *Philosophical Investigations*. I believe that its true force and significance have not really been absorbed into philosophy. To what extent this or that current theory of the mind is vulnerable to difficulties like those he raises is always a nice question that ought to be pressed more often and more persistently than it usually is.

It is a question some of us were raising about John Searle's *Speech Acts* in seminars in Berkeley in the late 1960s and early 1970s. That book was meant to develop and so to test the hypothesis that 'speaking a language is engaging in a (highly complex) rule-governed form of behavior',[1] and the question was just how far the scope of those rules was supposed to extend and what exactly it meant to say that the behaviour was 'governed' by them. Some of the rules are what Searle called 'constitutive', serving to define the different kinds of speech act we perform. Other rules are straightforwardly grammatical, distinguishing between a correctly and an incorrectly formed sentence. Still others are strategic or instrumental. We all comply with such rules in our talk, and we do so intentionally. At least in that sense we apply the rules, so we must somehow know what they are. The question was whether exercising that essential further knowledge or expertise or ability is in turn a matter of our engaging in rule-governed behaviour. If it is, we must in some sense know or grasp the rules we are following in doing that in turn, so the question arises again. It arises at each stage at which rule-following alone is invoked. Rules for following rules are no better than 'representations' allegedly showing how other 'representations' are to be understood. So what did the hypothesis that speaking a language is engaging in a rule-governed form of behaviour really amount to? Did it mean that our linguistic behaviour could be fully captured and so made intelligible by an appeal to nothing but rules alone? But how could that be? And if it could not, what import remained to the hypothesis that our

[1] J. R. Searle, *Speech Acts: An Essay in the Philosophy of Language* (Cambridge, 1969), 12.

speaking as we do is rule-governed? Our behaviour could not be *everywhere* governed or guided by rules.

These are large, intricate, and difficult problems. It was no shortcoming of *Speech Acts*, or of our discussions, that they remained unresolved. But in *Intentionality* Searle leaves no doubt where he now stands on these large questions, at least negatively. He endorses the regress argument and so explicitly rejects the hypothesis that 'all Intentionalistic mental life and all cognitive capacities could be entirely reduced to representations'.[2] That rejected view he identifies as 'the converse' of something he calls 'the hypothesis of the Background' which he therefore thinks there are good reasons to accept.

Strictly speaking, it would seem that what is established by the regress argument ought to be nothing more than the negative idea that 'representations' alone are never enough. Searle does seem to agree that the regress argument is sound. But he also finds other considerations even more convincing in supporting a 'hypothesis' to the effect that intentional states are 'underlain' by a 'Background' of 'skills, abilities, preintentional assumptions and presuppositions, stances, and nonrepresentational attitudes' (p. 151). That too he calls 'the hypothesis of the Background'. It appears to be a positive, substantive thesis that goes well beyond the negative point supported by the threat of a regress. It tells of a previously neglected domain that must be seen to figure in any fully adequate theory of the mind. Searle even sketches a 'minimal geography' of the newly exposed area, recommending a distinction between the 'deep' and the 'local Background', and between those aspects of it which have to do with 'the way things are' and those which have to do with 'how to do things' (pp. 143–4). He speculates about how best to study this 'Background' and how to understand how it works.

It is very difficult to describe, and therefore to understand, what sort of thing this 'Background' is supposed to be. I think Searle would be the first to insist that he has not really been able to explain it satisfactorily so far. But he is certain that it must be there and that it must be acknowledged and incorporated into any full account of human intentionality. And however little is known about it at the moment, he is certain that it must be regarded as 'mental'.

[2] J. R. Searle, *Intertionality: An Essay in the Philosophy of Mind* (Cambridge, 1983), 152. Page numbers alone in parentheses in the text refer to this book.

Failure to understand its nature and operation he finds to be the source of many philosophical problems which, when properly understood, will presumably simply go away.

I want to take up some of these points in the hope of encouraging Searle to say more. My ruminations accordingly focus at least as much on the general question of what can reasonably be expected of any positive treatment along these lines as on the detail of what Searle has already said. I simply take for granted the negative thesis that any theory invoking nothing but 'representations' or 'intentional contents' would be regressive and therefore inadequate. The question is what to do in the face of that inadequacy. It is a question about what a full account or theory of human intentionality is supposed to be, whether there is reason to think such a thing is possible, and whether it could be the key to important philosophical misconceptions if it were.

It is not easy to tell where the negative thesis leaves off and Searle's positive 'hypothesis' begins, or exactly how much the considerations he finds more convincing really support. One thing he appeals to is the way we acquire physical skills. It is certainly true that human beings must have some capacities or abilities in order to do anything, or even to learn to do anything. We could not walk if we did not have the ability to walk, and we could not even learn to walk, or acquire the ability to walk, if we did not have the further capacity to acquire that skill. In that sense there are conditions that must be fulfilled if we walk or if we acquire the ability to walk. Those capacities and abilities could therefore perhaps be said to lie in the background of what we do and to make our actions possible. The same is true of speaking a language, expressing our desires, communicating with others, and so on; there too there are many conditions that must be fulfilled if we do those things. Of course we can look for the sources or bases of our many capacities—muscle control, reflexes, balance, and so on in the case of walking, and other no doubt more complicated features of the organism in the other cases. But that does not seem to be what Searle has in mind when he speaks of studying the 'Background'.

What he says about physical skills that is meant to support or explain the positive idea of the 'Background' seems to be at most that learning how to do something cannot be understood as solely a matter of 'internalizing' a set of rules or instructions which become increasingly unconscious while functioning as 'representations' from which we read off what we are supposed to do. That view does seem clearly unacceptable, but what makes it unacceptable appears to be the threat of a regress. 'Representations' or rules alone could never be enough without some further rules for applying them. 'Practice makes perfect,' Searle says, 'not because practice results in a perfect memorization of the rules, but because repeated practice enables the body to take over and the rules to recede into the Background' (p. 150). This last phrase is puzzling. It suggests that for Searle there *are* rules in the 'Background', and if the 'Background' is essential to a proper account of physical skills, as he claims, it would seem that those rules would have to come into the story after all. And then the regress threatens. No 'Background' of rules alone would be enough.

If, as seems better, we drop that last phrase and say only that 'the body takes over', we would be saying simply that, with practice, we do acquire various physical skills. That is true, but it says nothing about doing it by being guided by rules, and nothing about a 'Background' that rules recede into either. Searle expresses the point perhaps best of all two sentences earlier when he says that as the learner gets better and better any rules he might have been given 'become progressively irrelevant' (p. 150). It is not that they recede into a 'Background' and function unconsciously, or even that they function as part of the 'Background' at all; they simply play no explanatory role in an account of what the person is doing or how he learns. But that, as it stands, is no more than a negative thesis. It could perhaps be said, positively, that certain capacities and abilities must be present, or else the body couldn't 'take over', but it is hard to find in this consideration alone a reason to believe that such capacities and abilities constitute a 'Background' as Searle understands it.

Another consideration that helps convince him of the need for his 'Background' is our understanding of the literal meanings of sentences. There are several different points here. One is that it is possible to grasp the meanings of each of a number of words without understanding an apparently grammatical sentence made up of those words alone. Another is that in understanding the literal meanings of those sentences that we do understand we tacitly take for granted a certain context or range of contexts; that 'the literal meaning of a sentence is not a context-free notion' (p. 145). Behind both points is the idea that not everything it takes for us to understand the literal meaning of a sentence can itself be made part of that literal meaning, so something more than literal meaning must be appealed to in accounting for our understanding of sentences.

The conclusion again seems to me undeniable, but what makes it so, as Searle himself argues, is the threat of a regress. If we try to state all the facts we think would suffice to fix the meaning of a given sentence, he says:

> those facts will be stated in a set of sentences, each with its own semantic content. But now those sentences themselves have to be understood and that understanding will require yet more Background. If we try to spell out the Background as part of the semantic content, we would never know when to stop, and each semantic content we produce will require yet more Background for its comprehension. (p. 148)

That is the regress argument, and it could be stated with no mention of what Searle here calls 'Background' (simply replace the word 'Background' throughout with the word 'sentences'). Such reasoning supports only the negative thesis that 'representations' or 'semantic contents' or sentences alone are never enough.

A third consideration he finds convincing is our immediate understanding of certain kinds of metaphor. We recognize what is meant by the phrase 'a lukewarm reception', for example, even though our understanding 'does not rely on any perception of literal similarity between lukewarm things and the character of the reception so described' (p. 149). Searle thinks that must be so because he thinks there simply are no such 'literal similarities' in this case. He might seem then to be allowing that if there were 'literal similarities' between the items in question our understanding of the expression might well be explained by appeal to rules we follow for interpreting metaphors on the basis of such similarities. He argues only that since not all metaphors are like that, we could not be relying on such rules in every case. But the regress argument shows that even in cases in which there are 'literal similarities' our understanding of metaphors cannot be explained by appeal only to rules we follow in interpreting them. Further rules would be needed to explain how we interpret those rules in turn. So we can't be relying on nothing but rules in any case.

With that negative conclusion in hand, we could even grant that there are some 'literal similarities' in the particular case in question. And in fact that seems to be true. Similarities, after all, are fairly easily come by, if you are allowed sufficiently abstract terms in which to express them. A lukewarm reception and a lukewarm thing could be said to be similar in at least this respect: the ardour with which the reception is carried off and the heat of the thing are both roughly half-way between the highest and the lowest degrees of it that we are normally familiar with. I do not suggest that this similarity provides us with a rule that we rely on in understanding the phrase "a lukewarm reception". But that is no reason to deny that the similarity is there. Nor do I suggest in general that rules alone can explain our understanding of something. That is the point that really matters for Searle's case for his 'Background'. But the regress argument is enough to establish the point, and in itself it is purely negative. It is not easy to see, then, what positive ideas of a 'Background' are added by what he says about metaphor, or indeed about the other two considerations he mentions.

It is perhaps better to turn to the general theoretical project Searle is engaged on and to the role he thinks an appeal to the 'Background' should play in an account of intentional phenomena.

One thing he does not want to say is that the 'Background' explains intentional phenomena in the way rules or 'representations' were said to do by the theories he rejects. It is not that, rather than relying on rules or 'representations' alone in our understanding of something, we rely instead or as well on the 'Background'. That would put the 'Background' into the foreground and would be the very opposite of what he has in mind. The threat of a regress undermines the idea that our intentional activities are guided by the 'Background' just as it does the idea that they are guided by rules or 'representations' alone. It implies that, in general, our mental activities are not in the relevant sense guided by anything at all. But still Searle thinks a 'Background', positively conceived, must somehow be invoked.

The idea from which his whole theory of intentionality begins is that 'every Intentional state consists of an *Intentional content* in a *psychological mode*' (p. 12). But even to understand how intentional states, so understood, are possible, the 'Background' must be brought in. Those elements that constitute the 'Background' are what 'enable all representing to take place' (p. 143); without them there would be no intentional states at all. Intentional states 'only are the states they are, against a Background of abilities that are not themselves Intentional states' (p. 143). So it appears that our understanding of intentional psychological phenomena generally depends on a grasp or acknowledgement of a 'Background' which makes them all possible.

This is perhaps one reason why for Searle the 'Background', whatever it is, cannot be made up of intentional contents possessed in some psychological mode. No set of intentional states could explain how *any* intentional states at all are possible. Whatever can be understood as an intentional state already requires the presence of a 'Background' for what Searle calls its 'functioning', for its determining 'the conditions of satisfaction' which make it the particular intentional state it is (p. 143). He therefore repudiates his own natural description of the 'Background' as made up of 'assumptions', 'presuppositions', or 'attitudes', since to have any of those, it seems, is to be in an intentional state. We can always select a particular part of the 'Background' and make its presence explicit by identifying it as an assumption or presupposition, but as soon as we have done that we can no longer think of it as part of the 'Background' as Searle understands it. It looks as if that is because invoking such intentional states could not do what he thinks an appeal to the 'Background' is meant to do. It could not help explain how there could be any intentional states at all. The explanatory function of the 'Background' would be lost.

He would prefer then to describe the elements of the 'Background' as 'abilities', 'capacities', or 'practices'. That is presumably to render them non-propositional, and so to avoid the danger of their slipping into the foreground as states involving a propositional content held in some psychological mode. But he finds even those descriptions inadequate in another way; 'they fail to convey an appropriate implication that the phenomena are explicitly mental' (p. 156). For Searle it is crucial that 'the Background consists of mental phenomena' (p. 154).

Even if the 'Background' must be 'mental', why is it not right to say that abilities, capacities, and practices are what make up the 'Background'? Aren't many of our abilities and capacities mental abilities and capacities? My ability to do long division in my head, for example, seems to be something purely mental. My ability to remember the English words for those things we typically sit on or those things we eat off also seems to be something mental. I don't just mean my competence in using the correct words on the appropriate occasions—although I don't see why that cannot be called mental as well—but my ability to remember what the correct English words are. Without abilities or capacities like that we probably could not think or get into any intentional states at all.

It could perhaps be argued that what disqualifies abilities from being part of the 'Background' that Searle insists must consist of 'mental phenomena' is that an ability is not a 'phenomenon', and it is not itself something mental, even if it is an ability to do something mental. When I do long division in my head, it might be said, the actual thoughts I have are all mental phenomena, but the ability I am exercising in thinking those thoughts in that activity is not itself something mental. This is a possible line of argument, but I don't think it can be what Searle has in mind. Or if it is, it is not enough.

For one thing, although it is true that an ability is not a 'phenomenon' in the sense of an occurrence, a state of affairs, or something that happens, he does not want to say that 'mental phenomena' in that sense are what the 'Background' does consist of. Particular mental occurrences or happenings do not make up the 'Background'; they are the sorts of things Searle thinks the 'Background' makes possible. So abilities and capacities are not to be disqualified as 'mental phenomena' because they are not occurrences or happenings.

Furthermore, to deny that an ability, even an ability to do something mental, is itself something mental would presumably mean that an ability to do something physical is not itself something physical either. The ability to walk or to ski would not be something physical any more than the ability to do long division in one's head would be something mental. Even if this were Searle's reason for denying that abilities and capacities are appropriately 'mental'—which I doubt—he would still have to explain why abilities and capacities so understood cannot be what makes up the 'Background'. Why must the 'Background' consist of something 'mental' rather than something that is neither mental nor physical? Again, I suggest that it is because of the explanatory role it is meant to play. Brute abilities or capacities alone could not do that job.

It is undeniable that we must have certain abilities or capacities if we are able to do anything at all, and so in particular if we think, speak, believe, wish, hope, and so on. In that sense there are human abilities and capacities that are necessary for our being in any intentional states. We might even identify some of the capacities lying behind particular kinds of intentional state by producing or imagining the absence of the capacity and then seeing which particular intentional states a person can no longer achieve. This sounds like a way to 'study the Background' as Searle thinks of it (p. 155), but he is reluctant to call such capacities or abilities part of the 'Background'.

It seems to me that the source of his reluctance could be the thought that the presence of such abilities and capacities, although necessary, would not really explain *how* the intentional states of which they are preconditions are possible. 'The Background provides a set of enabling conditions that make it possible for particular forms of Intentionality to function', Searle says (p. 157), but an appeal to the 'Background' seems meant to do more than simply bring that fact to our attention. The 'Background' has detail, articulation; it is somehow supposed to make intelligible to us precisely how we can get into the particular kinds of intentional state we can be in. It would not be enough to see only that there are, or even must be, such conditions; we must in addition be able to understand *how* those 'enabling conditions' enable us to have the forms of intentionality we have. Our being in intentional states must make sense to us, and it must do so in 'mental' or intentional terms. The presence of the 'Background' seems somehow meant to explain it in that special way. I think that is what Searle must have in mind when he insists that the phenomena in the 'Background' must be seen as 'explicitly mental' (p. 156).

I ascribe this general explanatory role to Searle's 'Background' on admittedly shaky grounds. It is the only thing I can find that would explain the conflict he feels among the various things he wants to say about it. He admits that 'there is a real difficulty in finding ordinary language terms to describe the Background' (p. 156), but there seem to be no technical terms that can be coherently introduced to describe it either. 'Practices', 'capacities', and 'habits' are not right, because they must somehow be understood as 'explicitly mental' phenomena. 'Assumptions' or 'presuppositions' are not right, because they imply that there are propositional contents which we entertain in some psychological mode. What is in the 'Background' must be thought of only as 'preintentional' or 'non-representational'—in other words, as 'assumptions' or 'presuppositions' that are not really assumptions or presuppositions at all.

Searle is fully explicit about his difficulty, but he seems to me to underestimate it. He says the price of trying to describe the 'Background' is 'metaphor, oxymoron, and outright neologism' (p. 157). But to me it does not look like a question of linguistic nicety or insufficient vocabulary; it looks more like contradiction. What are found to be the best terms to describe the 'Background' must immediately be qualified in ways that contradict their literal application. Terms like 'assumption' and 'presupposition', for example, 'must be literally wrong' (p. 156), although they otherwise seem to do exactly what reference to the elements of the 'Background' is supposed to do.

Searle asks a good question about his conception of the 'Background', but I do not find his answer satisfactory:

> The fact that we have no natural vocabulary for discussing the phenomena in question and the fact that we tend to lapse into an Intentionalistic vocabulary ought to arouse our interest. Why is it so? (p. 156)

His answer is that just as 'language is not well designed to talk about itself, so the mind is not well designed to reflect on itself' (p. 156); this means that 'the only vocabulary we have available is the vocabulary of first-order mental states' (p. 157). We are therefore tempted to think of the elements of the 'Background' as 'representations' or intentional states.

He does not say what is wrong with the linguistic resources we possess for talking about language or our mental resources for thinking about the mind. They seem pretty rich to me. But even leaving aside those dubious claims I don't think his answer goes far enough. What needs to be explained is why intentionalistic vocabulary is declared unavailable to us. Why would its use be a 'lapse'? It seems to be the most natural vocabulary for describing the phenomena in question. Searle agrees that when he lifts his mug of beer in a restaurant and is surprised by its near weightlessness, 'we would naturally say I *believed* that the mug was made of glass, and I *expected* it to be heavy' (p. 157). But he thinks that what we say in that case is wrong. He does not say why. He declares rather that he 'simply acted', but that does not seem to preclude an intentional description's being true of him. It is not wrong to say he was surprised; why doesn't the surprise betoken an expectation or other similar attitude? That seems to be the only way to make sense of it.

He acknowledges that 'we can and do, treat elements of the Background as if they were representations' (p. 157). As noted earlier, we might select a part of what Searle thinks of as the 'Background' and make its presence explicit as an assumption or belief or presupposition. That seems to be what happens in this case. But he insists that 'it does not follow from that, nor is it the case that, when these elements are functioning they function as representations' (p. 157). What we identify as an expectation was not necessarily 'functioning' as an expectation, or as any intentional state, when it was part of the 'Background'.

But even if that is so, it equally does not follow that when we do speak explicitly of someone who is surprised by the mug as having expected it to be heavy, what we are saying is not true. The most that follows is that we are not speaking of an element of what Searle calls the 'Background'. Or rather, we are not speaking of the expectation *as* an element of the 'Background'. That is because it is a condition of something's being an element of Searle's 'Background' that it not be described in intentional terms; if we report the presence of an intentional state we are not describing the 'Background'. But in describing the mug-lifter as being in the intentional state of expecting the mug to be heavy we could still be saying something that is true.

I have suggested that Searle excludes intentionalistic vocabulary from the description of the 'Background' because he sees that no set of intentional states could fulfil the explanatory function his 'Background' is meant to perform. The 'Background' must make intelligible to us how we come to be in any of the intentional states we are in, and it must do so in 'mental' terms. But once we put the demand in this way the conflict he points to seems inevitable. We want to understand how any of our intentional states come to be what they are; we want a theory of intentionality. Our abilities and capacities in themselves explain nothing; they are necessary, but their presence does not explain any particular exercises of them. But to use intentionalistic vocabulary and so to appeal to intentional states would mean that not all intentional states could be so explained. They would not be explained by anything lying 'behind' them; one such state would only be explained by some others. So no intentional states can be thought of as part of the 'Background';

and no brute non-mental or non-intentional phenomenon could be part of the 'Background' either, since they could never explain our being in the intentional states we are in.

My answer to Searle's question would therefore be that on the one hand we 'lapse' into intentionalistic vocabulary because we are looking for an explanation that will make the phenomena intelligible to us in that intentional way; but since the 'Background' is also something that is supposed to explain how any intentional states are possible, we see that it cannot be made up of intentional states in turn. There is therefore no vocabulary left for describing it at all.

The suggestion that he is imposing such explanatory demands on anything that could count as a 'Background' would help explain why Searle is so sure that a 'Background' as he understands it must be there, even if nothing fully satisfactory can be said about what it is. He would be giving expression to the almost irresistible thought that our having the kinds of intentional states that we do must after all be an intelligible phenomenon. If it is a fact that we are and can be in such states, there simply must be some explanation of that fact. The 'Background' will then turn out to be whatever could provide the right kind of explanation. But what could do that? No explanation in non-intentional terms could make intentional phenomena intelligible in the right way; no explanation in intentional terms could explain intentional states in general. The quest for a general theory of intentionality along these lines would seem to involve demands that cannot possibly be met.

The dilemma appears in its starkest form in Searle's brief application of his doctrine of the 'Background' to the solution or dissolution of traditional philosophical problems. He mentions the problem of 'realism' and argues that a proper understanding of the 'Background' shows that the question whether there exists a world independent of our representations of it is not even fully meaningful. If we think of 'realism' as a doctrine we hold or a hypothesis we can look for evidence for, we seem immediately faced with the problem of how we can ever show that it is true, or even reasonable. But for Searle:

> Realism, I want to say, is not a hypothesis, belief, or philosophical thesis; Realism is part of the Background in the following sense. My commitment to "realism" is exhibited by the fact that I live the way that I do, I drive

my car, drink my beer, write my articles, give my lectures, and ski my mountains. (p. 158)

There is not, he says, in addition to these manifestations of his intentionality, an additional hypothesis or belief that he holds to the effect that there is a world independent of his representations. 'My commitment to the existence of the real world is manifested whenever I do pretty much anything' (p. 159).

But if his *commitment* to 'realism' or to an independent world is what is manifested in his behaviour, then he must certainly have such a commitment, since he certainly does drink his beer, give his lectures, and ski his mountains. And what could it be a commitment to, if not to the existence of an independent world, or to the truth of the proposition that such a world exists? But if there is a problem of 'realism' at all—if thinking of 'realism' as something we believe or hypothesize leaves its truth or its reasonableness problematic—then thinking of it as something we are committed to would leave it equally problematic for us. The question would not have gone away.

The trouble comes, Searle thinks, from misconstruing the nature of the 'Background'. If we treat what is part of the 'Background', and is therefore 'preintentional', as if it were an intentional state or the 'intentional content' of such a state, the traditional difficulty immediately arises. But what Searle says is exhibited in the way he lives his life is described as just such an intentional state—commitment. So his *commitment* to an independent world could not be strictly speaking part of the 'Background'; no intentional states are in the 'Background'. At most what is in the 'Background' must be a 'pre-' or 'non-intentional' commitment. But then that could not be a commitment *to* anything; nor could it be a *commitment* to anything. Words simply fail us.

Even if the 'Background' did contain a commitment to something—to the existence of an independent world, say—the problem of 'realism' as Searle understands it would not be dissolved by appealing to that commitment. He thinks the problem of showing or demonstrating that there is an independent world is rendered meaningless by the fact that 'any *showing* or *demonstrating* presupposes the Background, and the Background is the embodiment of my commitment to realism' (p. 159). But even if our commitment to 'realism' is necessarily involved in trying to show or demonstrate anything, it does not follow that what we are thereby committed to is true, or that our commitment to it is reasonable. We could still wonder about the credentials of that presupposed commitment, just as we might wonder about the credentials of a belief in 'realism' or a hypothesis of an independent world. Talk of commitment rather than belief or hypothesis changes nothing, if there is a problem of 'realism' in the first place. The problem does not vanish even if our commitment to 'realism' is indeed presupposed in any attempt to show or demonstrate anything.

Searle seems to acknowledge this when he switches to speaking of 'realism', and not our commitment to it, as what is presupposed. The very posing of any question at all, he says, 'presupposes the preintentional realism of the Background' (p. 159).

> There can't be a fully meaningful question "Is there a real world independent of my representations of it?" because the very having of representations can only exist against a Background which gives representations the character of "representing something." This is not to say that realism is a true hypothesis, rather it is to say that it is not a hypothesis at all, but the precondition of having hypotheses. (p. 159)

What is here said to be a precondition of anyone's having any hypotheses, because it is a precondition of anyone's having any 'representations' or thoughts at all, is 'realism', or the existence of a world independent of our representations of it. Now we know that people do have many thoughts and hypotheses, so we know that the preconditions of their doing so must be fulfilled. So if we could know, as Searle here claims, that 'realism' *is* a precondition of there being any representations, we would be able to conclude that 'realism' is true, that there is a world independent of our representations of it. Far from the question's not being fully meaningful, an affirmative answer to it would be directly derivable from anyone's thinking anything.

This kind of response to the problem of 'realism' would require that it be proved, or at least made plausible, that the existence of an independent world is indeed a necessary condition of anyone's having any hypotheses, thoughts, or representations. Not only does Searle not attempt such a proof; he denies that one can be given. In insisting that the 'Background' must be 'mental' he explicitly rejects the idea that an independent world is itself part of the 'Background' and so is presupposed by our being in any intentional states.

Even if I am a brain in a vat—that is, even if all of my perceptions and actions in the world are hallucinations, and the conditions of satisfaction of all my externally referring Intentional states are, in fact, unsatisfied—nonetheless, I do have the Intentional content that I have, and thus I necessarily have exactly the same Background that I would have if I were not a brain in a vat and had that particular Intentional content. *That* I have a certain set of Intentional states and *that* I have a Background do not logically require that I be in fact in certain relations to the world around me . . . (p. 154)

This is meant to be true of all of us. That we are in intentional states, and that those states have the 'intentional contents' they have, does not on Searle's view imply that the world independent of us is any particular way rather than some other, or even that there is such a world at all. But if that is so, 'realism' itself is not part of the 'Background' that makes our intentional states possible; 'realism' says that there is a world independent of us. This is consistent in another way with what I am suggesting must be Searle's view of the 'Background'. The existence of an independent world would never be enough to explain how anyone could get into any intentional states with respect to it. A 'Background' that contained 'realism' in that sense would not be something 'mental' and so could not be the 'Background' as Searle understands it.

Appeal to a 'Background' containing 'realism' therefore would not work. But appeal to a 'Background' containing only a commitment to 'realism' would not eliminate the problem. Nor could it be literally correct to speak of the 'Background' that way, since the 'Background' does not consist of intentional states. So it seems that only something somehow in between the truth of 'realism' and a commitment to 'realism' could do the job. But what could that be?

In a recent discussion of Wittgenstein Searle identifies as the single most disappointing feature of the later work its opposition to philosophical theory, to 'the idea that we should be seeking a general theory or general explanation of the phenomena which puzzle us, specifically the phenomena of language and mind'.[3] He says his natural response to someone who says he cannot have a general theory of speech acts or of intentionality is to go out and prove that person wrong, as he has tried to do: 'to write general accounts of speech acts and of intentionality'.[4] But he also thinks

[3] Bryan Magee, *The Great Philosophers* (Oxford, 1988), 342–3.

[4] Ibid. 343.

the most powerful part of Wittgenstein's later work is its attack on the traditional idea that all our meaningful activities are the product of some inner theory—a theory of action and value by means of which we act, for example, or a theory of language by means of which we speak and understand the things we say. Wittgenstein by constrast reminds us that a great deal of what we do is 'biologically and culturally primitive'—we just do it.[5] Those 'animal reactions' he finds Wittgenstein appealing to Searle identifies as elements of his own 'Background'—'non-representational, non-theoretical mental capacities and dispositions'.[6] His doctrine of the 'Background' develops what he thinks is Wittgenstein's most important point.

Searle denies any inconsistency in his attitude to Wittgenstein, since he holds that the recognition of a non-theoretical set of background capacities is not inconsistent with developing a theory of language or of mind. 'The claim that we often in real life proceed without a theory is itself a theoretical claim',[7] he says. But that does not completely dispose of the threat of inconsistency. The claim that we often or even always proceed without a theory is not a 'theoretical' claim in the sense in which Wittgenstein is said to be opposed to philosophical theory. It is purely negative. It says nothing about how we do proceed, or what explains our proceeding as we do. It does not attempt to explain our behaviour at all. In that sense, it does not offer or promise a theory that would explain how language or thought or anything else is possible.

But Searle apparently does offer or at least aspire to such an explanatory theory. He does not content himself with pointing out that when we speak or think we do so (or even must do so) without applying a theory or following rules; he seeks a positive account of how we do proceed. His theory is that although we do speak and think and get into intentional states without a theory, we do not do so without a 'Background'. That is what makes it possible for us to proceed as we do, and only when we understand the workings of that 'Background' will we understand intentional phenomena.

Because of the threat of regress, that ingredient of Searle's theory of language or mind which is supposed to explain in general how our speech acts or our intentional states are possible cannot

[5] Ibid. 346. [6] Ibid. [7] Ibid.

be something that *guides* us or *directs* us to act in certain ways. We cannot be said to rely on the 'Background' in the way the rejected traditional theory says we rely on a theory or on rules. So the question is *how* an appeal to the 'Background' is supposed to make our being in intentional states at all intelligible to us. That is how the negative conclusion that we do not rely on a theory or on rules or on anything else that could guide us or direct us begins to raise the question whether there can be any general theory of speech acts or of intentionality that can do what Searle thinks such a theory should do. If it is supposed to explain intentional phenomena in 'mental' or intentional terms, then that negative conclusion does seem to be inconsistent with developing a general theory or a general explanation of the phenomena of language and mind.

The threat of a regress is not of course inconsistent with explaining any particular intentional phenomenon or set of such phenomena in intentional terms. The mug-lifter was surprised, and what partly explains his being in that state is that he was expecting the mug to be heavier. That helps make sense of his present condition in a way that no purely non-intentional cause could do. Even large classes of someone's, or everyone's, intentional states might be similarly explained by appeal to further intentional states not mentioned in the original class. We expand the beam of our intentional gaze to take in more and more such phenomena if they are connected in intelligible ways with those we want to understand.

In this way, perhaps no intentional phenomenon is necessarily beyond the reach of an explanation that would make it intelligible to us in the right way. But in fact and in practice we find a great deal about human behaviour that we do not or cannot explain further. But even the 'biologically and culturally primitive' reactions and ways of thinking at which our understanding typically stops and which are appealed to to explain other things we do are usually themselves intentional phenomena, described in intentional terms. We naturally raise our hands to avoid a blow. We naturally react to the gesture of pointing by looking in the direction of the line from wrist to fingertip. It comes naturally to us to understand the order 'Continue the series "+2"' by putting '1,002' after '1,000'. We have not left the domain of the intentional in describing ourselves and others in these ways.

This picture of understanding intentional states and other intentional phenomena does not require any 'Background' in Searle's sense. What is appealed to to explain intentional phenomena are other intentional phenomena, not 'pre-intentional' or 'non-representational' assumptions, presuppositions, stances, or attitudes. From what he says about 'realism' it looks as if one reason Searle resists this picture and seeks a non-intentional 'Background' is that he thinks certain philosophical problems would otherwise be inevitable and unsolvable. To say that when he is drinking his beer and skiing his mountains he is presupposing that there is a real world independent of his representations of it suggests to him that he knows that his beer and his mountains are there only if he knows that there is a real world. And Searle thinks that to know such a thing he would have to solve the problem of 'realism'.

But that would seem to me to be so only if there were not a perfectly innocuous way in which he does or can know that there is an independent world if he knows that his beer or his mountains are right there before him. Beer and mountains, after all, are objects that are independent of Searle's and everyone else's representations of them, so anyone who knows that fact will know that there are independent objects if he knows that beer or mountains are present. In this innocuous sense of presupposing, he can know the more general proposition (there are independent objects) is true by knowing that the more particular propositions (here is some beer; here is a mountain) are true. It would just be a matter of inferring the 'presupposition' from what presupposes it, or of moving from the more specific to the more general. I think Searle would insist, as he does in the mug-lifting case, that it is simply not true that he is presupposing or assuming the existence of an independent world. But I do not find that he has given a good reason for saying that. It does not follow from his theory of intentionality; all that follows is that no such presupposition could be part of the 'Background'. And simply granting that we do have such general beliefs or assumptions is not in itself enough to generate the problem of 'realism'.

I do not mean to suggest that this would be a way of trying to answer the philosophical problem of the existence of a world independent of our representations of it. That problem is meant to bring into doubt one's putative knowledge of particular facts about beer and mountains just as much as one's general presuppositions or assumptions about the world. If those particular bits of knowledge have been revealed as problematic, as the philosophical problem seeks to do, then even if Searle is right that our believing them does not presuppose more general beliefs about the world, the problem would remain. Nor would saying that they do presuppose general assumptions about the world be any help in explaining how they are known. The philosophical critique comes to encompass everything thought to be known about the world, particular and general alike. So if there is a question of 'realism' at all, the presence or absence of general assumptions or presuppositions about the world will not really matter. But that in itself does not show that it is always wrong to say that we have such general beliefs or make such general assumptions or presuppositions. If the philosophical problem of 'realism' could be defused or dissolved in some other way, it could be perfectly correct, and philosophically innocuous, to describe ourselves that way.

Even if its apparent potential for dissolving philosophical problems evaporated I think the real source of the appeal of Searle's 'Background' would seem to remain. It looks to be the only sort of thing that could possibly explain, in general, how any intentional states at all are possible. Since it is a fact of the world that there are beings who are in intentional states, we feel that there must be some explanation of that general fact. In that thought or aspiration we are making a stronger demand than the natural intellectual expectation that every intentional state should be, at least ideally, explainable. It looks more like the requirement that all intentional states should be explainable at once, and in the same way. No intentional states could be used to explain them, so the 'Background' must be 'pre- or non-intentional. But it seems that no non-intentional phenomena could explain them in the right way. This has all the hallmarks of a philosophical demand.

Is this really what a philosophical theory of intentionality is supposed to do? How could it? Must it explain the whole domain of the intentional in non-intentional terms? Could anything satisfy that demand? Whether Searle can give satisfactory answers to these large, intricate, and difficult problems depends on something we still do not understand well enough—what the 'Background' is supposed to be, or what kind of explanation he has in mind.

10

Quine on Exile and Acquiescence

My topic is Quine and the impossibility of exile. But it cannot be denied that by now he is something of an expert on the possibility of exile. Not that he has ever suffered that punishment himself, but he has probably visited more places on earth where it could be imposed on someone than anyone else. I speak here, however, not of such distant outposts as Pirapora or Unalakleet. The exile I have in mind would be much further away than they are, further even than the length of all of Quine's lifelong travels combined.

I have in mind what he has called 'cosmic exile'—the position of someone who would stand outside the 'conceptual scheme of science and common sense' and somehow philosophize about existence or the possibility of human knowledge or language or whatever it might be without any serious views of his own about reality.[1] Quine has always insisted on the impossibility of any such withdrawal from the human condition; he has stressed the inevitability of what he calls 'working from within'.[2] 'We cannot detach ourselves from [our conceptual scheme] and compare it objectively with an unconceptualized reality,'[3] he has written. To 'inquire into the absolute correctness of a conceptual scheme as a mirror of reality' we would have to 'talk about the world as well as about language, and to talk about the world we must already impose upon the world some conceptual scheme peculiar to our own special language.'[4] Yet, in the famous Neurath figure, 'we must not leap to the fatalistic conclusion that we are stuck with the conceptual scheme that we grew up in. We can change it bit by bit, plank by plank,

This essay was first published in P. Leonardi and M. Santambrogio (eds.), *On Quine* (Cambridge University Press, Cambridge, 1995).

1 W. V. Quine, *Word and Object* (Cambridge, Mass., 1960), 275.

2 W. V. Quine, *The Ways of Paradox and Other Essays* (New York, 1966), 239–41.

3 W. V. Quine, *From a Logical Point of View* (Cambridge, Mass., 1953), 79.

4 Ibid. 79, 78.

though meanwhile there is nothing to carry us along but the evolving conceptual scheme itself.'[5]

Quine had this picture before these words were written in 1950, and it continues today to express his idea of the special character of philosophy. It makes its procedures 'naturalistic' and its results 'immanent' and revisable. It makes philosophy continuous with natural science. There can be no 'detached', 'external' position from which to philosophize.

It is not easy to understand exactly what it is that we cannot do. I suppose that is always the way it is with impossibilities. The more you reflect on them the more unintelligible they become. We cannot speak without words; we cannot think about something with no terms in which to think of it; we cannot explain something while holding no views at all as to what is so. An exile in which we had thrown off even such domestic resources as these would be a very inactive exile indeed. What then have philosophers been after when in Quine's view they have aspired to 'cosmic exile' or have thought that they have achieved it?

One idea is what he calls 'first philosophy'. He has never said much about what that is supposed to be, but he is sure there is no such thing. He might have had in mind something that philosophers for many years certainly said they were doing, or said they ought to be doing: 'analysing' the concepts and principles of science or of everyday life. It was meant to be an a priori unpacking of the empty form or structure of our thought, or the discovery of the formal principles which any respectable enquiry must follow, quite independently of whatever 'content' might come to fill that form.

Quine has always rejected the idea of an enterprise that rests on or could provide us with knowledge independently of all experience. For him even the highest and most abstract reaches of logic and mathematics gain whatever support they might enjoy ultimately from their links with predictions of future observations. There is no purely a priori enquiry at all. And the idea that it might issue in 'analytic' truths, made true solely by the relations among concepts or meanings, could not explain how such an enterprise was possible even if it were. This is one of Quine's most famous doctrines. The confusions implicit in the very idea of analytic truth

[5] W. V. Quine, *From a Logical Point of View* (Cambridge, Mass., 1953), 78–9.

have become perhaps even more obvious to all philosophers in the forty years since 'Two Dogmas of Empiricism'.

Behind the appeal to analyticity was another project which Quine saw through from the beginning. That was the idea of somehow standing apart from everything that is true, starting out with nothing, or with nothing but a few expressions and some conventions for their employment, and then generating from those meagre beginnings alone something that is true, and so is true 'by convention'. That was the hope of those who saw 'analytic' truths as true solely by virtue of meaning and so completely empty and devoid of factual content.

Quine insisted as long ago as 1936 that a definition, even an arbitrary introduction of a new expression, does not itself generate truth. At best it serves to transmit truth from some antecedent truth to a new expression containing the novel term. 'What is loosely called a logical consequence of definitions is therefore more exactly describable as a logical truth definitionally abbreviated'.[6] Such truths could be true by convention alone only if the truths of logic are themselves true by convention alone. And in that case the 'conventions' could not be definitions; they must somehow generate truth, not just transmit it. The trouble here (making a long story short) is that there is no limit to the number of logical truths, so it would be a never-ending task to declare each of them true by fiat, one by one. The 'conventions' therefore must be general, and then logic will be needed to infer particular logical truths from the general 'conventions'. If nothing were logically true independently of our adopting certain 'conventions' there would be no way of generating all logical truths from any 'conventions' we might adopt. An attempted exile from all logical truth in the hope of somehow grounding it all anew would leave you nowhere, and with no way of getting anywhere.

In ontology, too, Quine has continually inveighed against conventionalistic disclaimers of serious commitment. A clear criterion was needed, but once it is accepted, and it is found that what you say carries commitment to certain abstract objects, for example, it is folly to suppose that you are not really saying that such objects exist. Nelson Goodman has praised Quine in this connection for his attachment to 'such sterling principles as: "Don't refer to what

[6] *The Ways of Paradox*, 72.

isn't"; "Don't suppose that merely by talking you are saying anything about anything"; but on the other hand, "If you do say something about something, don't think you can escape the consequences by saying you were only talking." '[7]

This last is in effect Quine's reprimand to Carnap. He had held that philosophical questions of what there is are not 'theoretical' questions which issue in assertions that are true or false; they are 'practical' questions about what sort of 'linguistic framework' to adopt. The question of whether there are any numbers at all, for example, is what Carnap called an 'external' question. It has no answer which is true or false; it is simply a question of whether to adopt certain linguistic forms, and it is to be settled pragmatically, by what proves expedient, fruitful, or conducive to the aim for which the language is intended. To accept a certain type of entity, for Carnap, 'means nothing more than to accept a certain form of language'.[8]

This for Quine is simply an effort to disclaim or ignore the consequences and commitments that go along with the employment of linguistic forms. It is, in his words, one more dodge 'whereby philosophers have thought to enjoy the systematic benefits of abstract objects without suffering the objects . . . : the suggestion that the acceptance of such objects is a linguistic convention distinct somehow from serious views about reality'.[9] This is the very case to which he applies the term 'cosmic exile' in *Word and Object*. It is true that the ontologist seems to speak of language. But to ascend to talking about linguistic forms rather than directly about the objects they are used to refer to is not to slip into exile or to avoid serious questions about reality. It does not make questions of existence into questions of language. Nor is it to abandon the test of expediency, fruitfulness, or conduciveness to the aims of science. Rather it is to extend that pragmatic test to all 'non-fiction genres',[10] including philosophy, and thus to see even ontology as part of the scientific enterprise.

The inevitability of 'working from within' is the key also to Quine's conception of epistemology—in a word, 'naturalized' epistemology. It asks how human beings come to believe and know the

[7] Introduction to W. V. Quine, *The Roots of Reference* (LaSalle, Ill., 1974), pp. xi–xii.

[8] R. Carnap, *Meaning and Necessity*, 2nd edn. (Chicago, 1956), 208.

[9] *Word and Object*, 275.

[10] Ibid. 275.

things they do, and it makes use of any knowledge we think we have already got about human beings and the world they live in that might help to answer it. It is thus part of science—the science of science. Philosophers in the past had hoped to explain our knowledge of the world without taking any of it for granted. They dreamed of a domain of neutral, unimpeachable data, and perhaps some a priori principles of confirmation, which together might serve to validate the whole body of scientific knowledge from the ground up. They were, or should have been, disappointed. Given their hopes, scepticism was the only reasonable conclusion. For Quine that was no surprise; their task was misconceived. There is no neutral ground on which a would-be validator can stand. To enquire profitably into the sources of our knowledge of objects is to operate within our current science, not outside it. 'No inquiry being possible without some conceptual scheme', for Quine 'we may as well retain and use the best one we know—right down to the latest detail of quantum mechanics, if we know it and it matters.'[11] Once again, exile would leave us nowhere, and with no prospect of getting anywhere. There is no Archimedean point.

It is thus clear that in all these areas the idea of 'immanence', of 'working from within', is of central importance for Quine. In ontology, in epistemology, everywhere in his philosophy, its unavoidability is what fixes the character of philosophical questions by drawing limits to the ways in which they can be answered. But now, when we come to Quine's understanding of what this very immersion or engagement itself amounts to, of what it is for us to be operating 'within' a particular 'conceptual scheme', or for a theory or a body of knowledge or a way of thinking or a language to be 'ours', I sense a certain falling away from the idea of the inevitability of starting from where we are. There is, I believe, a discernible resistance on Quine's part to a merely 'immanent' understanding of our possession of our own language, and a desire to stand aloof and describe our position in theses or doctrines which could be asserted, and would remain intelligible, from outside it. I have in mind Quine's doctrines of the indeterminacy of translation and of the inscrutability of reference. What is it like to understand those

[11] Ibid. 4.

theses as true of us and our language? Is it something we can really do, as it were, 'from within'? And will they have the kind of significance they are meant to have, if we can? This is slippery ground and I am not sure I can bring out the difficulty I think I see here. But let me try.

I will concentrate on the inscrutability of reference. It can be illustrated best by the device of the 'proxy function'.[12] For any two domains of objects, whatever they might be, if we have a function which assigns to each object of the one universe an object of the other, then the one set of objects can go proxy, referentially speaking, for the other. This is true of the Gödel-numbering of expressions in a formal system, for example: all truths apparently referring to objects of the one kind can be reconstrued as referring to objects of the other kind instead. So the thesis is that with no change of the truth-values of any whole sentences of our language, the references of the terms can be systematically permuted. To avoid suggestions of merely epistemic inaccessibility, the thesis is now better called the indeterminacy (rather than the inscrutability) of reference.[13]

What does it show about our understanding of the references of the terms we use in the language we speak? Can we be said to know what our terms refer to, or not? If not, what is it for us to be 'at home' in our own language? What do we find if we try to think of this thesis as true of the language we speak? Quine once feared that we find 'a certain dimness of reference pervading the home language itself'.[14] If, because of indeterminacy, it makes no sense for me to say of someone who asserts something that he is referring to rabbits, say, and not to undetached rabbit parts, or to rabbit stages, then it makes no sense to say it of myself either. This makes 'dimness' sound like understatement. It would be not just dim but completely indeterminate what we and our fellow speakers are referring to. To follow this line, it seems, would be to manoeuvre ourselves, as Quine put it,

> into the absurd position that there is no difference . . . between referring to rabbits and referring to rabbit parts or stages; . . . Surely this is absurd,

[12] Quine introduced the idea in his 'Ontological Reduction and the World of Numbers', *Journal of Philosphy* (1964). The essay is reprinted in *The Ways of Paradox*.

[13] W. V. Quine, *The Pursuit of Truth* (Cambridge, Mass., 1990), 50.

[14] W. V. Quine, *Ontological Relativity and Other Essays* (New York, 1969), 46.

for it would imply that there is no difference between the rabbit and each of its parts or stages. . . . Reference would seem now to become nonsense not just in radical translation but at home.[15]

The first step away from this quandary, Quine says, is to think of ourselves as 'at home in our language'.[16] Talk of reference would then be 'immanent'; it would be only because we speak from within some fixed scheme of reference that we can say determinately what our terms refer to, or indeed say anything at all. So here too it looks as if what avoids the quandary and explains how we can understand and speak of reference, or indeed of anything at all, is our familiar idea of the inevitability of 'working from within' a scheme of reference, what I am calling, in general, the impossibility of exile.

Or so it would seem. But we still have the indeterminacy of reference to contend with. We must acknowledge that there are several 'alternate denotations' for the familiar terms of our 'home language'—what Quine calls 'a grand and ingenious permutation of these denotations'[17] which would not alter the truth-value of any of the sentences we are disposed to assert. And that, in turn, shows that it is, in Quine's word, 'meaningless' to ask whether the English term "rabbit" refers to rabbits rather than to some ingeniously permuted denotation. Or at least it is 'meaningless to ask this absolutely; we can meaningfully ask it only relative to some background language'.[18] This ontological or referential relativity is what Quine then saw as the key to 'the resolution of our quandary'.[19]

I can see how it would be meaningless, or anyway impossible, to ask whether the term "rabbit" refers to rabbits or to something else, if you did not have some language in which to ask it, or if the words in which you tried to ask it did not themselves refer to anything determinate at all. But Quine says that we ask such questions only 'relative to' a background language; we cannot ask them 'absolutely'. I think he means to say more than that we can ask such questions only *in* some language, or only by knowingly using expressions which belong to some language. He says we can talk about reference only 'relative to' a background language. What does he mean?

As a response to the original quandary this seems to me to

[15] Ibid. 47–8. [16] Ibid. 48. [17] Ibid. [18] Ibid. [19] Ibid.

amount to sinking further into it. That also, I think, is how Quine came to see it. When we ask 'Does the word "rabbit" refer to rabbits?' he said someone could always counter by asking 'Refer to rabbits in what sense of "rabbits"?', thus launching a regress; and we need the background language to regress into.'[20] Now the speaker had presumably already resorted to a 'background language' to ask his question. So if the countering question raises an issue about the language used in that question, the 'background language' we now have to regress into will be a still different one. And we could go on to counter in turn by asking of the countering question itself: 'Refer to rabbits in what sense of "refer to rabbits"?' thus taking one more step down the regress. The situation Quine describes sounds desperate. But 'in practice', he says, 'we end the regress of background languages, in discussions of reference, by acquiescing in our mother tongue and taking its words at face value.'[21]

So here we arrive, finally, at the second idea in my title: acquiescence. In *Ontological Relativity* it is meant to be the way in which we are 'at home in our language'. It is the opposite of exile. It is what 'in practice' stops a potential regress and so avoids the 'nonsense' that reference would amount to if seen or talked about 'absolutely', somehow away from every 'home'. But what is it? How is 'acquiescing in our mother tongue' to be described? What is it to take the words of our home language 'at face value'?

It would seem that we could do so only if those words already have some 'value', something that we could 'take' and make use of. What Quine says about acquiescing in our mother tongue with respect to the reference of the word "rabbit" makes it sound as if it is simply a matter of our uttering the *sentence* 'The word "rabbit" refers to rabbits' when asked what that word refers to and being fortunate that no one comes along to ask an embarrassing question about what those words themselves refer to. But that sounds like nothing more than good luck, or saying something with our fingers crossed. It is not something that would stop a regress.

If the existence of an infinite regress of 'background languages' really would make 'nonsense' of all talk of reference by leaving it unfixed, then this way of 'acquiescing' at a certain point would not

[20] W. V. Quine, *Ontological Relativity and Other Essays* (New York, 1969), 49.
[21] Ibid.

alter that situation. We would just be refusing to face the 'nonsense' we are actually speaking when we try to say something about reference. We could specify the reference of the terms we are talking about only relative to those of the language we are then speaking, but Quine says that 'these can, at will, be questioned in turn'.[22] Wherever we happen to find ourselves at rest for the moment, all we would have to do is to contemplate ('at will') yet another 'ingenious permutation' of our references and we would be driven on again, one more weary step down the referential regress. That seems no way to understand what it is to be 'at home' in our language.

That was the quandary in the book *Ontological Relativity*, and in more recent writings Quine has tried to clear up, or to avoid, the obscurity. He now explains that what ontology or reference is relative to is not a 'background language' but a 'translation manual'. So to say that a foreign term "gavagai" denotes rabbits, Quine says, 'is to opt for a manual of translation in which "gavagai" is translated as "rabbit", instead of opting for any of the alternative manuals'.[23] Or, in general, 'To say what objects someone is talking about is to say no more than how we propose to translate his terms into ours.'[24]

Do these more recent clarifications help explain how we avoid the quandary threatened in *Ontological Relativity* by the possibility of an infinite regress? Quine explains the relativity of reference to translation manual by saying 'The translation adopted arrests the free-floating reference of the alien terms only relatively to the free-floating reference of our own terms, by linking the two.'[25] This still sounds desperate to me. How can linking the reference of an alien term to that of a term whose reference is 'free-floating' help specify the reference of that alien term? We might use yet another term to try to specify the reference of the term with the erstwhile 'free-floating' reference, but that still leaves all the references floating free. It looks like the same regress—or one just as long. Quine offers this reassurance:

The point is not that we ourselves are casting about in vain for a mooring. Staying aboard our own language and not rocking the boat, we are borne

22 Ibid. 51.

23 *Pursuit of Truth*, 51.

24 W. V. Quine, *Theories and Things* (Cambridge, Mass., 1981), 20.

25 Ibid.

smoothly along on it and all is well; 'rabbit' denotes rabbits, and there is no sense in asking 'Rabbits in what sense of "rabbit"?'[26]

This sounds like the point we need: the impossibility of exile, being 'at home' in our language, staying aboard it, and all's being well. But why, exactly, is there 'no sense' in asking 'Rabbits in what sense of "rabbit" '? What is it that bears us along and keeps everything going smoothly? It is what Quine allows himself to say about this that seems once again to cast us out of our own language—to send us, if not fully into exile, at least on the way to it at an accelerating rate. He immediately follows his reassuring words that all is well 'aboard our own language' with the explanation that 'Reference goes inscrutable if, rocking the boat, we contemplate a permutational mapping of our language onto itself, or if we undertake translation.'[27] Once again this suggests that 'all is well' only as long as we happen not to contemplate that 'ingenious permutation', or happen not to go in for translation. As soon as we do, we don't just rock the boat, we presumably throw ourselves right out of it. If we are not then floating free, it is only because we are in another boat which we will flip ourselves out of in turn as soon as we dare to contemplate the permutations still available to us there.

There is in this respect no difference for Quine between translating a foreign language and remaining at home and speaking only about our own. Even 'the home language can be translated into itself by permutations which depart materially from the mere identity transformation, as proxy functions bear out'.[28] If reference is relative to a translation manual, the troubling relativity must therefore be acknowledged at home as well. But—and here is the most recent solution—'if we choose as our manual of translation the identity transformation, thus taking the home language at face value, the relativity is resolved.'[29] This seems to say that, although what objects a given term refers to is relative to the translation manual chosen for translating that term, there is one manual—the 'identity transformation' which pairs each term off with itself—the choice of which 'resolves the relativity'.

I am not sure what it is to 'resolve' a 'relativity'. Can it mean that the reference of a term which is translated by 'the identity transformation' is *not* relative to a translation manual? Presumably not.

[26] W. V. Quine, *Theories and Things* (Cambridge, Mass., 1981), 20.
[27] Ibid. [28] *Pursuit of Truth*, 52. [29] Ibid.

But it does seem that choosing 'the identity transformation' manual is what is meant to stop the regress. So taking our words 'at face value' and being 'at home' in our language is for Quine a matter of our choosing the 'identity transformation' manual for translating the words of our home language.

I do not think this can be the whole story. Quine thinks we will show that we are 'at home' in the language in this way, and that we are adopting the identity transformation manual of translation, when we specify the references of our terms in what he calls 'disquotational paradigms analogous to Tarski's truth paradigm'.[30] Thus we say that the term "rabbit" denotes rabbits, the word "Boston" denotes Boston, and so on. Quine praises the 'disquotational account of truth' for explaining the truth of a mentioned sentence in terms that are as clear as the sentence itself. 'We understand what it is for the sentence "Snow is white" to be true', he says, 'as clearly as we understand what it is for snow to be white.'[31] "True" is in that sense transparent.

It would seem, therefore, that we would understand an analogous disquotational remark about reference only as clearly as we understand the terms used in that remark. So the sentence 'The word "rabbit" refers to rabbits' will explain the reference of that word to us only if we know what rabbits are. And someone's uttering that disquotational sentence would amount to saying that the word "rabbit" refers to rabbits only if he is referring to rabbits in using (not mentioning) that word in that sentence.

If the denotations of the terms were themselves free-floating or indeterminate, he would not succeed in specifying the reference of that term by uttering that sentence. In fact, he would not have said anything; he would just have uttered some sounds. Both disquotational T-sentences and disquotational sentences about reference need to be asserted with a certain meaning, or understood in some determinate way, in order to state or specify the truth-condition or the reference of the expressions they mention. It is this idea of understanding, or knowing what our words refer to, and not just uttering or being disposed to utter words, that Quine still, it seems to me, has left no room for.

Room must be found for it because 'taking the home language at face value', or being 'at home' in it in a way that avoids the

[30] Ibid. [31] Ibid. 82.

regress generated by referential relativity, cannot be simply a matter of our choosing 'the identity transformation' as a manual for translating words of the home language into themselves. Even if that is necessary, it is not sufficient. That is because understanding words, or even understanding a whole language, cannot be simply a matter of knowing how to translate. Let me illustrate what I mean.

Suppose I plan to travel eastwards and an obliging linguist friend supplies me with a term-by-term translation manual of Turkish into Urdu. I don't understand a word of Turkish, or of Urdu, but when I get to Istanbul, if I'm clever enough and I've got a good ear, I can be of great service to any monolingual Urdu speakers stranded there. I can give them a translation of each thing those to-us-incomprehensible Turks say or write. Someone who is bilingual between Turkish and Urdu could provide the same service, but he would understand what he hears and what he says, and I understand neither. But I might be as good a translator as he is. At any rate, that seems no more fanciful than the daunting task of radical translation.

Of course, if I'm not careful I might come to understand many of the Turkish expressions I hear. I might notice the circumstances in which they are uttered, or even (although it is difficult in Turkey) sometimes recognize what the people who utter them are doing, what they want, what they believe, and so on. But if I am careful to stick only to my service to Urdu speakers there is no need for me to do that. I might even occasionally help those Urdu speakers to learn a little Turkish, even though I know none myself. I might happen to be standing near a Turk when he utters a disquotational sentence which is the Turkish equivalent of "The word "rabbit" refers to rabbits." My translation of that sentence into Urdu could serve to tell my audience what one Turkish word refers to. Of course, my ear would have to be good enough to catch the quotation marks around that Turkish expression, and I would have to leave the Turkish word untranslated inside the quotation marks which I insert in the Urdu sentence. If I put everything into Urdu I would not be telling my audience anything they didn't already know. But if the Turks were liberal enough with their disquotational referential paradigms, and I were in the right places at the right times, I might have Urdu speakers in Istanbul learning Turkish like mad. But still I wouldn't understand a word.

Quine says 'To say what objects someone is talking about is to say no more than how we propose to translate his terms into ours.' Now I can say how I propose to translate the Turkish I hear into Urdu; I propose to use my manual. Suppose my friend were generous enough to give me not one but several different term-by-term manuals which could be used to pair off whole sentences of the two languages which speakers are disposed to assert. Then I can say 'Today is Tuesday so I propose to use manual number two.' When I look back on a full day of translating and point to the results, if I say 'I used manual number two all day; I translated this Turkish word with that Urdu word, this other word with that other one', and so on, I am not saying anything about what objects the Turks are talking about. I have no idea what they are talking about. Can what they are talking about be 'relative to' *my* choice of translation manual? Obviously not. What manual I choose does not even determine what objects I *think* the Turks are referring to. I have no view as to what they are referring to. I lack all understanding of the terms I am translating and the terms I am translating into. They are not terms of my own. That is why my ability to translate does not amount to understanding.[32]

Can we say that what objects the Turks are referring to is 'relative to' the choice of manual by translators who do understand the words into which they translate? Suppose I lend one of my manuals to each of two Urdu speakers. They can then understand what the Turks are saying. If the two manuals are different, the Urdu words each of them utters in translating a given Turkish sentence will differ. So what they *utter* is relative to translation manual. Is what they think a given Turkish term refers to also relative to their choice of manual? Will they disagree about what that word refers to? If they are both good translators, I think we cannot say that they will. If I eventually found a way to translate from Urdu into English, so I could understand my Urdu-speaking friends, I could not translate one of those speakers as saying to me that the Turkish word refers

[32] My example bears obvious structural similarities to John Searle's 'Chinese room' case ('Minds, Brains and Programs', *The Behavioral and Brain Sciences* (1980), 417–18; and elsewhere). Searle is there concerned with simulation of understanding, not translation. But just as he stresses the importance of the distinction between 'syntax' and 'semantics', what is crucial in my case is the distinction between having a translation manual for a language or a body of discourse and interpreting or understanding it. I do not draw from this negative point all the same positive conclusions about the mind as I think Searle does.

to rabbits and the other as saying that that same word refers to, say, rabbit stages. Rabbits and rabbit stages are not the same sort of thing. So I know that if the Turkish word refers to rabbits it does not also refer to rabbit stages. If I accept that it refers to rabbits, the most I can allow is that it only 'proxy-refers' (as I might put it) to rabbit stages. Since the objects are different, the relations that the word bears to the objects must be different. That is a constraint on my making sense of what my two trustworthy Urdu translators are saying to me. I could find no disagreement between them as to what the Turkish word refers to. That is because the words I would be translating them into are now words of my own. When I was blindly translating from Turkish to Urdu I had no views at all about the relations between the words I heard and the world.

The words must be 'mine', then, or I must be 'at home' with them. And that cannot be just a matter of their being words that I utter or words that I respond to systematically in some way or other, or even of my being disposed to utter them or to respond to them in that way. That much is true of all the Urdu words I have uttered, or have been disposed to utter, but I have not been 'at home' with them. I have not understood them. That is not because my utterances or my responses have not been intentional. They have; I have produced all those Urdu words with a definite intention. I intend to be of service in Istanbul. Nor would I be 'at home' in a language simply by choosing to translate the words of that language into themselves by means of 'the identity transformation'. That cannot be what it is to take words 'at face value'. If I have several different term-by-term mappings of Turkish into Urdu I can produce several different translation manuals of Turkish into itself. I could then choose 'the identity transformation' manual and use it to translate every Turkish utterance into itself. That would not be as useful a service to Turkish speakers as my earlier efforts were for Urdu, but if there can be said to be such a thing as 'homophonic translation', I would be doing it. But I would still not understand a word of Turkish.

Equipped with my bilingual manuals, I could mention Turkish expressions and say (in English now) what Urdu expressions translate them in each manual. With the manuals for translating Turkish into itself, I could say which Turkish expressions get paired off with which Turkish expressions. In the case of 'the identity transformation', that's easy. But I still would not know what any of those expressions means. Even if I hear a Turkish utterance which happens to be a disquotational sentence about the reference of a Turkish term, and I translate it correctly into Urdu, I would not know that what it says in either language is true, even if I know that the person I hear utter it does know it to be true, that is, even if I know that it is a true sentence. To know that what a sentence says about the reference of a certain term is true I must understand the words that are used to say what that mentioned term refers to. That is not knowledge merely of a relation of mutual translatability between two mentioned expressions.

It is the same with Tarski's T-sentences. They tell us the condition for a particular sentence's being true only if we understand the right-hand side of the biconditional. And no words are mentioned there. A corresponding disquotational paradigm about reference will tell us what the mentioned term refers to only if the words not mentioned but used in that sentence are 'ours', or we are 'at home' with them. We must know that the word "rabbit" as it is used in that sentence refers to rabbits, if that disquotational sentence is to tell us what the word "rabbit" refers to. That is not the sort of thing I know about any Turkish words. At most I know something about certain relations they bear to other words I can mention but not use.

It seems to me, then, that being 'at home' in a language, or having a language which is 'ours' in a way that stops the regress, must be understood as our knowing something about those words—something that is not itself just a fact about their relations to yet more words. I think Quine has always shied away from this idea because he thinks it would have to involve knowledge of or, even worse, acquaintance with, some entity which is the meaning of the word, or the meaning of a sentence. I don't see that anything like that must be involved, at least in any way we should want to resist. I know my neighbour's Social Security number, but that is not simply acquaintance with a number. It is propositional knowledge that such-and-such is the case. I think it is the case that the word "rabbit" refers to rabbits, and that the sentence "Snow is white" is true if and only if snow is white. And I think those are things that a great many people know. And if they know such things, then such things must be true. A language of which such things are true is what we all acquire as we learn to speak.

We English speakers are handed down or enter into a legacy

from former and current English speakers in which it is already true that the word "rabbit" refers to rabbits and that the sentence "Snow is white" is true if and only if snow is white. That is what prevents a regress. The language is there, and we find a 'home' in it, or in some other. Only if we are 'at home' somewhere can we say anything at all. Catching on to what words refer to and under what conditions sentences are true is what enables people who utter such sounds as "There's a rabbit" or "Snow is white" to be saying that there is a rabbit or that snow is white. Italians don't use those words; neither do Turks. But they all sometimes say that there is a rabbit or that snow is white. If there were no such facts about expressions at all, no one could ever say such things.

What, then, of what Quine calls the indeterminacy of reference? Don't we still have to acknowledge the possibility of a 'grand and ingenious permutation' of our references? Yes. But we must be 'at home' somewhere in order even to bring that off—to make it intelligible to ourselves. Someone who knows what objects the word "rabbit" refers to can devise a proxy function F which will associate with each of those objects a different object, the-F-of-a-rabbit. But he can do that only if he has got some way of identifying those objects for which he is going to introduce proxies. His language provides him with a means of doing that; the word he uses in identifying the original objects is a word that refers to rabbits. If he weren't able to refer to rabbits, or if his words didn't refer determinately to anything, he would not succeed in specifying the proxy function in the first place. He would not have specified the objects it is supposed to hold between. Once he has specified it, he can say that the word "rabbit" refers to rabbits, and also say that the word "rabbit" the-F-of-refers to the-F-of-rabbits. He contemplates a 'grand and ingenious permutation'. But that does not drive him out of his home language and down an infinite regress. He understands the permutation he is contemplating only because he knows that the word "rabbit" refers to rabbits.

We also must acknowledge that if there is such a proxy function F, then the word "rabbit" refers to rabbits if and only if the word "rabbit" the-F-of-refers to the-F-of-rabbits. But from that equivalence and the fact that a speaker knows that the word "rabbit" refers to rabbits it does not follow that the speaker also knows that the word "rabbit" the-F-of-refers to the-F-of-rabbits. His knowledge of the relation between his word and objects in the world is likely to include knowledge of its relation to those proxy objects only if he also knows, of a certain function, that it associates the two kinds of objects in that way. That is not something that is known by most speakers who know what "rabbit" refers to.

To say that we have knowledge of the references of our words is not to say that we can always be very helpful or even very articulate in saying what we know. Often the best we can do is to assert a disquotational referential paradigm. But even then we must know the references of the words we are using in that assertion. That knowledge too is propositional, but it need not be explicitly asserted or assented to by us. It is knowledge that is embodied in our capacity to use our words to say things and to respond appropriately to the sayings of others. It could be called a disposition, if you like. And the only evidence for it lies in the behaviour of human beings in interaction with one another; there is no place for an internal 'museum' of meanings. But I see no hope of understanding our knowledge of language as simply a matter of our being caused to utter certain sounds or to move in certain ways. The behaviour in question must be described using intensional terms like "says that *p*", "believes that *p*", and so on. It is a disposition or capacity to say things in some ways and not in others, for example, the disposition we English speakers have to say that there is a rabbit by uttering "There's a rabbit" and not by uttering "Ecco un coniglio", and the capacity we have to respond with appropriate understanding to some utterances we hear and not to others. That is the difference between my speaking a language I understand to those who understand me and my simply uttering sounds in Istanbul.

But now we come to a deeper reason why Quine would not look with favour on this idea. It involves attributing intensional states or attitudes to speakers as essential to understanding what it is for them to be 'at home', to speak and understand a language. Quine will find no virtue, or no inevitability, in starting 'from within' if what we must start from when we start from there is already couched in the intensional idiom. That is something he thinks we must get completely away from if we want to state only what is determinately true of the world. But I am suggesting that there is nowhere else for us to stand. An exile who tried to stand outside intensional and semantical notions altogether could not make the right kind of sense of language solely in terms of causes and effects of utterance and movements.

The closest Quine has come to acknowledging this is in his recent concession that the intensional idioms play an important role in the handing down, and hence in the learning, of language. The teacher typically must see that the learner perceives that it is raining if she is going to get her pupil to utter or to assent to a sentence to that effect in the right circumstances. She herself must therefore have mastery of the locutions '*x* perceives that *p*', '*x* believes that *p*', '*x* says that *p*', and so on—or corresponding mentalistic sentences in whatever language she happens to speak. What makes those sentences mentalistic is not reference to some hidden spiritual entity called a mind; it is the intensionality of the 'that *p*' locution when preceded by one of those verbs of attitude. Substitutivity of co-referring terms does to necessarily preserve truth. Such language is not reducible to the 'crystalline purity' of extensionality.[33]

Quine's acceptance of this Brentano thesis led him in *Word and Object* to infer the 'baselessness of intentional idioms' in an austerely scientific account of what he called 'the true and ultimate structure of reality', while conceding their everyday practical usefulness, even indispensability.[34] Now in *Pursuit of Truth* the indispensability, and not the 'baselessness', is stressed, and even seen as a reason for 'treasuring' the intensional idioms;[35] language probably could not have developed without them. But still they are not to be employed in what Quine now calls 'a global theory of the world, . . . accounting for all events'.[36] We can use those idioms separately, alongside the austerely extensional account, for covering some of those same events in an intensional way. That is what I am urging we must do if we are going to understand what it is for us to be 'at home' in our language. We must take competent speakers and hearers to know certain things about the meanings of their words, and so we must acknowledge the determinate facts of meaning, reference, and truth conditions which they appear to know.

That people say things and understand what others say in certain ways are just as much facts of the world which we know we live in as the fact that trees grow or the planets revolve. Without the inten-

[33] *Pursuit of Truth*, 71.
[34] *Word and Object*, 221.
[35] *Pursuit of Truth*, 71.
[36] Ibid. 72.

sional idioms we could not even state those facts of language or make them intelligible to ourselves. At most we could describe and explain physical events of human mouths opening and closing, human organisms moving in certain ways, and so on. Just as Quine's naturalized epistemology in general does not aspire to an understanding of science which is any better than the science which is its object, so we cannot expect our understanding of the mental as such to be any better than the intensional notions in terms of which we must understand it; there too we must 'work from within'. But if we must employ intensional idioms to make the right kind of sense of what human beings so obviously do, how can we pretend that in doing so we are not stating facts of the world—facts which, starting 'from within' and from where we are, we must acknowledge? An adaptation of Goodman's sterling principle seems to me as applicable here as Quine would agree that it is in ontology: If there is no way of accounting for everything that is true in the world without accepting truths expressed in intensional terms, then when you do succeed in saying something true about human beings in those terms, don't think you can escape the consequences by saying you were only talking.

11

Mind, Meaning, and Practice

In one of his harshest judgments on philosophy Wittgenstein observes: 'When we do philosophy we are like savages, primitive people, who hear the expressions of civilized men, put a false interpretation on them, and then draw the queerest conclusions from it.'[1] He does not document the extent to which this actually goes on in philosophy, or where it goes on, if it does. When he makes the remark he has been discussing possibility. In that case perhaps he has a point. It might also apply to much of what is said in philosophy about thought, meaning, and understanding—in short, about the mind. When we reflect philosophically on those 'mental' or 'intentional' ways of speaking in which we describe so much of what we do it is easy to start down a path, no one step of which is exactly 'savage' or 'uncivilized', but which ends up with something 'queer' in the sense of being completely and irretrievably mysterious.

I want to look at one—but only one—way in which Wittgenstein thinks this happens, and what he does, or suggests, to counteract it. It can start with puzzlement over the meanings of words. Not with wondering what some particular word means, but with wonder at the very phenomenon of meaning. Words as we encounter them are sounds or marks, but obviously not all sounds or marks are meaningful. Leaves make sounds in the wind, and a snail makes marks in the sand. It is not even their being produced by human beings that makes sounds or marks meaningful. Humans also produce sounds and marks which have no meaning, and often do so intentionally. As Wittgenstein puts it, mere sounds or marks on their own seem 'dead'.[2] Those that are meaningful are uttered or produced

This essay was first published in H. Sluga and D. Stern (eds.) *The Cambridge Companion to Wittgenstein* (Cambridge University Press, Cambridge, 1996).

[1] L. Wittgenstein, *Philosophical Investigations*, tr. G. E. M. Anscombe (Oxford, 1953), §194. Parentheses in the text containing '*PI*' refer to this book.

[2] L. Wittgenstein, *The Blue and Brown Books* (Oxford, 1958), 3. Parentheses in the text containing '*BB*' refer to this book.

with meaning. They are meant in a certain way, while other sounds and marks are not. Meaningful sounds and marks are responded to in certain particular ways, with understanding. They have a kind of 'life' which is not shared even by sounds or marks that happen to be signs or indications of something else, as the marks on the trunk of a tree are signs of its age, or the faint sound of a train is an indication of its distance from the hearer.

So far it seems undeniable and unproblematic that many sounds and marks are meaningful and are responded to with understanding and many are not. It is when we take the next, apparently natural, step that trouble looms. We ask 'How do the marks made on paper as a person writes differ from the marks made by a snail as it crosses the sand?' and it seems natural to take that as the question 'What has to be added to otherwise "dead" marks or sound to give them "life" and so to make them meaningful?' The thought is that meaningful sounds or marks differ from others in being *accompanied* by something. They either produce something, or are produced by something, that is not present among the causes or effects of merely 'dead' signs. That added something is what is thought to give the signs their 'life', and we come to think of it as something that can occur only 'in the mind'.

It seems that there are *certain definite* mental processes bound up with the working of language, processes through which alone language can function. I mean the processes of understanding and meaning. The signs of our language seem dead without these mental processes; and it might seem that the only function of the signs is to induce such processes, and that these are the things we ought really to be interested in. . . . We are tempted to think that the action of language consists of two parts; an inorganic part, the handling of signs, and an organic part, which we may call understanding these signs, meaning them, interpreting them, thinking. (*BB* 3)

Once we have the idea of these two distinct parts of the 'action of language' it is almost inevitable that we will focus on the 'mental' or 'organic' part. That will seem to be what 'we ought really to be interested in' because 'inorganic' or 'dead' signs alone, or the mere addition of 'inorganic' signs to 'dead' signs that are already there, could never give signs 'life' or meaning. Something completely different, it seems, must be added. 'And the conclusion which one draws from this is that what must be added to the dead signs in order to make a live proposition is something immaterial, with properties different from all mere signs' (*BB* 4). 'Mental' goings-on such as understanding, meaning, interpreting, and thinking are the sorts of things that have to be added. And because they belong to the 'live' or 'organic' part of language, and cannot be understood as involving only material and so 'dead' signs, it seems that they 'take place in a queer kind of medium, the mind; and the mechanism of the mind, the nature of which, it seems, we don't quite understand, can bring about effects which no material mechanism could' (*BB* 3).

The effects are special in all the ways that thought and meaning are special or unique in the world. A thought, which is something mental, can 'agree or disagree with reality' (*BB* 4). Nothing merely material or 'inorganic' can do that. You can think of someone, or 'mean' him when you say something, even if he is thousands of miles away, or dead, or doesn't and never did exist. You can believe what is not so, and fear something that could not even possibly be so. '"What a queer mechanism", one might say, "the mechanism of wishing must be if I can wish that which will never happen"' (*BB* 4).

To understand these familiar phenomena as special activities or operations performed by or occurring in 'the mind' would be to draw what Wittgenstein calls the 'queerest conclusions' from a false interpretation imposed on the expressions civilized persons use to talk about thought, meaning, understanding, and other 'mental' goings-on. It is what leads us to think of something called 'the mind' as the repository or *locus* of such activities, and so to think of it as an agent, or a thing or at least as a kind of place, and to think of it as hidden or 'inner' in some way, despite our having no idea of its even approximate dimensions or location.

We know where the brain is, and it is inner in the straightforward sense of being inside the skull. No doubt we could not think, mean, or understand anything if the brain were not there or did not function more or less as it does. We have the language of chemical reactions, electrical impulses, protoplasm, and so on with which to describe the operations of brains, but for what is said to go on 'in the mind', or what 'the mind' does, we need 'mental' or 'intentional' or psychological ways of speaking. Events that go on literally inside skulls remain as devoid of meaning, or as 'dead' in Wittgenstein's sense, as most events that occur outside skulls. If thought, intention, or understanding are needed to give otherwise 'dead' objects or events 'life' or meaning of the relevant 'mental' kind, then because they possess special features apparently not shared by any 'inorganic' or 'dead' material mechanism, those activities or operations will have to be seen as taking place in a special, and so a mysterious or occult, medium.

The general strategy of Wittgenstein's resistance to this apparently natural line of thought is to show that the puzzlement which we wrongly interpret to be about the nature of a medium is really a puzzlement 'caused by the mystifying use of our language' (*BB* 6). The mystification is due to our thinking of thought, meaning, and understanding as something that *accompanies* the handling of sounds, marks, or other objects. Wittgenstein tries to expose that disastrous assumption by showing that *whatever* might be thought to accompany the use of a sound or mark would be nothing better than another 'dead' mark or object or event. He does this by first inviting us to replace whatever 'mental' thing is thought to accompany the handling of physical signs with something which is itself overt and accessible. If the presence 'in the mind' of an image of a red flower is what is thought to be essential to a person's meaning or understanding the English words "a red flower", think instead of the person holding a picture of a red flower in his hand. If an inner act of interpretation or understanding is thought to take place in his mind when he hears and understands the phrase, think instead of the 'outer' act of his drawing his finger from left to right across a chart with the words "a red flower" on the left and a picture of a red flower (or even a real red flower) on the right. Wittgenstein says that 'we could perfectly well, for our purposes,' replace every allegedly 'inner' or 'mental' object or process with some such 'outer' object or act (*BB* 4). 'Our purposes' here refers to his aim of exposing the futility of appealing to a mysterious or occult 'inner' medium. It is futile because an external chart or picture or other object would be in itself no help in giving meaning to a written sign.

> why should the written sign plus the painted image be alive if the written sign alone was dead?—In fact, as soon as you think of replacing the mental image by, say, a painted one, and as soon as the image thereby loses its occult character, it ceases to seem to impart any life to the sentence at all. (It was in fact just the occult character of the mental process which you needed for your purposes.) (*BB* 5)

'Your purposes' here are those of expressing the apparently natural puzzlement about thought, meaning, and understanding.

Much more would need to be said to identify and to explain the force of each of the steps that are thought to lead to these deep and compelling misconceptions. My goal here is to understand Wittgenstein's opposition to them, and what he suggests should take their place. It is summed up in his now-famous remarks:

> But if we had to name anything which is the life of the sign, we should have to say it was its *use*. (*BB* 4)

> The sign (the sentence) gets its significance from the system of signs, from the language to which it belongs. Roughly: understanding a sentence means understanding a language. (*BB* 5)

> For a *large* class of cases—though not for all—in which we employ the word 'meaning', it can be explained thus: the meaning of a word is its use in the language. (*PI* §43)

It should be clear from the target against which these slogans are directed that the use of an expression, or the system of expressions within which it has a use, are not to be thought of as something merely accompanying the expression and thereby somehow endowing it with meaning or 'life'. Nor should we think that Wittgenstein is here trying to identify something that can be called 'the meaning' of a particular word. He is not pressing the question 'What is the meaning of a word?' in the sense of 'What is that thing that is a word's meaning?' Rather he is here summing up a response to the concern with the general meaningfulness of words with which we began—with what distinguishes meaningful sounds or marks from those which are 'dead' or mean nothing. The answer does not appeal to anything going on in 'the mind'; those sounds or marks are meaningful which have a distinctive role or use in a system of signs like a human language.

This is only a summary or capsule answer. There is no suggestion that the use of an expression is something that is easy to describe or explain. In fact, it can be felt that for certain philosophical purposes it cannot be fully or satisfactorily explained at all. I will come back to that idea.

The slogan 'the meaning is the use' has been understood and appropriated in a number of different ways, not all of them helpful in understanding Wittgenstein. An expression's having a use has sometimes been explained as there being conditions under which the expression can be correctly or justifiably or appropriately applied—'criteria of application'. Someone who knows the meaning of an expression would therefore know how and when to apply it to something, and when not. As an explanation of the notion this does not take us very far. For one thing, only certain words are properly said to be applied to something; for example, the word 'peacock' when I say of something directly before me 'That is a peacock.' Even in that remark the words "That" and "is" are not in the same way applied to anything, but they too contribute distinctively to what is said. And when I say 'A peacock roaming my garden would certainly enliven the scene' not even the word "peacock" is applied to something in the same way as before; there is nothing of which it is then being asserted that it is a peacock. Nor are the other words in that remark applied to anything, but they too are meaningful, so they too must have uses in Wittgenstein's sense.

The 'use' or 'application' of whole sentences has similarly been thought of as the conditions under which they can be truly or justifiably or appropriately asserted or used assertively. This view suffers from comparable difficulties and limitations. Many sentences we utter and understand are never used to make assertions. Of those that sometimes or often are so used, they also appear unasserted and still have a meaning and so a use. Uttering a sentence with meaning, or understanding a sentence, is something much richer than simply being able to assert or acknowledge the truth of what a sentence says. If the notion of 'application' is widened to include not only assertion but all other fully sentential speech acts, and to include among words not only predicates but all other expressions needed to form whole sentences, we are left only with the unhelpful observation that an expression's having a use is a matter of there being conditions under which it can be correctly or justifiably or appropriately used in communication.

It is closer to Wittgenstein's conception of the use of an expression to think of it as the distinctive role of the expression in all those human activities in which it is or might be employed. This can be seen as a generalization of the idea, present in Frege and the *Tractatus*, that the meaning of an expression is displayed in the contribution it makes to the truth or falsity of all the sentences in which it can appear. The new direction of thought in which Wittgenstein was moving on his return to philosophy in 1929 goes beyond truth-conditions and purely linguistic items like sentences to encompass an utterance's contribution to whatever human beings manage to do in uttering or responding to it.

The meanings of the expressions "Slab", "Pillar", "Block", and "Beam" of the 'complete primitive language' described in *PI* §2 can be seen in that way. Their whole use lies open to view; we can see exactly what role the utterance of each of them plays in the lives of those people. Even if we think of the expressions as sentences, there is no need to think of them as being used to make assertions, or even to predicate something of certain objects. They none the less have 'life' or meaning in a way that no other sounds or marks do in that community. Of course, the difference that the utterance of a particular sound or mark makes in everything people do cannot always be so easily described, or perhaps even described at all in reasonably complete terms, especially in the kinds of languages and lives that we are all familiar with. The point so far is only the very general fact of a difference between a sound or mark's having a use or role in human activities and its having no such role. The sounds of the leaves in the wind and the snail's marks in the sand are 'dead' and without a use in that sense.

It is in this light that we are to understand Wittgenstein's observation that a sentence or expression has 'life' 'as part of the system of language' (*BB* 5), and that understanding a sentence means understanding a language. Understanding a language, in turn, 'means to be master of a technique' (*PI* §199). The 'technique' involved is the technique of acting and responding linguistically in appropriate ways, of being a human language speaker, and so being capable of the sorts of activities and reactions that language makes possible. The builder in language-game §2 knows how to get the building-stones he needs; the assistant understands him and brings the right stones. In that case, being master of a language means being master of only one or two very simple 'techniques'—perhaps too few for it to qualify as a language at all. Real life as we know it involves many more. The kinds of things that human beings can do in and with language are virtually limitless.

Whatever the actions or activities or responses involving language might be, in order for someone to have mastery of certain techniques there must be such a thing as carrying out those techniques, or doing the things in question correctly. In order for the builder to have mastered the technique of ordering the kind of building-stone he needs, there must be a way of ordering a certain kind of building-stone. There must be something he has mastered. This is nothing more than the platitude that there must be some difference between performing an action of a certain kind and not performing it, between engaging in a certain activity and not engaging in it. If not, there would be nothing to master. Someone who calls out 'Slab!' or 'Pillar!' randomly from time to time has not mastered the 'technique' that the experienced builder follows in the community Wittgenstein describes. A would-be assistant who simply jumps up and down in distinctive ways on hearing a builder's utterances has not understood those utterances correctly. He has not mastered the technique of passing stones to the builder as he needs them and orders them.

This shows that there must be such a thing as the correct way of using or responding to a sound or mark that has meaning or a use. Exhibiting mastery of a technique involves doing the thing correctly. This could be put by saying that one who utters or responds to an utterance correctly is following the rule for the use of that utterance. That is not to imply that the person consults some rule book or set of instructions. It means only that the person utters or responds to the expression in the right way. Wittgenstein does not object to talk of rule-following. It is his exploration of the only ways in which this undeniable condition of mastery can be satisfied that is meant to lead away from any appeal to a mysterious inner realm or medium as essential to understanding thought, meaning, and understanding.

For someone's performance to be the correct way to do something there must be some standard or pattern to which it conforms. For the use of linguistic expressions, those standards can be provided ultimately only by the ways in which the expressions are in fact used. Nothing else could give a particular, distinctive significance to an expression; meaning is not something a sound or mark carries with it in itself, independently of how it is used. Of course, an expression can be endowed with meaning, or its meaning can be explained, by the use of other expressions, but those expressions in turn must have a use and be used correctly if the explanation is to succeed. That requires that there be some way in which those expressions are used, some regularities or general practices to which an individual speaker's performance can conform or fail to conform.

> It is not possible that there should have been only one occasion on which someone obeyed a rule. It is not possible that there should have been only one occasion on which a report was made, an order given or understood; and so on.—To obey a rule, to make a report, to give an order, to play a game of chess, are *customs* (uses, institutions). (*PI* §199)

Someone who stands near a partly built building and shouts out 'Slab!' is not thereby giving an order if there has been no practice of sounds' having been uttered and responded to for certain purposes in certain regular ways in the past. Someone who carries a stone to a building site shortly after hearing such a shout has not thereby understood it to have a particular meaning if there is no general practice of responding to it or to other sounds in that way. The sound 'Slab!' would simply have no 'life' or use in those circumstances, or at any rate it would not have the use and so the meaning it has in language-game §2.

From Wittgenstein's description of what he calls that 'complete primitive language' we can see what those expressions mean in that community, what those who use them correctly mean by them, and what those who understand them understand them to mean. In thinking of that situation in the ways we do, we do not need to add to the description any supposition to the effect that some objects or acts appear in mysterious 'inner' regions called the 'minds' of those people. We know what they are doing, and we can see from the description of their practice alone how their use of those sounds contributes to it. They build, and the particular ways in which they build involve communication between a builder and his assistant. In §6 Wittgenstein explains how children of that community might be brought up to perform those actions, to use those words as they do so, and to react in the right ways to the words of others. Even if that training involves 'ostensive teaching' of the expressions in the presence of the different kinds of stones, it would be no help to think that that 'ostensive teaching' succeeds by producing a connection between the sound and some act or item 'in the mind' of the pupil. The teaching is successful if the pupil learns to carry the right kinds of stones to a builder, or to order the stones he needs if he is a builder. That is the only 'connection' the teaching has to establish, since whoever receives the teaching and uses and responds to those sounds in the right ways understands them and knows what they mean. Even if the 'ostensive teaching' did always produce some object or act 'in the mind', no such thing would be sufficient for meaning or understanding, since the very same 'ostensive teaching', and so the production of the very same thing 'in the mind', could have brought about a quite different understanding of those sounds. For example, if pupils were trained not to carry a slab to the building but rather to break another kind of stone into pieces when they hear the sound 'Slab!', that sound would then have a different meaning in those circumstances—it would not be an order for a slab. But what happened in the 'ostensive teaching', and what object was produced 'in the mind' as a result of that teaching, might have been just as they are in the case Wittgenstein describes. It is in people's capacities or abilities to use and respond to sounds and marks in the right way that their meaning and understanding them resides.

It is perhaps easy to feel that the 'primitive' situation described in *PI* §§2 and 6 and even 8 is not rich or complex enough to be a case of a full-fledged human language. The range of behaviour involving those sounds is so limited it might seem that automata could be trained to engage in it without thinking, meaning, or understanding anything. But even if that is so, the lessons illustrated schematically in that simple case might be carried over to more realistically complex linguistic behaviour.[3] Anyone in our society who systematically responds to questions of the form 'What is *x* plus *y*?' by giving the sum of *x* and *y* shows that he understands the word "plus" to mean *plus*. That is in fact how the word is used in English. Someone who knows what it means and understands it has mastered the 'technique' of using that word—the 'technique' of asking for, giving, and in other ways talking about the sum or the addition function in English.

Saul Kripke, in a provocative and influential book,[4] has elaborated a 'skeptical' view according to which there is no such fact as a person's meaning *plus* by "plus", or understanding that word as used on particular occasions to mean *plus*. On that view, given all the applications of the word that a person has made or responded to in the past, and everything there is or could be 'in his mind', it is still not determined what he means by the word "plus"; it is

[3] 'Our clear and simple language-games are not preparatory studies for a future regularization of language—as it were first approximations, ignoring friction and air-resistance. The language-games are rather set up as *objects of comparison* which are meant to throw light on the facts of our language by way not only of similarities, but also of dissimilarities' (*PI* §130).

[4] Saul A. Kripke, *Wittgenstein on Rules and Private Language* (Cambridge, Mass., 1982).

compatible with all those facts that he means and understands by it something different from *plus*. This view represents a challenge to the very idea of 'the rule for the use of an expression'. It applies just as much to general practices or customs as it does to individual applications of a 'rule'. Many different 'rules' are all said to be compatible with everything that has actually happened in the community and every item that has ever been in anyone's mind up to any given point, yet many of those 'rules' differ from one another in what they imply would be the correct move the next time. That *this* rather than *that* is the correct move at a particular point is therefore held not to be fixed by any past or present fact. There is therefore no such fact as a person's (or everyone's) following *this* particular rule rather than some other; there is no such unique thing as *the* rule by which a person (or everyone) proceeds. This has the unsettling consequence that there is no such fact as an expression's meaning one thing rather than another, or a person's understanding it one way rather than another. 'It seems that the entire idea of meaning vanishes into thin air'.[5] Kripke finds this 'skeptical' view in Wittgenstein; or at least the problem to which it seems such a discouraging answer he finds to be 'perhaps the central problem of *Philosophical Investigations*'.[6]

One thing that casts doubt on the attribution of this 'skeptical' view to Wittgenstein is that it involves something that Wittgenstein forcefully and repeatedly rejects. Kripke describes the problem as that of finding a fact that constitutes a person's meaning or understanding an expression in one particular way rather than another, and he holds that any such fact must somehow 'contain' within it some 'directions' or 'instructions' to the person to say or do things in a certain way in virtue of meaning or understanding the expression in the way he does.[7] That is because, for Kripke, there must be something that 'justifies' a person in doing what he does when, for example, he says '125' in answer to the question 'What is 68 plus 57?'; he cannot just be proceeding 'blindly'. The right answer to give is '125' if "plus" means *plus*, but the problem is to say what fact it is that shows him, or shows anyone, that that is what that expression means on this occasion, as opposed, say, to Kripke's *quus*.[8] If

[5] Saul A. Kripke, 22. [6] Ibid. 7. [7] Ibid. 11.

[8] '*x* quus *y*' denotes the sum of *x* and *y* if *x* and *y* are both less than the highest numbers for which the function has actually been computed; if not, it denotes 5. It is imagined for purposes of the example that for '68 plus 57' on this occasion only the second condition is fulfilled.

there is such a thing as his meaning or understanding "plus" to mean *plus* on that occasion, or his following the rule according to which the correct answer to give to such questions is always the sum, what is it that determines that that is the meaning he understands it to have, or that that is the rule he is following? The 'skeptical' answer is: nothing does or could determine that. So there is no such thing as meaning or understanding an expression in one particular way rather than another.

Wittgenstein would certainly endorse the idea that there could be no item in the person's mind, or anywhere else for that matter, that instructs the person, or tells him what to do, in the sense that its presence there guarantees that the person understands the expression "plus" to mean *plus*. That is just the point brought out by the 'ostensive teaching' of builders and their assistants in *PI* §6. With a different training in using and responding to the expression, the very same 'ostensions' and the very same item produced by them in the speaker's 'mind' would bring about a quite different understanding of the expression. What an expression means is to be found in its use, not in any fact or item which is supposed to give it or specify its meaning. Disconnected from any particular ways in which it would be correct to use or to respond to it, any such fact or object on its own would be at best only one more 'dead' sign. That is the key to recognizing the futility of appealing to an object or item in the mind or anywhere else. The 'skeptical' view concludes from the failure of any such appeal that there is no such thing as an expression's meaning or being understood to mean one thing rather than another. Wittgenstein on the contrary brings out how and why it cannot be a condition of an expression's meaning what it does, or of its being correctly understood in one way rather than another, that there be some object or item or fact that instructs its users or determines what they are to do and so in that way justifies their responses. Nor is that a condition of there being such a thing as the rule by which they proceed, or a 'technique' or practice of which they are masters.

We make sense of what happens in the community described in language-game §2 by understanding them to be following the rule, or engaging in the practice: when a builder calls out 'Slab!' he is ordering a certain kind of building-stone—let us call it in English a slab—and assistants who understand that expression correctly carry a slab to the builder when they hear that sound. A builder who orders a slab in that way on a particular occasion, and an assistant who carries him a slab when he hears that order, conform to the general rule or practice for that expression. They are using and responding to 'Slab!' correctly. That there is that practice in that community is what the fact that "Slab!" means what it does there amounts to. Similarly, that English speakers follow the rule that when asked 'What is *x* plus *y*?' it is correct to give the sum, is part of what the fact that "plus" means *plus* amounts to. Someone who speaks English and conforms to that general practice on a particular occasion understands that word to mean *plus*.

The 'skeptical' view holds that there are no facts of meaning or understanding an expression in a particular way—that there is no difference in what happens or what is so in the world between a person's or a community's meaning one thing by a certain expression and their meaning something different by it. Nothing in anyone's 'mental history' or 'mental history of past behaviour' establishes that by "plus" someone means *plus* rather than *quus*, for example.[9] On the 'skeptical' view there is no fact anywhere which is the fact that "Slab!" is an order for a slab in language-game §2, or that "plus" means *plus* in an English-speaking community. 'There can be no such thing as meaning anything by any word'.[10]

Now it must be admitted that there are a great many facts about the past behaviour of a community or an individual in connection with a particular expression which do not together imply—and so cannot be taken to be equivalent to—the fact that that expression means what it does or that the community or the individual understands it in one particular way rather than another. The introduction of concepts like Kripke's *quus* helps to bring that out. There are many facts of what has actually gone on in the community described in language-game §2 that are perfectly compatible with assistants' now doing something different on hearing 'Slab!' and builders' accepting what they do with approval or without objection. Perhaps from now on when they hear 'Slab!' they will break into pieces whatever stone lies next to a slab in the stone pile, or they will carry to a builder what we call a block, not a slab, and builders will make appropriate use of what is brought. This could be so if the community simply started using "Slab!" in a different way, and so changed its meaning. But, more importantly, it could

[9] Kripke, *Wittgenstein on Rules*, 21. [10] Ibid. 55.

be so even if "Slab!" continues to mean the same as it has meant before. If the rule those speakers have been following is something like: when a builder calls out 'Slab!' he is ordering a slab if it is before time *t* but otherwise he is ordering a block, then our original understanding of them would be wrong. It would be wrong even though every correct response in the past has involved carrying a slab to a builder. On the alternative rule or practice, it would not be correct, after the time in question, for an assistant to carry a slab to a builder on hearing 'Slab!'

The same is true of the English word "plus". Even if every particular answer every English speaker has ever given to questions of the form 'What is *x* plus *y*?' has been the sum of *x* and *y*, it does not follow that those who understand the expression correctly will give the sum tomorrow, even if "plus" continues to mean the same as it has meant in the past. Nor does it follow that the sum will be the right answer to give. If "plus" meant *quus*, and tomorrow we were asked a question of the form 'What is *x* plus *y*?' about numbers beyond those which have actually been computed so far, it would not be correct to give the sum as the answer even though every right answer to such questions in the past has been the sum. In that sense it is possible for something other than the sum to be the right answer, given all those facts of past behaviour.

To say that it is possible for a slab to have been delivered, or for the sum to have been given, every time in the past, and yet it not be correct tomorrow to deliver a slab, or to give the sum, even though the meanings of "Slab!" and "plus" have not changed, is to say that it is possible for those facts of past behaviour to have been as they are and for those speakers not to be following the rule that "Slab!" is an order for a slab, or that "plus" means *plus*. What is not possible is for those to be the rules they are following and it not be correct to deliver a slab, or to give the sum. Whether a community or an individual is following a particular set of rules or not is a contingent matter of fact. It is possible for us to be wrong about what rules they are following. But in identifying the rules or practices they are following we thereby specify, if only implicitly, what a correct response or a proper understanding of the expressions in question would be.

The fact that there are many descriptions of what has been so or has gone on in the past which do not together imply, and hence are not equivalent to, intentional or semantical statements like ' "Slab!"

is an order for a slab' or '"Plus" means *plus*' does not show that there is something more to an expression's meaning what it does, or a response to an expression's being correct, than the expression's being used in a certain way in the community. It is a matter of how that 'use' or rule or practice is to be described. What an expression or a speaker means, or what rule for an expression an individual or a group of speakers is following, or what is a correct application of or response to an expression, are not equivalent or reducible to facts which are not themselves specified in similarly intentional or semantical or normative terms. The 'use' of an expression as it is relevant to meaning is the distinctive role the expression plays in the activities in which human beings utter it and respond to it as they do. Those actions and responses can help identify that meaning only if they are seen and understood as intentional; to ascribe them to those agents is to ascribe attitudes with intentional contents. A description in non-intentional terms of what happens whenever certain sounds are uttered or certain marks are made would not say what human beings are doing with those sounds or marks. It would leave the sounds and marks 'dead' or without 'life' or meaning. Facts of what human agents are intentionally doing are not equivalent or reducible to facts merely of physical or physiological happenings specified in non-intentional terms.

This intentional character of thought and action and language is indispensable to our understanding them in the ways we do. An order, for example, is something with particular content; fulfilling the order requires that what was ordered be done. That is what gives the order its particular identity. An order for a slab is fulfilled by bringing a slab. That gives the standard of correctness of response for those who understand the utterance. We certify the correctness of that response in saying that those who make the utterance are ordering a slab.

> 'An order orders its own execution.' So it knows its execution, then, even before it is there?—But that was a grammatical proposition and it means: If an order runs 'Do such-and-such' then executing the order is called 'doing such-and-such'. (*PI* §458)

An order to do such-and-such orders no more than what is specified in its content. Even if every slab ever brought in response to orders in language-game §2 has in fact been grey and has weighed less than ten pounds, it does not follow that what was ordered on all those occasions were grey slabs weighing less than ten pounds, or that it would not be in accord with such an order to deliver a black slab that weighs more. Similarly, it is not simply the fact that every correct answer to 'What is *x* plus *y*?' in the past has been the sum that determines the correctness of giving the sum in answer to such a question this time. Every correct answer might in fact have been the sum even though the sum was not what the question asked for. As things are, it is correct to give the sum because "plus" means *plus*; asking in English 'What is *x* plus *y*?' is asking for the sum of *x* and *y*.

The 'skeptical' view represents the challenge: if those alleged facts of meaning, correctness, or accord with a rule cannot be identified with or shown to be equivalent to anything that actually happens or is so in the world, what could they possibly amount to? But to put the objection in that way is to expose the assumption or prejudice that lies behind it. It assumes that it never happens or is never so in the world that, for instance, a builder orders a slab and an assistant obeys the order, or that someone asks for the sum of two numbers and someone else gives the right answer. What can be said in support of that assumption?

The possibility of 'quus'-like interpretations of sounds or marks or other items does succceed in refuting any view of meaning or understanding which requires that there be some item in a speaker's or hearer's 'mind' which tells him what to do in using or responding to an expression. No such item could determine the speaker's or hearer's response, or its correctness. If the item that was present when a speaker hears 'What is *x* plus *y*?' meant *plus* it would 'tell' him to give the sum, but if that same item was present and meant *quus* it could 'tell' him to give the answer '5'. Introduction of further items to try to settle the matter would lead to a regress.

But if the requirement of 'instruction' or 'guidance' has been dropped from an account of meaning or understanding, as for Wittgenstein it must be, what support remains for the 'skeptical' view? The possibility that "plus" might mean *quus* shows only that facts of meaning or understanding or correctness of response do not follow from and so are not reducible to any non-intentionally described goings-on, no matter how complex or long-standing. All the non-semantical or non-intentional facts of what has happened or what has been so in the world up to any given point are compatible with different and conflicting intentional or semantical or normative statements. Given all those past facts, an utterance of 'Slab!' in language-game §2 could be an order for a slab or it could be an order for a slab if it is before time *t* and otherwise for a block; uttering 'What is *x* plus *y*?' could be asking what is *x* plus *y* or it could be asking what is *x* quus *y*. But that does not directly imply that there simply are no such semantical or intentional facts of meaning or understanding or of responses' being correct. Nor does it show that "Slab!" 's being an order for a slab is not something that ever happens or is so in the world, or that nothing that could be so in the world is incompatible with its being an order for a slab if it is before time *t* and otherwise for a block. We take it to be true of the community described in language-game §2 that "Slab!" is an order for a slab. If that is so, then what is so in that community is incompatible with "Slab!" 's being an order for a slab if it is before time *t* and otherwise for a block. If it is true that "plus" means *plus*, that rules out its meaning *quus*. Those incompatibilities are essential to the very point of an appeal to 'quus'-like terms; at most one of the conflicting intentional or semantical statements can be true. But that does not imply that *none* of them is true. So it gives no support to the 'skeptical' view that there are no facts at all of what speakers or expressions mean, or of how or whether they are correctly understood.[11]

That conclusion could perhaps be reached on the further assumption that non-intentionally specified facts are somehow the only facts there are, or that they are privileged in some way. But to make that assumption with no further support would seem to be nothing but prejudice. If statements of one kind are not equivalent or reducible to statements of another kind, it does not in general follow that the irreducible statements say nothing and are neither

[11] The blanket introduction of "quus-like" terms without further restriction would have devastating effects on our efforts to understand or learn anything, not just about meaning and understanding. If the possibility that someone means *quus* rather than *plus* by "plus" shows that there is no such fact as his meaning anything at all by it, then there would also be no such fact as our having confirmed an empirical generalization or having any more reason to believe one thing rather than its opposite, as Nelson Goodman showed (*Fact, Fiction, and Forecast*, 2nd edn. (Indianapolis, 1965)). By parallel reasoning it could be shown that there is no such fact as a person's performing an action of some determinate kind (e.g. walking, rather than walking-if-observed-before-time-*t*-and-otherwise-flying), and even no determinate facts at all (e.g. there is a tree in the meadow, rather than there is a tree-if-observed-before-time-*t*-and-otherwise-a-hippopotamus in the meadow).

true nor false. Mathematical truths, for example, are not reducible to non-mathematical truths, but that is no reason to conclude that there are no mathematical truths. It shows only that they are different from non-mathematical truths in ways that presumably can be described and understood. Similarly, statements about what expressions mean, or how they are understood, or about the correctness of certain responses to them, are not equivalent or reducible to non-semantical or non-intentional descriptions of what goes on when certain sounds or marks are made. It shows only that they differ from non-semantical or non-normative statements in ways that presumably can be described and understood.

Intentional or semantical remarks like '"Slab!" is an order for a slab' or '"Plus" means *plus*' are things we say and mean and understand every day. To explain what they mean and how they differ from other statements would be to understand and describe their use; that is what determines that they have the meanings they do. Saying '"Slab!" is an order for a slab' serves to identify what "Slab!" means in the community in language-game §2, and so to distinguish its use or meaning from that of "Pillar!", "Block!", and "Beam!", which each have different uses in that language. '"Plus" means *plus*' says what a certain English expression means, and so distinguishes its use or meaning from that of other expressions like "minus" or "times". We make similarly intentional remarks about what an individual speaker means or understands on a particular occasion. A builder who calls out 'Slab!' means it as an order for a slab, an assistant who hears him and delivers a slab understands that order correctly. A pupil who answers '125' when asked 'What is 68 plus 57?' has correctly understood "plus" to mean *plus* (and has also got the sum right). It seems that we would be unable to make the right kind of sense of the familiar phenomena of speaking and meaning and understanding without thinking of them in these ways. We would be restricted to describing a series of sounds and marks and movements without seeing them as having any particular 'life' or meaning.

The 'skeptical' view must somehow account for these familiar remarks about the meanings of expressions or speakers' understanding of them while none the less holding that they do not say what they seem to say and are neither true nor false. Kripke suggests that on Wittgenstein's conception of 'use' there is a way of doing that. It is matter of describing the conditions under which such things are 'legitimately assertable', and showing that 'the game of asserting them under such conditions has a role in our lives'.[12] Our social interaction with others depends on our trusting and relying on them in many ways, so it is not surprising that 'the "game" of attributing to others the mastery of certain concepts or rules' is important to social life.[13] This is especially clear in child-rearing, education, and training, for example. Someone who has performed successfully in a sufficient number and variety of tests is deemed to have mastered the concept of addition and is accordingly 'admitted into the community as an adder; an individual who passes such tests in enough other cases is admitted as a normal speaker of the language and member of the community'.[14] Those who are incorrigibly deviant in certain respects are to that extent excluded. In extreme cases they cannot participate in the community or in communication at all. The 'game' of ascribing concepts and understanding to speakers is to be understood as a complex activity of social 'admittance' and 'exclusion'.

It is certainly in accord with Wittgenstein's conception of meaning as use to include in the description of the use of expressions an account of what human beings are doing in using them as they do and what point or role those activities have in the lives of those people. But what has been said so far along the lines Kripke suggests falls short of a full and adequate description of the familiar use of those expressions. For one thing, it does not explain what is being done or said in remarks about a general practice in a community and not about an individual speaker's performance. To say ' "Slab!" is an order for a slab in language-game §2' is not to 'admit' some speakers into one's linguistic community, or to encourage or approve of anyone's behaviour in any way. To say ' "Plus" means *plus*' is not to 'admit' anyone into the English-speaking community either. Such remarks appear to be descriptions of what goes on in a certain community; what those who use and understand the expressions correctly are doing and saying.

Even though to say of a particular person 'He understands "plus" to mean *plus*' can be a way of 'admitting' that person into the community, that is not enough to identify what the speaker is thereby saying about the person, or in what way or in what respect he is 'admitting' him into the community. We might say of a person who

[12] Kripke, *Wittgenstein on Rules*, 78. [13] Ibid. 93. [14] Ibid. 92.

has passed certain other tests 'He understands "minus" to mean *minus*', and thereby 'admit' him into the community in a certain respect. But 'He understands "plus" to mean *plus*' does not mean the same as 'He understands "minus" to mean *minus*.' Those two remarks do not have the same use. In uttering one of them a speaker is not doing in every respect the very same thing as he is doing in uttering the other. What is missing so far from the description of their uses is any indication of the difference between the two remarks.

Conformity to the general practice in the community is what determines the correctness of a person's employment of or response to expressions. But to say of someone who is deemed to have shown himself master of the concept of addition 'He understands "plus" to mean *plus*' is not simply to say of him that his employment of "plus" conforms to that of the community. It might also be said of him 'He understands "minus" to mean *minus*' on the grounds that his employment of that expression conforms to that of the community as well. To say that he uses and responds to an expression as others do is not in itself to say what particular meaning he or they understand that expression to have. Nor do I specify that meaning if I say of him only that he uses the expression in the same way as I do. A remark like 'He understands "plus" to mean *plus*' does specify that meaning. Saying only that he uses and responds to "plus" as I or as others do in the community does not. To say that we 'admit' him because he conforms to community practices in his use of both "plus" and "minus" therefore does not explain how his use of one of those expressions differs from his use of the other. It does not say what my or the community practices in question actually are. We can of course go on to say that in that community, or as I use them, "plus" means *plus* and "minus" means *minus*. That then does serve to specify how he uses and understands them, if he conforms to those practices. But that is a statement about the meaning of certain expressions, or how they are understood. It says more than simply that there is a consensus in the community, or with me, in the use of those expressions.

In trying to describe the 'game' or practice of 'admitting' certain people into the community—which on the 'skeptical' view is all that anyone is doing in saying things like 'He understands "plus" to mean *plus*'—Kripke says the person 'is admitted into the community as an adder', as someone who 'has grasped the concept of addition',[15] or as giving the right answers to "addition problems".[16] That does serve to specify a particular respect in which the pupil is 'admitted' into the community. But it does so only by attributing to those who thereby 'admit' the pupil a recognition or acknowledgement that, not only does the pupil's use conform to that of the community, but also in the community "plus" means *plus*. The 'skeptical' view cannot allow for any such specific recognition or acknowledgement, since it would be recognition of something which on that view has no truth-conditions and so is neither true nor false. The 'skeptical' view denies that there are any such facts. But without some such particular specification of a pupil's understanding there can be no adequate explanation of the differences in use and so in meaning between remarks like 'He understands "plus" to mean *plus*' and 'He understands "minus" to mean *minus*.' The 'skeptical' view gives no satisfactory account of such remarks.

Wittgenstein's reminders of the way in which the meanings of expressions are determined by their use in the community, and the correctness of an individual's understanding is determined by his conformity to that practice, stand opposed to any appeal to an 'inner' or 'mental' object or item as essential to understanding the facts of meaning, understanding, and thinking. Even if there is no good reason to accept the 'skeptical' view that there are no such facts to be understood or accounted for, consideration of the challenge represented by that paradoxical view none the less brings out a very important point. It is that how someone means or understands certain expressions, or what those expressions mean in the sense of what are the rules or practices for their correct employment in a community, are facts which in general cannot be adequately specified except by using the very concepts that the speakers in question are thereby said to be masters of. Because we know what an order is, and can pick out a certain type of stone we call a slab, we can say that builders in language-game §2 who utter 'Slab!' are ordering a slab. Equipped as we are with the concept of addition, we can say what a pupil who responds to certain utterances in distinctive ways has mastered; he has got the concept of addition, he understands and gives the right answers to addition problems, he understands "plus" to mean *plus*. If we were restricted

[15] Ibid. 92. [16] Ibid. 96.

to saying without interpretation only what utterances a speaker responds to, what distinctive movements of his body are caused by those utterances, and what utterances he himself is thereby disposed to make in different circumstances, we could not make the right kind of sense of what he is doing in responding and uttering as he does. No description which falls short of identifying *what* speakers mean and understand by the expressions they utter and hear, and *what* they are doing and saying and understanding when they utter and respond in those ways, will succeed in fully specifying the meanings of those expressions or the thought those speakers have in using them as they do. We have access to facts of meaning and understanding that the 'skeptical' view denies only because we already possess concepts and thoughts that are embodied or expressed in those very facts.

This is important, if correct, because it suggests that the paradoxical 'skeptical' view derives much of its appeal from a recognizable sense of philosophical dissatisfaction or disappointment it is possible to feel in the face of a more robust, non-'skeptical' view of meaning and thought. Wittgenstein's writings reveal an intimate familiarity with that dissatisfaction.

When we see the richness, complexity, and intricate interrelations among the rules, techniques, and practices that determine the meanings of even some of the apparently simplest things we say and understand, there seems little or no hope of our gaining a single commanding view and describing those rules or practices perspicuously once and for all. There is no difficulty for us in using the expressions and following the rules as we do. The difficulty is in stating clearly and fully what those uses or practices are. That is one of the apparent dissatisfactions of the appeal to nothing more than 'use' as an explanation of meaning. It is not just a matter of complexity. It is that in giving descriptions of the practices we and others engage in we must employ and rely on the very concepts and practices and capacities that we are trying to describe and understand. One reason it is difficult to describe them correctly is that we see right through them, as it were; they are too close to us to be seen for what they are. This inability to command a clear view of our concepts, and the apparently natural tendency in philosophical reflection to wrongly assimilate the use of one kind of expression to that of another, is for Wittgenstein a continuous source of philosophical problems.

The conclusion can be philosophically dissatisfying or disappointing in another, and deeper, way. If facts of what expressions mean, of the correctness of certain ways of understanding them, or of the rules by which speakers and hearers proceed, can in general be expressed only in semantical or intentional statements which make use of the very concepts that they attribute to those they describe, then they would seem not to be the kinds of facts that could ever explain how language or meaning in general is possible, or what facts or rules human beings rely on, as it were, to get into language in the first place, from outside it. That can seem to leave the phenomena of meaning, understanding, and thinking as philosophically mysterious as they would be on the hypothesis of an occult mental medium. No explanation of thought or meaning in non-semantical or non-intentional terms would be available. That can be felt as deeply dissatisfying.

Much of Wittgenstein's later philosophy deals in one way or another with the aspiration or demand for a different and potentially more illuminating kind of explanation of meaning. There is rich material for philosophical 'treatment'. His investigations bring out in as many ways as possible how nothing does or could 'instruct' or 'guide' us in speaking or in understanding the speech of others. Nothing could 'tell' us how to speak, or how to understand what others are saying. Meaning or rules can be told or explained only to those who know how to speak and understand what is said. We get into language at all, not by following instructions or explanations of how to do it, but only because we share enough natural responses, interests, and inclinations with those who already speak. Nothing 'deeper' or intellectually more satisfying is available, or would help. We recognize what builders in language-game §2 are doing, and understand them to be ordering a slab. We understand what those who respond to addition problems in certain ways are doing, and see that they understand "plus" to mean *plus*. 'The common behavior of mankind is the system of reference' by means of which we understand each other (*PI* §206). Mankind is a talking species. Such essentially linguistic practices as 'commanding, questioning, recounting, chatting, are as much part of our natural history as walking, eating, drinking, playing' (*PI* §25).

12

The Theory of Meaning and the Practice of Communication

Near the end of his essay 'A Nice Derangement of Epitaphs' Donald Davidson, writing in English, concludes that 'there is no such thing as a language'. Some people have stopped reading at that point. But that is not all he wrote—even in that very sentence. What he says is: 'there is no such thing as a language, not if a language is anything like what many philosophers and linguists have supposed.'[1] I take this as my text. I want to explore what I think Davidson is getting at here. I find it very important—and something that a great many philosophers continue to miss, or even to deny.

To explain what he means by saying that a language is nothing like what many philosophers and linguists have supposed, we have to ask what they have supposed. Those Davidson has in mind have supposed that, as he puts it, 'communication by speech requires that speaker and interpreter have learned or somehow acquired a common method or theory of interpretation—as being able [*sic*] to operate on the basis of shared conventions, rules, or regularities'.[2] He thinks that supposition must be wrong, because 'no method or theory fills this bill'.[3] If communication by speech required such a method or theory, there would be no such thing as communication by speech.

So when he denies that there is such a thing as a language as many philosophers and linguists have thought of it what he is denying is that there is such a thing as 'linguistic competence as often described'.[4] The main culprit in descriptions of linguistic

This essay was first published in *Crítica*, 30:88 (April 1998).

[1] D. Davidson, 'A Nice Derangement of Epitaphs', in R. Grandy and R. Warner (eds.), *Philosophical Grounds of Rationality: Intentions, Categories, Ends* (Oxford, 1986), 174.

[2] Ibid. [3] Ibid. [4] Ibid.

competence is again an assumption that he puts this way: 'The systematic knowledge or competence of the speaker or interpreter is learned in advance of occasions of interpretation and is conventional in character.'[5] That is what he thinks has to go. It is an idea he argued against in his paper 'Communication and Convention' as well.[6] 'We must give up the idea of a clearly defined shared structure which language-users acquire and then apply to cases,'[7] he says. In short, 'we should give up the attempt to illuminate how we communicate by appeal to conventions.'[8]

Now what exactly is being denied here—and so what is being positively said or implied about how we do communicate? There is no question that people communicate by speech; many people are very good at it. But there also seems to be no question that those who are good at it are competent, even fluent, in some particular language. What is the bad way of thinking of that competence that Davidson is warning us against? Is it wrong to think that a person's competence in a particular language is, as he says, 'learned or somehow acquired'? Surely not. Is it wrong to think of a person's competence as 'learned or acquired in advance of occasions of interpretation'? Well, no. I acquired my competence in English in advance of the 'occasions of interpretation' that I have been presented with in, say, the last ten years. I could speak English just as well ten years ago as I can now. And there will be, I hope, a great many 'occasions of interpretation' yet to come, in my future. So my present competence has been acquired in advance of all of those occasions. But was my competence in English 'learned or acquired in advance of' *all* 'occasions of interpretation'? I don't think so. It was only because the people around me said things in English on certain 'occasions of interpretation' in my surroundings, and because I had to catch on to what they were saying on those occasions, that I became competent in English. If no one had ever said anything in my presence, I probably would not have acquired any particular linguistic competence at all.

Is that something that many philosophers and linguists would deny? Some would say that an infant is born with a general capacity for language, perhaps even a 'language module', in advance of

[5] D. Davidson, 161.
[6] In his *Inquiries into Truth and Interpretation* (Oxford, 1984).
[7] 'A Nice Derangement of Epitaphs', 174.
[8] Ibid.

exposure to the sounds of any particular language, and in that sense has a prior capacity to acquire particular languages by exposure. But does anyone hold that competence or fluency in English or Spanish or any other particular language is acquired in advance of all 'occasions of interpretation'? Again, I don't think so.

What is more relevant to what I think Davidson is concerned with is to ask whether, as he puts it, a speaker's competence is 'learned in advance of occasions of interpretation and is conventional in character'. It is the idea that we can 'illuminate how we communicate by appeal to conventions' that he thinks we have to get rid of—that we 'operate on the basis of shared conventions, rules, or regularities'.

What *is* the idea that we have to get rid of here? Is it the thought that speakers who communicate share certain rules or regularities in their speech, or that their speech conforms to certain shared conventions? I don't think that can be it. Speakers of English do communicate with one another, and I think they can also be said to follow certain rules or regularities in their speech. For instance, most English speakers on the whole follow the rule for pluralization: generally speaking, add 's'. The rule for forming plurals is different in Italian. Of course, the rule I stated is only rough; there are many exceptions. But it is not that no precise rule can be formulated, in this or in any other case. Davidson does express doubts about whether all English speakers do follow the same rule for pluralization,[9] but in general I don't think that in denying that we operate on the basis of shared conventions, rules, or regularities he means only that precise and exceptionless rules or regularities about English are not to be found. He does say that we must give up the idea of a 'clearly defined shared structure which language-users acquire and then apply to cases', but I think the emphasis there is on a clearly defined structure's not being shared and *applied to cases*, rather than on its not being shared and clearly defined.

After all, Davidson is the person who introduced, and who has done more than anyone else to promote, and to make vivid and promising, the idea of what he has called a systematic 'theory of meaning' for a particular natural language—say, English. That theory would ideally take the form of a recursive theory of truth

[9] Ibid. 172.

for that language, and would reveal the meanings of particular expressions by showing how a finite supply of elements can be put together to generate an indefinitely large number of new expressions with particular meanings by the application of a finite number of rules. That the correct meanings of English expressions can be generated in that way by those rules is to be shown by an empirical theory of English. So to be true, the theory and its rules must capture the way English speakers actually speak.

That is just what we would expect, since there is nothing else for a theory of meaning of a particular language to capture. What words or expressions mean in English can depend on nothing more than how those expressions are used by speakers of English. So the statements expressing the theory of meaning for English will be true only if English speakers actually speak in the ways they describe. The statements of the theory will be in that sense true generalizations—they will express what can be called regularities (and why not rules?) in the speech of English speakers. Of course, like most generalizations, they will be only approximately true, or true under a certain idealization. Many particular utterances by what are otherwise English speakers will deviate from them. But that does not mean that the structure that the theory ascribes to English is not 'clearly defined'. Nor does it mean, I think, that at a certain level of generality the regularities or rules are not shared. They are shared in the sense that the same regularities or rules are true of the speech of a great many people. It is only because that is so that they can be said to constitute of a theory of meaning for English.

I don't think Davidson denies, or has reason to deny, any of this. Surely he has not abandoned his central idea of an empirical theory of meaning for English. For the same reason I don't think he has reason to deny that there are shared *conventions* of English, given what I think he wants to stress about communication and linguistic competence. There might be to some extent simply a terminological difference here. I think there can be said to be a convention of, for instance, driving on the right in the United States and driving on the left in England. Of course, by now, it is required by law, but I don't think that means it is not conventional. If it is, then there are two different conventions in effect with respect to driving in two different English-speaking communities. Similarly, I think there is only one convention in effect in both those communities in English speakers' using the word "and" to express conjunction, say, or in using the word "bed" for something to sleep on, or in expressing the thought that snow is white by uttering the sentence "Snow is white". Spanish speakers have different conventional ways of doing those things. They share different conventions.

What I think Davidson does want to insist on about communication and linguistic competence is that, as he puts it, we do not '*operate on the basis of* shared conventions, rules, or regularities'. That does not mean that there simply are no such things as conventions or rules, or that if there are they are not shared. The important idea is rather that whatever conventions, rules, or regularities there might be, they do not have the kind of role in communication that many philosophers and linguists have supposed. We do not 'operate on the basis of' them.

Even if there is a clearly defined—or at least potentially definable—structure of a language that many speakers share, those language-users do not communicate with each other by taking that general structure and applying it to cases. Davidson will grant that we can think of a clearly defined theory of meaning for a language as a kind of machine which, when fed any arbitrary expression of the language, will grind out the meaning of that expression. But speaking and understanding what is said—in a word, communicating—is not just a matter of grinding out the meanings of expressions in that way. To think that an appeal to conventions or rules or theory can illuminate how we communicate is perhaps to suppose that it is. But communication involves more than the meanings of expressions. It is a matter of a person's saying something, and of one person's understanding what another person says.

That is what Davidson brings out by focusing first on malapropisms, mistakes, and misuses of words that none the less do not impede communication. When Mrs Malaprop in Sheridan's play utters the words 'a nice derangement of epitaphs' she is describing something as a nice arrangement of epigrams. That is what she means, and we know that that is what she means—just as we understand her when she describes someone as 'the very pineapple of politeness' or says someone else is 'as headstrong as an allegory on the banks of the Nile'. Those are English words, but the meanings we rightly ascribe to her remarks are not the meanings that an empirical theory of meaning for English would grind out by applying to the words she utters the principles or rules of that theory. The theory would have her speaking of epitaphs, pineapples, and allegories, but we know better. The point is—and of course it does not depend on malapropisms—that we often understand what people say even when the words they use standardly mean something different from what we take the person to mean in uttering them on a particular occasion. If we have never heard those particular words used with those particular meanings before, we can still understand what is said. We can even understand someone when we have never heard any of his words used with any meanings at all before, and so have no idea what they mean.

Two people do not have to share a language, or share the same words with the same meanings, in order to communicate successfully. So it is not true, as many philosophers and linguists have apparently supposed, that communication by speech *requires* that speaker and hearer share a common set of conventions, rules, or regularities. If they do not, they can still understand each other, but obviously they do not do so by the application of a clearly defined, or even loosely defined, theory of meaning for a language they share, or even a theory of meaning for one or another of the different languages that each of them happens to be master of.

Direct application of a theory of meaning for English would give the wrong answer in Mrs Malaprop's case, even if we had such a theory and it was completely precise. It would be what Davidson calls a 'standing' or 'prior' theory: a general characterization of the meanings of expressions in the language which we might possess in advance of being presented with any 'occasions of interpretation' from Mrs Malaprop. When she speaks, we interpret her with what Davidson (somewhat oddly, to my ear) calls a 'passing' theory: something that works at the moment for the particular utterance she has made. That is, we assign meanings to some of her words as used on that occasion which differ from the meanings assigned to those words by the standing or prior theory of English. But we do not assign those passing meanings to her words by applying to her utterances a general theory of meaning—even a passing theory of meaning. That is why speaking of a passing *theory* can be misleading. There is nothing more to having or employing what Davidson calls a passing theory of a person's utterance than interpreting or understanding that utterance—correctly identifying what the speaker is saying. That is a transient achievement; it says only what the speaker meant by certain words on that occasion. It has no predictive power. She might mean something completely different by those same words the next time. If she is Mrs Malaprop, she probably will. But still, if we are good at understanding, we will be able to find out what she means the next time too.

We, as speakers and hearers and interpreters, understand what people are saying on particular occasions. We do so by identifying what they intend to say, even if they use their words in deviant ways or in ways that we are otherwise unfamiliar with. But such interpretation is no mechanical procedure carried out in accordance with, and in that sense guided by, rules or conventions formulated in advance and simply applied to the case. It involves skills, or strategies, which we all have. Our ability to understand one another as we do is part of, and ultimately not easily distinguishable from, our knowing our way around in the world generally. And there are no rules or directions for doing that. There are better and less good ways of doing it, depending on what is at stake, but there is no way of formalizing a set of procedures, or teaching a set of instructions, that would be guaranteed to churn out the right answer each time, any more than there is an algorithm for discovering anything else about the world.

I think it is Davidson's idea that what holds for the understanding of malapropisms, mistakes, and misuses of words, which is what I have been talking about so far, holds as well when we happen to share the language with the speaker, and the words we hear are just the words we expect to hear, and we assign them the meanings they are assigned by a theory of meaning for the language in question. Even then we are interpreting and understanding what a person is saying; we do not simply insert the utterance into a meaning-generating machine and read off the output. Even if we had such a theory of meaning, and so such a machine, and everything it said about the particular language in question was correct, it would not *follow* from the fact that it assigns a certain meaning to an expression in that language that someone using that expression on a particular occasion uses it with that meaning. That doesn't follow even if the person's only language is the language in question. Something more than, or something different from, what a theory of meaning for that language would tell us is needed in order for us to understand what anyone is saying when he uses the words that the theory of meaning tells us the meanings of.

This is the important point, or fact, that I think Davidson wants to insist on. It is a point, or a fact, which many people seem to resist, and so are led into great difficulty, or paradox. The point is that what we have just seen to be true of interpreting malapropisms and misuses—namely, that a theory of meaning for the language is not enough when the intended meaning differs from the meaning assigned by the theory—is also true of interpreting standard, non-deviant utterances, when the intended meaning is the same as what the theory of meaning says it is. Even then, in Davidson's words, there is 'no learnable common core of consistent behaviour, no shared grammar or rules, no portable interpreting machine set to grind out the meaning of an arbitrary utterance'.[10]

Philosophers who resist or deny that will concede that a theory of meaning does not suffice for the interpretation of speakers whose uses of words deviate from the standard uses that the theory describes. But they deny that it follows that a theory of meaning does not suffice when speakers' uses of words *are* in accord with the uses the theory describes. After all, any particular utterance can be deviant on a particular occasion, so the general theory will not be sufficient for interpretation when that happens, but it is not possible for *all* or *most* uses of an expression in a natural language to deviate in meaning from what a correct general theory of meaning for that language assigns to it. Since the way expressions of the language are actually used is all there is for an empirical theory of meaning for that language to capture, repeated and widespread so-called 'deviation' from the meanings assigned by the theory would simply mean that the theory in question is wrong. It would not accurately describe the way those expressions are in general used. Most speech in a given language *has to* be in accord with what a correct theory of meaning for that language says. So if we apply that correct theory of meaning to utterances in that language, we will be right most of the time.

This last point is certainly right. And perhaps from the fact that something more than a theory of meaning is required in deviant cases it does not strictly *follow* that something more is required in standard, non-deviant cases as well. But still, I think the conclusion

[10] 'A Nice Derangement of Epitaphs', 173.

is true; a theory of meaning alone does not suffice for interpreting speech, even in the normal case in which a single, widely shared language is being used correctly.

That is because speaking, or communicating, involves saying something, which is a case of doing something, and no theory of meaning for a language can tell you what a person is going to do or how he is going to do it, and no such theory alone can tell you what a person is doing on a particular occasion, or how he is doing it. It can tell you what the words he utters mean, and so it can tell you, conditionally, what he would mean or what he would be saying *if* he were speaking literally or using his words with the meanings they standardly have in his language. But what a speaker is actually up to on any given occasion is something that a hearer has to recognize or figure out, even if he knows the speaker's language, or even if he has a theory of meaning for that language. I don't mean that it is difficult to recognize what our fellow human beings are doing, or that in the normal case it represents any kind of challenge at all. I mean only that a theory of meaning for a person's language does not alone tell us what the person is saying on any occasion.

That seems hard to deny. And perhaps no one would deny it. But if it is undeniable it is because a theory of meaning for a language is being understood as a theory the statements of which are true if the expressions of the language in question are in fact in general used in the ways those statements say they are. In that sense the theory describes a general practice; it is about what goes on in general. Whether a particular person's utterance on a particular occasion conforms to those general statements or not is always a further question. And that question cannot be answered by a general theory of meaning for the person's language.

As I said, that seems hard to deny. But many philosophers will object that a theory of meaning as we have been understanding it so far is too modest, or that a philosophical account of meaning and understanding should give us more. That is, many appear to aspire to an account of meaning that will tell us what someone means when he utters certain words. That is something we usually come to know when we hear someone speak, and many philosophers appear to think of that knowledge as something we derive from our knowledge of the language, or of the meanings of words, or of the meaning of something.

Michael Dummett, for instance, has long maintained that 'a theory of meaning is a theory of understanding'. One thing he has meant is that, as he put it, 'what a theory of meaning has to give an account of is what it is that someone knows when he knows the language, that is, when he knows the meanings of the expressions and sentences of the language'.[11] Just as it stands, that seems like a reasonable demand. And I think, and I think Davidson thinks, that a correct theory of meaning as we have been understanding it so far could be said to do that. Competent speakers of English know the meanings of the (or most of the) expressions and sentences of English, and if a theory of meaning for English accurately reveals those meanings by showing how the meanings of some expressions are related to and built up out of the meanings of others in the systematic way that a recursive theory describes, then that is what competent speakers can be said to know about the meanings of those English expressions. They know what those expressions mean, and they know they are related in those ways. So the theory does give an account of what someone knows when he knows the language.

But Dummett thinks that a theory that does only that much would be too modest to provide what he calls a 'philosophical understanding' of meaning. He thinks it would not explain communication and understanding because he thinks speakers' knowledge of their language is what *enables* them to speak and understand one another. As he more recently puts the point, 'A speaker's employment of his language rests upon his knowledge of it; his knowledge of what the words and sentences of the language mean is an essential part of the explanation of his saying what he does.'[12] Now being an 'essential part' of the explanation of a speaker's saying what he does does not perhaps go beyond the more modest idea of a theory of meaning as we have been thinking of it so far. There might be other equally 'essential' parts of the explanation of a speaker's saying what he does. But Dummett appears to be demanding more of a theory of meaning when he holds that a speaker's employment of his language 'rests upon his knowledge of it'. He thinks a person's knowledge or mastery of his language should *explain* his giving particular meanings to his utter-

[11] M. Dummett, 'What is a Theory of Meaning? (I)', in his *The Seas of Language* (Oxford, 1993), 3.

[12] *The Seas of Language*, p. xi.

ances and should *explain* his understanding the meanings of the utterances of others. That is why he thinks a satisfactory theory of meaning for a language should do more than just tell us what competent speakers of that language in fact know.

This is what imposes more ambitious demands on a theory of meaning for a language than we have been supposing so far. It is not easy to see exactly what these additional demands are—or, once they are made clearer, whether they could ever be fulfilled. A satisfactory theory on this richer conception should also include an account of what having knowledge of the language 'consists in'—or, as Dummett also puts it, it should explain how that knowledge of the language is 'delivered' to the speaker.[13] If his knowledge of the language is what enables a speaker to say things in that language and to understand the utterances of others, and if his speaking and understanding as he does 'rests on' that knowledge, then the theory must explain (in Dummett's words) 'how possession of the . . . knowledge operates to guide, prompt, or control the speaker's utterances', or 'how the knowledge is applied when the occasion for its application arises'.[14] Particular applications of the knowledge—particular utterances in the language, or understandings of particular utterances of others—are to be shown to be drawn out of, or derived from, one's knowledge of the language. So any theory of meaning that captures the knowledge one has in knowing a language should account for that fact. A theory that simply stated how speakers of that language in general actually speak, or under what conditions the expressions they use are true—and in that sense what they know—would not do that.

I think Dummett's thought is that if to describe someone as knowing a language were simply to say that his speech instantiates and in that sense conforms to the statements of a correct theory of meaning for that language, then attributing such knowledge to a speaker would just be a way of describing his behaviour. As Crispin Wright, following Dummett, once put it, such a minimal ascription of knowledge would not 'supply the needed contact of the theory with the . . . speakers' actual performance'.[15] In talking of speakers' knowledge in only that modest sense 'there is no real suggestion of

[13] Ibid. [14] Ibid.

[15] Crispin Wright, 'Rule-Following, Objectivity and the Theory of Meaning', in S. H. Holtzman and C. M. Leich (eds.), *Wittgenstein: To Follow a Rule* (London, 1981), 110.

[what Wright calls] an internalized "programme". All that such talk need involve is that speakers' practice fits a certain compendious description.'[16] And that is felt not to be enough. Dummett in a similar vein requires that we think of knowledge of the language as what he calls a 'mechanism'[17] or a 'piece of internal (mental) equipment'[18] by which speakers are 'guided' or 'controlled' in saying what they say and in interpreting the utterances of others. That is what he thinks the philosopher interested in meaning and understanding should account for. If that is what mastery or knowledge of a language is, and if a theory of meaning for a language is a theory of what a speaker knows when he knows that language, then a theory of meaning should explain how the contents of that 'piece of internal equipment' are 'delivered' to a speaker to 'guide, prompt, or control' his utterances and his interpretations of the utterances of others.

This might look like just a different conception of a theory of meaning for a language, or stronger requirements for what Dummett thinks of as a 'philosophical understanding' of meaning. But for Dummett and others it is more than that. It is the basis of an objection to all theories of meaning expressed in terms only of truth—or perhaps I should say of truth understood non-epistemically.

Dummett thinks a theory of meaning for a person's language should explain the person's mastery of the language, and that 'this explanation must embody an account of what it is to have the concepts expressible in the language'.[19] And a theory of meaning in terms of truth or truth-conditions alone, he thinks, fails to do that. It will say such things as that in English the predicate ". . . is a bed" is true of an object if and only if that object is a bed, or that the sentence "Snow is white" is true if and only if snow is white. But that is to make use of the very concepts that are said to be expressed by the words whose meanings or truth-conditions the theory states. That is something that Davidson right from the beginning has said is only to be expected from a truth-conditional theory of meaning.[20] Only someone who knows what a bed is could learn

[16] Ibid. [17] *The Seas of Language*, p. xii.

[18] M. Dummett, 'What Do I Know When I Know a Language?', in his *The Seas of Language*, 97. [19] Ibid. 99.

[20] See e.g. his 'Semantics for Natural Languages', in his *Inquiries into Truth and Interpretation*, 56.

from that explanation what the predicate ". . . is a bed" means, and only someone who knows what snow is, and knows what it is for something to be white, could grasp the meaning of "Snow is white" from the fact that that T-sentence is derivable in the theory.

When the language under study is different from the language in which the theory of meaning is stated, a truth theory looks in a way more helpful. In that case, there could be a kind of explanation of a person's mastery of a language. Someone who speaks English might, theoretically at least, come to know Spanish by consulting a theory of meaning for Spanish that is expressed in English. In Spanish, he finds, ". . . es una cama" is true of an object if and only if that object is a bed, "La nieve es blanca" is true if and only if snow is white, and so on. His mastery of Spanish would be explained by his knowledge of a theory of meaning for Spanish, but only because he already possesses the concepts that he is learning to express in Spanish. And his possession of those concepts is embodied in his prior mastery or knowledge of English. Obviously his mastery of English would not be explained in the same way by attributing to him knowledge of a truth theory of meaning for English expressed in English. Any such theory uses concepts to state the meanings or truth-conditions of expressions in the language, but it does not explain what it is to have those concepts. So having knowledge of such a theory would not be enough to explain a speaker's employment of his language.

Dummett accordingly demands of a theory of meaning that the knowledge of the meanings of expressions that it attributes to a speaker should *explain* a speaker's performance in speech and interpretation. It would have to be a knowledge of meanings that a speaker's application of his language to particular occasions in some sense 'rests on'. It would have to be knowledge that 'operates to guide, prompt, or control the speaker's utterances'. But in order to explain it in the right way, a theory of meaning would have to be an 'account of the understanding of a language that makes no appeal to the prior grasp of the concepts that can be expressed in it'.[21] So it would have to attribute to a speaker an 'internalized programme', or 'mechanism', or 'piece of internal (mental) equipment' which 'delivers' appropriate particular utterances or interpretations of utterances to the speaker without requiring him to

[21] 'What Do I Know When I Know a Language?', in *The Seas of Language*, 99.

possess or grasp in advance the concepts that are expressed in the words he is being guided in the application or interpretation of.

This raises large and complex questions. I can deal briefly with some, and only sketchily with others. Does a theory of meaning for a language stated in terms of truth alone fail to meet these demands of Dummett's? As far as I can understand those demands, I think it does fail to meet them. Is that a fatal defect in a truth theory of meaning, or an objection to the enterprise of constructing such a theory? I cannot see that it is. A correct truth-conditional theory of meaning describes what speakers of a particular language know by stating or revealing the meanings of the expressions they understand and competently use. In speaking as they do, speakers *exhibit* the competence that the theory describes. But that competence is not something from which each exercise of it is somehow extracted or generated by application of the rules or principles of the theory. To have the competence or knowledge in question is simply to speak, or to have the ability to speak, in accord with the general practice that the theory describes.

Does that mean that a speaker's knowledge of his language cannot *explain* his performance in the language? Well, what needs to be explained in a particular context, and what it takes to explain it, seem to me highly variable. If I am travelling with a friend in Turkey and he is having a much better time than I am, I might ask myself why. What explains his great success in interacting with all those Turks, or the ease with which he communicates with them, whereas I am getting nowhere, and no one is paying any attention to me? The explanation is that he knows Turkish. His knowledge of the language is what explains his performance, and my ignorance of it is what explains mine. But that does not mean that his successful performances are churned out of some reservoir or mechanism called 'knowledge of Turkish', any more than mine are churned out of a reservoir or mechanism called 'ignorance of Turkish'.

The fact that it attributes no such mechanism is not an objection to, or a shortcoming of, a theory of meaning in terms of truth. It couldn't be. Having knowledge of the meanings of all the expressions in a language is not enough to determine what a speaker means in making a particular utterance. That is just the point Davidson insists on. There is no 'portable interpreting machine set to grind out the meaning of any arbitrary utterance'. If such a machine, or knowledge of a language so understood, were required for communication and understanding, there would be no such thing as communication and understanding. If competence or mastery of a language had to be understood in that way, there would be no such thing as competence or mastery of a language. In other words, 'there is no such thing as a language, not if a language is anything like what many philosophers and linguists have supposed'.

This raises deeply obscure questions about the source, the nature, and the reasonableness of Dummett's demands. I am very uncertain about this. What do Dummett and those who seek a more epistemically oriented account of meaning really want? And why? They want a theory of meaning or understanding that would ascribe to speakers something that explains, in the sense of containing, generating, or guiding—and so giving meaning to—the particular utterances they make. But whatever plays that role must be a body of knowledge: something that speakers know. But if a person knows something, he must understand the content of that knowledge; he must have or grasp the concepts used in expressing what he is said to know. That is precisely why Dummett thinks a truth-conditional theory of meaning could not explain a speaker's performance; to have the knowledge that such a theory attributes, a speaker would have to understand, and so already possess, the concepts used in the T-sentences that the theory states.

So what must be in the mind of a speaker that would explain his performance in the right way is something he knows and understands, but it must also genuinely guide or control him, so it cannot rely on or presuppose his possession of the very concepts in the expression of which it is guiding or controlling him. So it cannot guide him only in the way in which instructions in English could tell someone how to say things in Spanish. A theory of meaning of the sought-for kind is supposed to apply to a person's mastery of his first, or only, language. This makes it look as if it must attribute knowledge that instructs or guides a speaker in saying and understanding things in the very language in which it instructs or guides him. But no knowledge or information could guide or instruct a person in coming to possess the very information that is supposed to be guiding him in that way.

Dummett concedes, of course, that it cannot be demanded of a theory of meaning for a language that it should be capable of conveying 'every concept expressed by a word in the language to one who does not possess it; some concepts must be taken as basic'.[22] And there will be others that 'cannot by their nature be conveyed by means of a verbal explanation'.[23] But for the rest, a condition of adequacy for a theory of meaning for a language appears to be that it should convey to someone who does not know the language or possess most of the concepts expressible in it an understanding of the expressions of the language, and so possession of those concepts. This makes it look as if Dummett's demands could be met only by a theory or body of information that tells a person how to speak, or what words to apply on what occasions, and it must do so without presupposing that he has any prior knowledge or understanding of what he would be doing or saying by using those words in those ways on those occasions.

This is perhaps what seems to recommend rejection of a truth-conditional theory of meaning in favour of a conception 'according to which the meaning is to be explained in terms of what is taken as *justifying* an utterance',[24] and why 'assertibility conditions' are thought to be essential to an account of the meanings of sentences. The idea appears to be that to know the meaning of a sentence is to be able to recognize the conditions in which to use it or apply it. But if that knowledge of those 'assertibility conditions' does not make use of or presuppose a grasp of the concepts that would be expressed in the application or utterance of that sentence under those conditions, the most it could tell a speaker is that under those recognizable conditions the application or assertive use of the sentence would be justified. But in uttering a sentence a speaker will be making an assertion only if he knows what that sentence means, or what assertion he is making. And his knowledge only of the conditions under which he can justifiably utter a certain sentence assertively does not tell him that. That is something that a truth-conditional theory of meaning for a language could tell someone: what assertion he would be making if he uttered a certain sentence and meant by it what it means in the language. But it could tell that only to someone who already understood and so possessed the concepts expressed in the assertion. For a person who lacks those concepts and that understanding, the sentence would be no

[22] *The Seas of Language*, p. viii. [23] Ibid.

[24] M. Dummett, 'Can Analytical Philosophy be Systematic, and Ought It to Be?', in his *Truth and Other Enigmas* (Cambridge, Mass., 1978), 452.

more than a string of words or marks. Something that told him when he would be justified in uttering those words or writing those marks assertively would not tell him what assertion he would be making if he did that. And it would not guide him in making any particular assertion either.

I confess bewilderment about the idea of meaning as embodied in the so-called 'assertibility conditions' of an expression, and about how even a theory of meaning that did make use of that notion could do what Dummett appears to demand.

In Wittgenstein's later treatment of such notions as meaning and understanding there is a sustained attack on the idea of a person's knowledge or understanding of meaning as a state or mechanism from which his acts or performances spring as from a reservoir[25] and which generates or guides, and in that sense explains, particular manifestations of that knowledge or understanding. He thinks there is what he is inclined to call 'a curious superstition' or 'a kind of general disease of thinking which always looks for (and finds)' such a mechanism.[26] But no equipment, no item or formula or expression in the mind—or anywhere else—could guide us or instruct us in its applications unless we understood it or it expressed something we know or believe. It could not show or tell us what to do if it meant nothing to us. So one thing it could not tell us is how to understand or interpret it. There must therefore be a way of interpreting or understanding something which is not a matter of following instructions or being guided in one's interpretation or understanding.[27] This is just what makes it look as if Dummett's demands could never be fulfilled. To understand something is to be capable of manifesting that understanding; it is not necessarily to grasp or understand something that generates or guides those manifestations.

This, I believe, is what Wittgenstein is getting at when he says that when we have attained 'greater clarity about the concepts of understanding, meaning, and thinking' it will then become clear what can lead us—and did lead him, he says—'to think that if anyone utters a sentence and *means* or *understands* it he is operating a calculus according to definite rules'.[28] The point is not that

[25] L. Wittgenstein, *The Blue and Brown Books* (Oxford, 1958), 143.

[26] Ibid.

[27] See e.g. L. Wittgenstein, *Philosophical Investigations*, tr. G. E. M. Anscomke (Oxford, 1953), §201.

[28] Ibid. §81.

such a person is operation a calculus according to 'indefinite' rules instead. The point is that he is not operating a calculus or mechanism at all. This is fully in accord with Davidson's verdict that 'there is no portable interpreting machine set to grind out the meaning of any arbitrary utterance'.

But the demand for a mental mechanism or reservoir remains. In a curious twist, Crispin Wright found in the later work of Wittgenstein what he thinks of as 'a number of *prima facie* challenges to the idea' of a theory of meaning for a language expressed in terms of truth-conditions—or perhaps a theory expressed in any terms at all.[29] In fact, he perceived 'a very fundamental tension' between what Wittgenstein says about meaning and understanding and 'thinking of language as amenable even to description by the sort of theory envisaged' by Davidson.[30] But this alleged challenge or tension arises only from Crispin Wright's and Dummett's requirement that any such theory of meaning must attribute to speakers of the language some knowledge the possession of which will '*explain* the potentially infinitary character of mastery of . . . the natural language'.[31] A theory that captures that mastery must *explain* a speaker's knowledge or recognition of the meanings of novel sentences in his language, and not simply describe that mastery and attribute it to speakers.

Wittgenstein does indeed oppose that conception of a mental mechanism that generates and in that sense explains particular instances or applications of one's mastery. But that does not threaten or challenge the idea of a theory of meaning for a natural language that does not require or attribute any such mechanism or explanation. Even less does it threaten the views of someone who denies that there is any such mechanism.

In a further twist, Saul Kripke has found in Wittgenstein an argument for the paradoxical or sceptical conclusion that there is no such thing as a person's meaning one thing rather than another by any utterance that he makes. What Wittgenstein does argue is that there could be no item the mere presence of which in the mind or anywhere else determines that it has a certain meaning or determines that I mean such and such when I utter a sound with that

[29] 'Rule-Following, Objectivity and the Theory of Meaning', 112.
[30] Ibid. 114. [31] Ibid. 111.

thing present in my mind. That will imply that nobody ever means one thing rather than another when he utters something only if one further assumption is made. Kripke sometimes appears to make that assumption, or to be tempted by it, although he quite rightly does not claim to find it in Wittgenstein.

He says he sometimes has

> something of an eerie feeling. Even now as I write, [he says] I feel confident that there is something in my mind—the meaning I attach to the 'plus' sign—that *instructs* me what I ought to do in all future cases. I do not *predict* what I *will* do . . . but instruct myself what I ought to do to conform to the meaning . . . But when I concentrate on what is now in my mind, what instructions can be found there? . . . What can there be in my mind that I make use of when I act in the future? It seems that the entire idea of meaning vanishes into thin air.[32]

Kripke says Wittgenstein accepts this conclusion; it is part of 'a picture of language based, not on *truth conditions*, but on *assertability conditions* or *justification conditions*'.[33] There is no fact as to whether Jones means addition by the word "plus", but the use and therefore the meanings of sentences like "Jones means addition by the word 'plus'" can none the less be explained in terms of their 'assertability conditions'. They in turn are to be understood only as the conditions of 'acceptance' or 'rejection' of Jones as a member of the linguistic community, not as conditions under which someone who uttered such a sentence would say something true about what Jones means. The sceptical conclusion is that there is nothing that is true or false as to what Jones means.

But when Kripke says that meaning vanishes, or that no one ever means anything, we should keep reading, just as we had to keep reading when Davidson said there is no such thing as a language. It is the very idea of something in the mind that instructs or guides a person's meaning or understanding what he does that Wittgenstein exposes as a widespread philosophical illusion. But without that idea, the sceptical or paradoxical conclusion cannot be reached in the way Kripke reaches it. So what Kripke actually establishes in the name of Wittgenstein is equivalent to what can be put in a

[32] Kripke, *Wittgenstein on Rules and Private Language* (Cambridge, Mass, 1982), 21–2.

[33] Ibid. 74.

way that brings it closer to the text from Davidson with which I began: 'there is no such thing as a person's meaning something, not if meaning is anything like what many philosophers have supposed.'

13

Private Objects, Physical Objects, and Ostension

David Pears's *The False Prison* stands out as a subtle, intricate pursuit of closely interwoven themes at the centre of Wittgenstein's philosophy, both early and late. It is impressive in its presentation of the continuity of those preoccupations, and of Wittgenstein's unwavering attachment to them even while transforming his ways of dealing with them eventually into a new and radically different way of proceeding in philosophy. That makes it difficult to find natural points of entry into the book anywhere after the beginning of volume i. What has gone before is essential to a proper understanding and criticism of what is to be found at any given point, and of what is to come. That is how it is with the thought of any great philosopher.

But Pears singles out 'the private language argument' as 'the centrepiece of *Philosophical Investigations*',[1] and therefore presumably as a centrepiece of Wittgenstein's whole later philosophy.[2] He gives that argument a very good run for its money through the closely argued central chapters of volume ii of *The False Prison*. He sees it 'a self-contained unit',[3] and in three different ways. It is brief and can be cut neatly out of the rest of *Philosophical Investigations* and evaluated on its own. It is a *reductio ad absurdum* argument, so it can succeed only if its premisses can be independently identified and the absurdity of the conclusion traced back to one or more of them. And it applies only to a language for

This essay is to appear in D. Charles and W. Child (eds.), *Essays on David Pears and Wittgenstein* (Oxford, 2000).

[1] David Pears, *The False Prison: A Study of the Development of Wittgenstein's Philosophy* (Oxford, 1988), ii. 361.

[2] Philosophy of mathematics, which is barely touched on in *Philosophical Investigations*, was of at least equal concern to Wittgenstein in his later work as questions of mind and language. A rich banquet can be expected to have more than one centrepiece.

[3] Pears, *The False Prison*, ii. 329.

sensations (or other 'mental' phenomena) whose connections with the physical world have been severed, not to a language for physical objects, or language in general.

What is under attack in the argument Pears has in mind is the idea that there could be a language of a certain kind, carefully described by Wittgenstein as follows:

> The individual words of this language are to refer to what can only be known to the person speaking; to his immediate private sensations. So another person cannot understand the language.[4]

The 'so' in the last sentence indicates that the impossibility of another person's understanding the language is a consequence of what its words are supposed to refer to. So the argument is directed not simply against the possibility of a language that only one person can understand, but against a language whose words are to refer only to a person's 'immediate private sensations'. Some idea of what that is supposed to be is given in §256, where a language is said not to be appropriately 'private' if 'my words for sensations [are] tied up with my natural expressions of sensation'.

> But suppose I didn't have my natural expression of sensation, but only had the sensation. And now I simply *associate* names with sensations and use these names in descriptions.[5]

Pears understands the sensations in question to be 'completely detached from everything in the physical world',[6] and he finds in §258 of *Philosophical Investigations*,[7] or perhaps only in its last three sentences,[8] an argument against the possibility of a language to talk about them. That paragraph begins with an attempt to set up an association between a sign and a certain sensation by 'impressing on myself the connection between' them.

> But 'I impress it on myself' can only mean: this process brings it about that I remember the connection *right* in the future. But in the present case I have no criterion of correctness. One would like to say: whatever is going to seem right to me is right. And that only means that here we can't talk about "right".[9]

[4] L. Wittgenstein, *Philosophical Investigations*, tr. G. E. M. Anscombe (Oxford, 1953), §243. Parentheses in the text containing '*PI*' refer to this book.

[5] *PI* §256.

[6] Pears, *The False Prison*, ii. 328.

[7] Ibid. 213–14.

[8] Ibid. 328.

[9] *PI* §258.

The argument Pears finds here is meant to show that in the imagined language there would be no distinction for the putative speaker between applying a word to a sensation-type correctly and applying it incorrectly.[10] This would mean that the speaker, 'would not be able to set up a descriptive language'[11] by giving himself 'a kind of ostensive definition of sensation-types'.[12] He 'could not reidentify phenomenal types' or 'learn to use words for them'.[13] With no distinction between seeming right and being right,[14] 'what is done as it is for the doer, and what is done as the successful achievement . . . are collapsed together', with the result that 'in the sense of "doing" in which doing is a practice, nothing is done'.[15] Therefore no language for referring to 'immediate private sensations', so understood, is possible.

The special richness of Pears's investigation lies in his relentlessly pressing the question of exactly how this conclusion is reached. Why must a putative speaker of such a language fail?

> If sensation-language is completely detached from the physical world, what exactly is the crucial loss which leaves us without a distinction between seeming right and being right?[16]

He thinks it is not easy to find an answer to the question in the text of *Philosophical Investigations*.[17] He mentions two possible answers. The first says that the putative speaker of the imagined language would be left with no way to distinguish between seeming right and being right because he would be unable to check his judgements of sameness from one occasion to another by asking other people. The second answer says it is because he would have lost any chance of checking his judgements 'on standard physical objects'[18] that he would not be able to make the distinction. The first answer draws on one feature of a 'private' language: the fact that nobody other than the speaker could understand it. The second appears to focus on something more fundamental: the kinds of things the words of such a language are supposed to refer to.

Pears argues for the second answer. He thinks the 'crucial loss' occurs because 'sensations' are 'completely detached from everything in the physical world'.[19] That is why they could not be referred to or talked about. But why not? His answer is that the putative

[10] Pears, *The False Prison*, ii. 328. [11] Ibid. 354. [12] Ibid. 213.
[13] Ibid. 416. [14] Ibid. 361. [15] Ibid. 422. [16] Ibid. 361.
[17] Ibid. 333. [18] Ibid. 362. [19] Ibid. 328.

speaker could not fulfil what can be seen to be a necessary condition of learning to use the words of his language to mean something. And that can be seen in turn from the necessary conditions in general of anyone's acquiring a skill or learning how to do something correctly.

> Learning is possible only if there is a standard of success which the pupil can apply to what he does in order to improve his performance. . . . If he lacked any criteria of objective error, any progress that he made would not be attributable to learning but to a miracle.[20]

> we cannot even try to acquire a skill without a usable criterion of successful performance.[21]

A 'usable criterion' here appears to be understood as a test: some operation the performance of which would tell or indicate to the learner that he has performed correctly. The test or indication must be decisive:

> There must be a discoverable difference . . . between his merely feeling that he has got it right this time and his actually getting it right.[22]

Speaking a language is a particular kind of skill. And acquiring the skill of using a word to mean something, or learning how to use it correctly from occasion to occasion, is possible 'only when there is an independent criterion for "the same again"'.

> This independent criterion is available for physical objects and their properties, and also for anything which has an identity connected with the identities of physical objects and their properties. But it is no longer possible to reidentify phenomenal types when all their connections with the physical world have been severed, and so it is no longer possible to learn to use words for them.[23]

Referring to sensations and their properties 'on the private stage of the mind' is not like referring to physical objects and their properties 'in the external world'.[24] A speaker is not related to them 'in anything like the way' in which he is related to the properties of physical objects.[25] 'Standard physical objects which could be assumed to provide the same stimulation on different occasions of perception'[26] would give a speaker something independent to appeal to.

[20] Pears, *The False Prison*, ii. 344. [21] Ibid. 345. [22] Ibid. 344.
[23] Ibid. 416. [24] Ibid. 354. [25] Ibid. 357. [26] Ibid. 362.

The point . . . is that physical objects stand out from their background and endure, and that is why we are able to set up a descriptive language by isolating them and sorting them into types.[27]

[The] mind can get a purchase on physical properties independently of their background, but it cannot get any purchase on the properties of sensations when they are completely detached from the external world. To put the point in another way, physical objects supply us with constancies against which we can push when we are acquiring proficiency with a vocabulary for describing them, but detached sensations do no such thing.[28]

In the 'private language', sensations are 'something completely detached from all physical criteria'.[29] That assumption is the culprit to which Pears thinks the absurdity of the conclusion is to be traced. So the 'crucial loss' suffered by a putative speaker of a language for sensations completely severed from the physical world is the absence of any 'usable' or 'viable' criterion or test for the correctness of his applications of words to the items he means to talk about. Physical objects, by contrast, can provide criteria for "the same again" that enable a speaker to distinguish his being right in applying a word from its only seeming to him that he is right.

Since such a stable criterion could be used whether or not there were other people around,[30] even a completely solitary speaker who had no other people with whom to check his judgements of sameness would not suffer the debilitating loss that a speaker of the 'detached sensation' language would suffer. So the first answer to the question of the 'crucial loss', which mentions only the impossibility of corroboration by others, must be rejected. The absence of other people would be no loss for someone who can check or 'calibrate'[31] his judgements on 'standard physical objects', and get the 'reassurance'[32] he needs from them alone.

I would like to express some doubts, both about this argument and about whether it is to be found in Wittgenstein. I think a different answer to the question of the 'crucial loss' is more strongly supported by what he says. I think it is a better answer, not only in avoiding those doubts, but in incorporating much that Pears rightly stresses while going beyond his account in ways that are more in

[27] Ibid. 354–5. [28] Ibid. 357–8. [29] Ibid. 350.
[30] Ibid. 362. [31] Ibid. 334. [32] Ibid. 372.

accord with what he too describes as fundamental and pervasive features of Wittgenstein's later philosophy.

As for the argument itself, considered on its own, how convincing is it? The first premiss—that in order to acquire a skill you must be able to apply a test that will indicate to you that you are doing the thing correctly—seems to me doubtful as a generalization. As long as your repeated efforts are in fact correct, and you learn to act in those ways whenever it is appropriate, you will be doing the thing correctly even if you don't know how to apply a test to tell you that you are doing it correctly. With many skills, there is nothing but practice to help you. The only 'test' of successful performance is the extent to which you succeed in doing what you are trying to do. A person could acquire many skills and capacities while lacking a capacity to apply tests to his performances to see whether he is doing them correctly.

I think that is true of speaking a language. A person can learn to speak correctly and mean something by what he says without knowing how to check to find out whether he is speaking correctly or meaning what he says. Correct applications of his words, intentionally produced, are enough for his saying and meaning what he does by his utterances. So the second premiss—that an independent criterion for "the same again" is needed in learning to use a word correctly—also seems to me doubtful, and for the same reason.

The argument draws a sharp contrast between words for physical objects and words for sensations 'completely detached from all physical criteria'. But if a person is very good at applying the same word to what he takes to be a physical object of the same kind from occasion to occasion, why could he not also be very good at applying the same word to what he takes to be a sensation of the same kind from occasion to occasion, even if those sensations are 'completely detached from the physical world'? Even if he does not identify what he feels through any connections it might have with the physical world, what prevents him from carrying over to his sensations a recognitional capacity he has shown he possesses with physical objects?

The objection appears to be that with words for such sensations there could be no decisive check—no 'independent criterion'—of the correctness of their application. But if the person is careful and reliable elsewhere, why can't he be just as careful and reliable with his 'detached' sensations? If he is, then his having carefully applied a word to one of his sensations would mean that it had passed the decisive test. To insist that the test must indicate that his sensation really is of a certain type, not merely that it seems to him as if it is, is to add nothing. After careful consideration, what a reliable speaker might declare is that he has a sensation of a certain type, not that it seems to him as if he has.

If it is objected that he could arrive at such a categorical verdict only by making an inference from the way things seem to him to the way they are, and that he could have no decisive or independent test to guarantee the soundness of that step on any particular occasion, then the contrast with physical objects would be lost, and it would be impossible to speak meaningfully about anything. That things are a certain way does not follow from the fact that they seem that way to someone, and if in applying a word to something a test is always needed to guarantee the step from its seeming to be applied correctly to its actually being applied correctly, no one could ever apply any word correctly to anything. To know that any particular test had turned out positively, a further test would be needed to indicate that it really did turn out that way, and did not just seem to. And a further test would be needed of that test, and so on without end. There is nothing peculiar to sensations, even 'detached' sensations, in this familiar regress.

There is no threat of regress if it is granted that physical objects are in fact of certain types, and that we can sometimes just see, and so know, that an object is of a certain type, without inferring it from the way it seems. But why can we not equally grant that sensations are also in fact of certain types, and that we can sometimes just feel, and so know, that a sensation is of a certain type? If what a person judges on such an occasion is that he has a sensation of the same kind as he has had before, and not simply that it seems to him that he does, the fact that *we* cannot independently tell whether he is right does not mean that he cannot be right, or that he cannot tell that he is right.

I think the argument that Pears calls 'the private language argument' is weak because it concentrates too exclusively on the possibility of talking about certain kinds of things. It turns on what a person would have to do to succeed in talking about sensations whose properties are completely detached from the physical world, but it does not question sufficiently deeply what those 'immediate private sensations' are supposed to be, or whether there are such things. If it is conceded—or not denied or even questioned—that there are such things, and that we have them, the only thing left for the argument to do would be to show that we could not learn to talk about them. But by then it seems to me too late. The general considerations about language are too weak in themselves to establish such a strong negative conclusion.

None of this means that the argument Pears presents is not Wittgenstein's argument. But I think there are good reasons to doubt that this is the best interpretation of the treatment of the idea of 'immediate private sensations' in *Philosophical Investigations*. Pears himself draws attention to some of those reasons. He even stresses some of the important general considerations which lie behind them. But in the end I think his interpretation does not do full justice to those ideas.

In introducing volume ii of *The False Prison* Pears draws attention to a set of ideas that must be at the heart of any adequate understanding of Wittgenstein's philosophy.

> One of the recurrent themes of *Philosophical Investigations* is that we cannot give a word a meaning merely by giving it a one-off attachment to a thing. What is needed is a sustained contribution from us as we continue to use the word, an established practice of applying it in a way that we all take to be the same. . . . [T]he indefinitely prolonged sequence of correct applications of a word cannot be fixed unequivocally by any example or set of examples. . . . Nor can we eliminate this latitude by falling back on something in our mind, like a picture or a rule or a mental act. . . . The correct continuation of a series can be determined only by what we, who continue it, find it natural to do. So if our contribution is ignored, it will not be possible to pick out the right continuation from the others. Anything will pass as correct, and the distinction between obeying the rule and disobeying it will collapse. This distinction must be based on our practice, which cannot be completely anticipated by any self-contained thing. We do not, and cannot, rely on any instant talisman.[33]

These thoughts are central to the way Wittgenstein's later philosophy surpasses the *Tractatus*, and to the way it would subvert much subsequent philosophy as well, if properly recognized. Pears explains that they are not always easy to see or to keep in mind in the detail of Wittgenstein's work. His writings are difficult to follow because he is often responding to 'shadowy adversaries' operating

[33] Pears, *The False Prison*, ii. 208–9.

largely behind the scenes,[34] but with whom he himself never loses contact. The targets are philosophical theories or conceptions or inclinations which all in one way or another violate this basic fact about meaning.[35]

There is at the very least a certain tension between the fundamental importance Pears rightly attaches to these very general, far-reaching ideas about meaning, and the central position he gives to what he sees as an independent, self-contained argument in §258 of *Philosophical Investigations*. That argument appears to turn only on very general considerations about acquiring skills, and on what is needed for someone to learn to use a word in the same way each time. In what it says is required there is no reference to 'an established practice of applying it in a way that we all take to be the same'. A solitary speaker is said to be capable of isolating physical objects from their background, sorting them into types, and setting up a descriptive language to talk about them, all on his own.

Pears, characteristically, raises what looks like a serious difficulty for his interpretation on just this point. Given that the private language argument as he describes it is central and relatively self-contained, there is 'a very general question about Wittgenstein's later philosophy of language: "Why so much emphasis on activity, practice, and use?" . . . Speaking a language is obviously something that we do, but why is that so important?'[36] He gives only what he calls a quick answer: it is because that way of looking at language puts it firmly in its place within the world, and is 'the best corrective for a bad habit of thought which is endemic in Western philosophy—the inveterate tendency to narrow down the mind's access to reality, constricting it to point-to-point contact'.[37]

That answer is perhaps correct as far it goes, but I think it is too quick and too general. It does not go far enough to explain how the appeal to practice and use actually functions at particular points. Nor does it explain why it appears to be absent from a central argument of *Philosophical Investigations*.

I think Pears would say that an appeal to practice or use is not absent from the private language argument as he sees it.[38] The

[34] Ibid. 222. [35] Ibid. 223. [36] Ibid. 420. [37] Ibid. 421.

[38] 'A practice can be established only when there is an acknowledged connection between a sequence of attempts and a sequence of independently checkable achievements' (ibid. 422).

speaker he imagines can give himself an ostensive definition of words for kinds of objects, and set up a descriptive language for talking about them, because he has an independent check on the correctness of his applications of those words. His going on to apply those words to things, his occasional checking, his saying things about the objects he has learned to talk about—all this can be described as a practice, as something he does. His words would have the use he has given them in the practice he has set up. But according to the argument, nothing comparable can be said about someone trying to talk about sensations completely detached from the physical world, because no reliable checks are possible with them. So for Pears there is an appeal to a practice, but no appeal to, or need for, a *communal* or *shared* practice, in order for language to be possible.

But what exactly is the practice of Pears's solitary speaker? What does he do? Pears says he sorts physical objects into types and gives himself a kind of ostensive definition of words for objects of certain kinds. He can do that because he can pick out physical objects from their background. The words he introduces to speak of them are presumably not to be thought of as proper names or individual labels attached singly to only one object each, since the speaker is said to apply the same word to different objects of the same kind. But this immediately raises the question 'Which kind?' And how does the speaker determine which kind of object his word is to apply to on its next application?

This is a question Wittgenstein begins to raise very early in *Philosophical Investigations*, even before he explicitly takes up the idea of ostensive definition in §27. It is a question about words of all kinds, not only words for sensations, and its implications run through the whole discussion of meaning and understanding and continuing a series according to a rule that extends up to §242. Uttering a sound or writing down a mark in the presence of an object, or a series of them, does not alone determine what would be a correct application of that word on the next occasion. To say that it will be correct to apply the word only to objects that are the same as the original object or objects is to say nothing. Every two or more things are the same in some respect or other.

Nor would it help to appeal to what the speaker is concentrating his attention on in the original cases, or to what he intends. The question is how he does that. Even if he is concentrating on a conspicuous physical object in front of him when he pronounces a certain word, what is it for him to have the colour of the object in mind, say, and not its shape? That is to ask what determines that the word he introduces is to be a word for things of a certain colour rather than things of a certain shape. The object alone does not fix it, nor does any series of objects, and it cannot be accounted for by any item in the mind. That is precisely the point of what Pears identifies as a recurrent theme of *Philosophical Investigations*: 'we do not, and cannot, rely on any instant talisman', and 'the meanings of our words are not guaranteed by any independent pattern already existing in the world and waiting for language to be attached to it'.[39]

Of course, ostensive definitions of words can be given, even with a single instance. A person can even give one to himself. But they work only if the person to whom the definition is given knows what kind of word is being defined.

> So one might say: the ostensive definition explains the use—the meaning—of the word when the overall role of the word in language is clear. Thus if I know that someone means to explain a colour-word to me the ostensive definition 'That is called "sepia"' will help me to understand the word.[40]

Someone who already knows how colour-words are used can learn by ostension to use new colour-words with that same 'overall role'. And someone familiar with that 'role' can intend a new word of his to be a word for a colour with which he is presented. In each case a 'place' for a word of that kind is already prepared within the speaker's abilities.

This is the background to the question Wittgenstein asks about a would-be speaker about 'immediate private sensations'. To raise the question, he concedes that, although it would be impossible for others to teach such a child the use of a sensation-word, 'let's assume the child is a genius and itself invents a name for the sensation':

> But what does it mean to say that he has "named his pain"?—How has he done this naming of pain? . . . When one says 'He gave a name to his sensation' one forgets that a great deal of stage-setting in the language is presupposed if the mere act of naming is to make sense. And when we speak of someone's having given a name to pain, what is presupposed is the

[39] Pears, *The False Prison*, ii. 363. [40] *PI* §30.

existence of the grammar of the word "pain"; it shews the post where the new word is stationed.[41]

This comes immediately before the central passage of §258. The speaker there is imagined to give himself an 'ostensive definition' that 'serves to establish the meaning' of a certain sign by impressing on himself 'the connection' between that sign and a sensation he has at the time he utters it or writes it down. Again, Wittgenstein's question is 'What kind of connection?' It is supposed to be a connection that establishes how that sign is to be correctly used in the future. But a word can be 'connected' with one and the same thing in many different ways. To say that 'in the present case I have no criterion of correctness' is to observe that nothing has so far been done to determine which future applications of that sign will be correct and which not. Not even what kind of word it is to be has been fixed. That is perhaps why 'one would like to say' that whatever is going to seem right to me is right. But to make that remark would not be to say (taking it literally) that if an application of the word seems right to me then it is right. It would be no more than a somewhat indirect way of pointing out that so far there can be no question of right or wrong about any application at all.

The point of there being 'no criterion of correctness' cannot be simply that there is no *test* that the speaker can rely on to tell him that his application of the sign is correct. There is so far nothing for any such test to be a test *for*. Nothing has been done to fix what *being* correct is or would be. What would a test for correctness try to ascertain? Correct as what, as having what meaning? The 'overall role' of the sign has not been specified; there is so far no 'post' at all at which it is 'stationed'. It is just a mark written or a sound uttered on a certain occasion. Nothing can be said about what kind of mark it is, or what it means.

Wittgenstein carries this line of thought further in §261 by asking what reason there is even for calling the word a sign for a *sensation*. The fact that it was written or uttered when a sensation was present is not enough. If the 'ostensive definition' attempted in §258 *is* understood as a definition of a sensation word—if that is the 'post' at which the new word is to be 'stationed'—then the attempt to set up a language of the kind originally described will

41 *PI* §257.

have been abandoned. "Sensation" is a word of our common language, and as we ordinarily use it, our words for sensations are tied up with our natural expressions of sensation.[42] But the speaker of the language to be imagined is to have no natural expression of the things his words refer to; they are something that 'can only be known to the person speaking'.

So whatever the grammar or role of the words he introduces is to be, they will not be sensation words as we ordinarily use them.

> And it would not help either to say that it need not be a *sensation*; that when he writes "S" he has *something*—and that is all that can be said. 'Has' and 'something' also belong to our common language.[43]

If in our common language the uses of 'has' and 'something' in the relevant senses are also tied up with natural expressions of the 'something' that the person 'has', those words could not serve that would-be speaker's purposes either.

The negative point here is that the role and therefore the meaning of the words in the imagined language have not been determined or even suggested by anything described so far. There is no 'criterion of correctness' in the sense that there is nothing for the correct application of those words to be.

> It might be said: if you have given yourself a private definition of a word, then you must inwardly *undertake* to use the word in such-and-such a way. And how do you undertake that? Is it to be assumed that you invent the technique of using the word, or that you found it ready-made?[44]

If you found it ready-made, there must already have been a way of using a word with that kind of 'overall role', and therefore with that kind of meaning. And your applications of a word with that kind of meaning will be correct only if they are in accord with that ready-made way of using it.

That is the 'crucial loss' suffered by the imagined would-be speaker about his 'immediate private sensations'. His words cannot have the role or grammar of the ordinary sensation-words we are all familiar with. Our sensation-words are tied up with natural expressions of sensation, and so are disqualified. Even the words 'has' and 'something' of our common language are unavailable to him for his purposes. What is left? When such a would-be speaker is imagined, what exactly is being imagined? What idea remains of

[42] *PI* §256. [43] *PI* §261. [44] *PI* §262.

'his purposes'? Nothing that has been described so far makes the signs he writes down intelligible, or even indicates that they mean anything at all. Wittgenstein, apparently sympathetic to this plight, says 'So in the end when one is doing philosophy one gets to the point where one would like just to utter an inarticulate sound.' But he follows immediately with the insistence that even 'such a sound is an expression only as it occurs in a particular language-game, which should now be described'.[45]

The use of the sound in the language must be described, because only in that way can it be made intelligible to us, so we will know what it means and what someone who uses it is expressing. If we understand the meaning of a sound so described, it is because we recognize its role in linguistic communication that we can understand. We 'domesticate' it. If nothing in the description enables us to do that, it remains an inarticulate or unmeaning sound. The would-be speaker means nothing. It is an understatement to describe him as suffering a 'loss'.

The point applies equally to the would-be solitary speaker about physical objects as Pears describes him. If he sets up his language completely from scratch, there are presumably no 'overall roles' already in place for the words he introduces to fulfil. Without that stage-setting, he alone will have to give them their roles. But nothing is said to indicate what the words he introduces in the presence of physical objects are to mean, or what he does to give them one meaning rather than another. Simply uttering a certain sound whenever an object of a certain kind is present fixes nothing. To say that he learns to apply the same word to all those objects that give him 'the same stimulation on every occasion of perception' is no help. Blue and round objects of the same size might be assumed to give the same stimulation, but blue objects and round objects and objects of the same size are three different kinds of object, and the words for them pick out different kinds of things and so differ in meaning. This solitary speaker is said to be in a good position because he can 'calibrate' his reactions or judgements or skills on 'standard physical objects'. But which reactions or judgements? In the absence of a way in which his words are to be applied, or a specification of the kinds of word they are supposed to be, there would be nothing to check or 'calibrate'.

[45] *PI* §261.

The positive point is that the 'criterion of correctness' of a person's application of a word is conformity with a practice of using words in that way, with that kind of meaning. There is nothing else for a word's being used correctly on a certain occasion to be. Sounds or marks do not carry their meanings or the conditions of their correct application somehow within themselves. Of course, not every word requires prior usage of that very word in order to be applied correctly. If we have a language, we can explicitly formulate a rule according to which a certain word is to be used, even if that rule has never been formulated, and no word has ever been applied in conformity with it, before. But that formulation will have the meaning it has, and so will prescribe that new use, only because of the way the words it contains have been and actually are used.

The point is completely general, and is not restricted to words for sensations. Wittgenstein makes it earlier in a now-famous passage strikingly parallel to §258, but long before 'private sensations' have even been mentioned.

> And hence also "obeying a rule" is a practice. And to *think* one is obeying a rule is not to obey a rule. Hence it is not possible to obey a rule "privately": otherwise thinking one was obeying a rule would be the same thing as obeying it.[46]

What is here said to make it impossible to obey a rule 'privately' in applying one's words to things is not that the objects to which the words are to be applied are 'detached from all physical criteria', so there can be no independent test of correctness. It is rather that there must be such a thing as a rule in order for anything that goes on to be in accord with it or not. To say there must be a rule is to say that there must at some point be practices of doing things in certain ways—actual cases exhibiting what we call 'obeying the rule' or 'going against it'[47]—in order for there to be a standard against which the correctness of any particular moves can be determined. That is the very general observation from which this conclusion ('hence') is drawn.

> It is not possible that there should have been only one occasion on which someone obeyed a rule. It is not possible that there should have been only one occasion on which a report was made, an order given or understood;

[46] *PI* §202. [47] *PI* §201.

and so on.—To obey a rule, to make a report, to give an order, to play a game of chess, are *customs* (uses, institutions).

To understand a sentence means to understand a language. To understand a language means to be master of a technique.[48]

There could not be only one person who followed a rule only once—only one occasion of rule-following, ever[49]—since without any rules already in effect, whatever a person did on a single occasion would not be a case of rule-following. That is the point of Wittgenstein's question about a would-be speaker without rules to conform to: what would it be for anything he did to be correct or incorrect? Even if he 'performed' many times, over and over, what determines what those performances would have to be like in order to be correct? If some rules have been followed by some people already, the correctness of his performances, or even of a single performance, could be assessed against them. But if the solitary would-be speaker is imagined as starting from scratch, with no rules or practices already in effect, there will have been no actual cases of anyone's following any rule or doing anything correctly. To insist that it would be enough for him simply to start applying the same word to the same kind of thing again and again does not answer the question. It does not fix what it would be for anything he does to be correct or incorrect.

There will be an answer to the question if there is some practice or institution against which, or in the light of which, his performances can be assessed. I think we can perhaps just imagine the abstract possibility of a solitary speaker who has never encountered another human being. The idea that he simply 'invents' uses for all his words is hard to accept, but leaving aside the question of how he acquired his abilities, I think we can make sense of the possibility of a such a speaker to the extent to which we can make sense of the uses his words are said to have. If it is stipulated that he uses some words for the colours of things, some for the shapes of things, some for sensations, and so on, then I think he is being described as speaking a language.[50] We would have no idea how he

[48] *PI* §199.

[49] Pears, *The False Prison*, ii. 381. Pears reads the sentence 'It is not possible that there should have been only one occasion on which someone obeyed a rule' so that it 'requires a person to do whatever is going to be described as "obeying a rule" more than once' (p. 378). But surely it means only that it is not possible for there to have been only one occasion on which anyone obeyed a rule.

[50] The main difficulty in making sense of this speculation is what the speaker is imagined to be doing in order for it to be true of him that he uses certain words for

came to do it; it would be a kind of miracle. But if his usage was described fully enough in a way we could make sense of, we would have to admit—however miraculous it seemed—that he was indeed speaking of such things. If he used English, or German, or French words to speak of them, I think we would even have to admit that he was speaking English, or German, or French. We could imagine meeting him and carrying on a conversation with him in one of those languages.

As far as I can see, there is nothing in this possibility that is incompatible with what Wittgenstein says about the need for a practice in order for there to be correct and incorrect applications of words. There are, after all, such practices as speaking of the colours of things, and of the shapes of things, and of sensations, and speaking English, or German, or French. If this solitary person can be seen as speaking a language, it is not because he can check his judgements of sameness against physical objects that are somehow available to him, but because he is described as engaging in some of those familiar practices that only language-speakers are capable of. What is astonishing about him is that he does so without ever having come into contact with any of those practices.

Pears opposes what he calls a 'social theory of rule-following'. That was the first, rejected, answer to the question of the 'crucial loss'. But that question was about what a speaker needs in order to check his judgements of sameness of the application of his words, and so to distinguish between seeming to be right and being right in those applications. Pears thinks the absence of shared practices with other people would not leave a speaker with no possible checks, as long as he still had physical objects, so the 'social theory' is wrong. But Wittgenstein's view of the need for a shared practice, and of what would be 'lost' without one, is not a 'social theory of rule-following' in that sense. It says nothing about the need for checking one's judgements of sameness of application. It is a view about the conditions of there being such a thing as correct applications of words. Without some practice or rules, there would be

the colours of things, others for the shapes of things, and so on. Uttering certain sounds only in the presence of such features of things would not be enough. I think we would have to see him as saying things that have some internal structure or complexity, so that one performance is connected in intelligible ways with other possible performances, and he can be seen as having concepts that he deploys in different ways. It is not clear whether or how his actions could exhibit such abilities with no linguistic interaction with other people.

nothing for any judgement of correctness of application to be a judgement of. Correct as what?

The importance of the possibility of a solitary speaker for Pears is that it represents someone who in his solitude could 'set up his language alone, and check the regularity of his use of words on standard physical objects'.[51] If that were possible, he thinks it would show something important about the possibility of language. It would show the 'sufficiency of standard physical objects'[52] as a 'stabilizing resource' for keeping the speaker's 'vocalizations on the rails',[53] and so making language possible. Pears finds Wittgenstein 'evasive about the need for other people',[54] and is disappointed that he never explicitly takes up the question 'we all want to hear him answer':[55] whether the availability of physical objects is alone sufficient for the possibility of language. Nor does he prove, or even directly argue for, the thesis that shared practices or institutions are necessary in order for words to be applied correctly, and so for language to be possible.

To appeal only to community practices seems to Pears complacent; to stop there is to miss something. It suggests that 'a community of language-speakers, taken collectively, is not answerable to anything outside the circle of its own agreed practices',[56] and it ignores the question of 'what keeps the vocalizations of the whole linguistic community on the rails'.[57] That is why the possibility of a solitary speaker about physical objects is important and revealing: 'it isolates a resource which certainly underpins the practice of the community'.[58] To ignore or evade that possibility, as Pears thinks Wittgenstein does, is to miss that important fact about language.

It is easy to feel such disappointment if you seek in Wittgenstein an impossibility proof which establishes the necessary conditions of the possibility of language and so explains why our language is secure. But the upshot of those very general ideas about meaning that constitute a recurrent theme of Wittgenstein's later philosophy is that the demand or search for such a 'stabilizing resource'

[51] Pears, *The False Prison*, ii. 334.
[52] Ibid. 375. [53] Ibid. 387. [54] Ibid. 381.
[55] Ibid. 381. I take this to be equivalent to Pears's question 'Is what is called "obeying a rule" something that it would be possible for only *one* man to do?', since he thinks the solitary speaker he imagines could 'calibrate' his judgements on physical objects alone.
[56] Ibid. 387. [57] Ibid. [58] Ibid. 388.

to 'underpin' our language and keep us 'on the rails' is a will-o'-the-wisp. That desire is what lies behind so many of those 'shadowy adversaries' which the later works try in different ways to expose. There could be no such 'resource'. Nothing could do what such a 'talisman' is apparently required to do. No set of objects—even physical objects—to which words are to be applied, and nothing in the minds of those who would apply them, could 'stabilize' or 'underpin' those applications from outside all language that is used to talk about them. There could be nothing that a community's using its words in the ways it does could be 'answerable to' in that sense.

That is not because there are no physical objects, or that they do not give 'the same stimulation' on different occasions of perception, and not because there is nothing in the minds of people who would apply words to them; but because nothing in the world or in the mind could play such a guiding or stabilizing role unless it *meant* something to the people whose actions are to be 'stabilized' or 'underpinned' by it. Yet something's having such a meaning for them could not itself be fixed by some further 'stabilizing resource', but only by something that those people in fact do: by what Wittgenstein calls 'a consensus of *action*: a consensus of doing the same thing, reacting in the same way'.[59]

Pears acknowledges, even insists on, the importance of the point for Wittgenstein.

> How could a philosopher step outside factual language and find any independent support for it? Isn't that precisely the kind of theory of meaning that is rejected in the long investigation of rule-following which develops out of the critique of the *Tractatus* in *Philosophical Investigations* and leads into the private language argument?[60]

The answer is 'Yes'. I think this shows that what Wittgenstein does in those passages from which Pears extracts 'the private language argument' must be understood in some other way.

Starting in §243 of *Philosophical Investigations*, he takes up what looks like a challenge to the idea that 'it is impossible to obey a rule "privately"'. In §258 we are invited to try out the idea of a language whose words 'refer to what can only be known to the person

[59] Quoted by Pears (p. 446) from *Wittgenstein's Lectures on the Foundations of Mathematics*, ed. C. Diamond (London, 1975), 184.

[60] Pears, *The False Prison*, ii. 388.

speaking; to his immediate private sensations'. The method followed is what Wittgenstein calls 'the method of §2'[61]: consider a language for which the description given is really valid. When we try to do it, we find either that the possibility dissolves, or that anything we can say that makes sense to us fails to capture the idea. We are left with an urge to utter an inarticulate sound. Dissatisfied, we can, and probably will, try again, and again, to capture the 'inner' or 'private' object that is accessible only to ourselves.

This is just what is to be expected from a philosophy whose aims and effects are as Pears has described them:

> The other will be led by gradual transitions from something which he does want to say, but which is really, if he could only see it, nonsense, to something else which consistency forces him to say, and which he will immediately recognize as nonsense. This analysis will move slowly from one carefully chosen linguistic example to another, and its purpose will be to retrieve the other. He must be brought back to our actual linguistic practices, and, if he is brought back to them, it will be with an understanding of them which he could not have achieved without his excursion into the dreamworld of language.[62]

It is not as far as it might seem from what Wittgenstein in the *Tractatus* declared to be 'the correct method of philosophy':

> The correct method of philosophy would really be the following: to say nothing except what can be said, i.e. propositions of natural science—i.e. something that has nothing to do with philosophy—and then, whenever someone else wanted to say something metaphysical, to demonstrate to him that he had failed to give a meaning to certain signs in his propositions. Although it would not be satisfying to the other person—he would not have the feeling that we were teaching him philosophy—*this* method would be the only strictly correct one.[63]

[61] *PI* §48.

[62] David Pears, *Wittgenstein* (London, 1971; 2nd edn. with postscript 1985), 176–7.

[63] L. Wittgenstein, *Tractatus Logico-Philosophicus*, tr. D. F. Pears and B. F. McGuinness (London, 1961), 6.53.

INDEX